D0811623

THE AIR FORCES

Other National Historical Society Publications:

THE IMAGE OF WAR: 1861-1865

TOUCHED BY FIRE: A PHOTOGRAPHIC PORTRAIT OF THE CIVIL WAR

WAR OF THE REBELLION: OFFICIAL RECORDS
OF THE UNION AND CONFEDERATE ARMIES

OFFICIAL RECORDS OF THE UNION AND CONFEDERATE NAVIES
IN THE WAR OF THE REBELLION

HISTORICAL TIMES ILLUSTRATED ENCYCLOPEDIA OF THE CIVIL WAR

CONFEDERATE VETERAN

THE WEST POINT MILITARY HISTORY SERIES

IMPACT: THE ARMY AIR FORCES' CONFIDENTIAL HISTORY
OF WORLD WAR II

HISTORY OF UNITED STATES NAVAL OPERATIONS IN WORLD WAR II
by Samuel Eliot Morison

HISTORY OF THE ARMED FORCES IN WORLD WAR II
by Janusz Piekalkiewicz

A TRAVELLER'S GUIDE TO GREAT BRITAIN SERIES

MAKING OF BRITAIN SERIES

THE ARCHITECTURAL TREASURES OF EARLY AMERICA

For information about National Historical Society Publications, write:

The National Historical Society, 2245 Kohn Road, Box 8200,
Harrisburg, Pa 17105

THE ELITE
The World's Crack Fighting Men

THE AIR FORCES

Ashley Brown, Editor
Jonathan Reed, Editor

Editorial Board

Brigadier-General James L. Collins, Jr. (Retd.)
Former Chief of Military History, US Department of the Army

Ian V. Hogg
Authority on smallarms and modern weapons systems

Dr. John Pimlott
Senior Lecturer in the Department of War Studies,
Royal Military Academy, Sandhurst, England

Brigadier-General Edwin H. Simmons (Retd.)
US Marine Corps

Lisa Mullins, Managing Editor, NHS edition

A Publication of
THE NATIONAL HISTORICAL SOCIETY

Published in Great Britain in 1986 by Orbis Publishing

Special contents of this edition copyright © 1989 by the
National Historical Society

All rights reserved. Printed in the United States of America.
No part of this book may be used or reproduced in any manner
whatsoever without permission except in the case of brief
quotations embodied in critical articles and reviews.

Library of Congress Cataloging-in-Publication Data
The Air Forces / Ashley Brown, editor ; Jonathan Reed, editor.
  p.   cm.—(The Elite : the world's crack fighting men ; v. 12)
  ISBN 0-918678-50-1
  1. Air forces—History. 2. Air warfare—History. I. Brown,
Ashley. II. Reed, Jonathan.   III. National Historical Society.
IV. Series: Elite (Harrisburg, Pa.) ; v. 12.
UG630.A3813   1990
358.4'009—dc20   89-12201
                                                       CIP

CONTENTS

INTRODUCTION

It would be hard to find a more glamorized field of service than the air corps of the world. Flying dazzlingly high above the clouds to swoop down upon an enemy, aces going one-to-one in virtually the last single combats in warfare, and even the bombers facing desperate odds against fighters and anti-aircraft fire, all adds up to a heroic and highly romanticized kind of warfare. Behind the movie-screen drama, however, it is also among the most dangerous ways for men to make war, which is why many of the truly Elite have always sought out THE AIR FORCES.

Consider the Luftwaffe airmen of the Kampfgeschwader 200 unit, formed specifically to carry out hazardous air missions behind enemy lines. They dropped agents in night air flights, trained crewmen for supposed suicide bomber runs, and even attempted to land assassins behind Russian lines with a plan to kill Stalin.

For another kind of bravery, there was the Soviet 586th Fighter Air Regiment, piloted by women. The Russians were the first to send women into aerial combat, and where they met enemies in the skies, they held their own. Lydia Litvak, in the short year before she was shot down and killed, claimed 12 German fighters and one bomber as kills.

The American "Jolly Green Giants" in Vietnam, flying their rescue helicopters, faced incredible odds as they hovered over downed U.S. aircraft, one man hanging from a steel lifeline as he was winched down to bring up dazed and wounded airmen, while crew mates held off enemy ground troops from the chopper.

All of their stories and more are told in THE AIR FORCES. From the Spanish Civil War through the fighting in the Falklands, wherever brave airmen have challenged the skies as well as their foes, THE AIR FORCES follows them. Pakistanis, Israelis, Soviets, Germans, Americans, and more . . . national ties and allegiances fall by the wayside in considering the individual feats of brave men and women who have gone the extra distance to stand with THE ELITE.

**When the Germans
launched Operation
Barbarossa in June 1941, the
Soviet Air Force, although
having a frontline strength
of over 10,500 aircraft, was
ill-prepared to meet the
onslaught of the 2770
aircraft fielded by the
Luftwaffe. By any standard,
most of the Soviet designs
were obsolete and, despite
a process of modernisation,
pilots were unable to meet
the Luftwaffe on anything
like equal terms. Less than
half the Soviet combat
strength in the west
consisted of modern types;
the rest were clearly out-
dated.
The brunt of the Luftwaffe's
attacks were borne by units
of the Leningrad, Baltic,
Kiev, Odessa and Western
Special Districts. Each
consisted of between 600
and 1400 aircraft of all types;
by 23 June, their
commanders were
admitting to the loss of some
1200 planes. The Western
Special Military District,
with its headquarters in
Minsk, received the
greatest mauling. One of its
units, the 9th Composite
Division, lost all but 63 of its
409 aircraft.
After three months of bitter
fighting, Hitler ordered the
Wehrmacht to capture
Moscow. Over 1200 of the
Luftwaffe's aircraft were
moved into the area to
support the operation, codenamed 'Typhoon'. Scraping
the bottom of the barrel to
oppose this thrust, the
Soviets were able to field
less than 400 aircraft.
Despite initial successes,
Typhoon ground to a halt,
the German forces crippled
by the Russian winter.
Remarkably, the Red Army
went over to the counter-
attack on 5 December,
supported by some 350
aircraft. Despite appalling
weather, the pilots flew over
50,000 sorties in defence of
Moscow, with 1254 men
winning awards. The
Luftwaffe's loss of 1400
aircraft marked a turning
point in the air war.
Above: The Soviet Army
Aviator's badge.**

**Locked in a deadly air war with the
Luftwaffe, the pilots of the Soviet
16th Guards Fighter Regiment lived
up to their creed to fight to the last**

ON 22 JUNE 1941, the German armed forces unleashed
a devastating Blitzkrieg on Russia. During the opening phase of the operation, codenamed Barbarossa,
wave after wave of the Luftwaffe's bombers, dive-
bombers, and fighters pulverised targets along a
front stretching from the Baltic to the Black Sea.
Caught unprepared, the Voenno-vozdushnye Sily
(Soviet Air Force) suffered appalling losses.

By the evening of the first day's fighting, the
Luftwaffe's victory claims stood at 1811 enemy aircraft destroyed for the loss of only 35 of their own.
Moreover, although the greater number of these
aircraft had been destroyed on the ground, when
Soviet fighter pilots did give battle in the air, their
obsolescent aircraft and poor tactics were no match
for the Luftwaffe's battle-hardened fighter forces.

Yet this view of the combat capabilities of the
Soviet fighter pilot took no account of the very real
handicaps of poor equipment, inadequate training,
and a command structure paralysed by fear and
suspicion in the aftermath of Stalin's purges. Under
such conditions, it was remarkable that in the dark
days of 1941-42 there were individual Soviet fighter
pilots and a select number of fighter regiments that
distinguished themselves in action.

One unit that was held in especially high regard
was the 55th Fighter Regiment, commanded by
Lieutenant-Colonel N.V. Isayev. Later to gain greater fame as the 16th Guards Fighter Regiment, it was
flying MiG-3 interceptors in the Odessa Military
District at the outbreak of the war, and was, as stated
by the official history of the Soviet Air Force in the
Great Patriotic War, 'rightly considered to be one of
the finest air regiments'. However, the MiG-3,
although a more modern design than the Polikarpov
I-153s and I-16s which equipped the majority of the

FORWARD TO VICTORY

Soviet fighter units, was not a particularly successful aircraft. It was difficult to fly, poorly armed and, because it had been intended for the high-altitude bomber interception role, did not perform well at the low and medium levels where most air combats took place.

Therefore the 55th Fighter Regiment had to rely on the courage and tenacity of its pilots in combat, rather than any advantages gained from the qualities of its aircraft. Three of the unit's airmen particularly distinguished themselves in the early air battles. The high quality of leadership displayed by Isayev was recognised by the award of the Hero of the Soviet Union, the highest Russian military decoration, and one of his squadron commanders, Captain Anatoly

Sokolov was a combat veteran of air battles over Manchuria with the Japanese Army Air Force in 1939. Sokolov was remembered by Senior-Lieutenant Alexander Ivanovich Pokryshkin, the most promising member of his squadron, as 'a splendid pilot' and 'a calm, cool-headed fellow, both on the ground and what is more important in the air'.

The Soviet fighter regiments each comprised some 40 aircraft during the early months of the war, although experience soon showed this to be rather too cumbersome to

Main picture: Soviet fighters take off from a rudimentary grass airstrip to do battle with the Luftwaffe. Clockwise from top: Heroes of the Soviet Union. Kankeshev Ahmet Haptal, credited with six victories in nine days; Alexander Pokryshkin, winner of the award on three occasions; N.V. Isayev, Commander of the 55th Fighter Regiment; and Grigory Rechkalov, a former miner, who scored 22 kills.

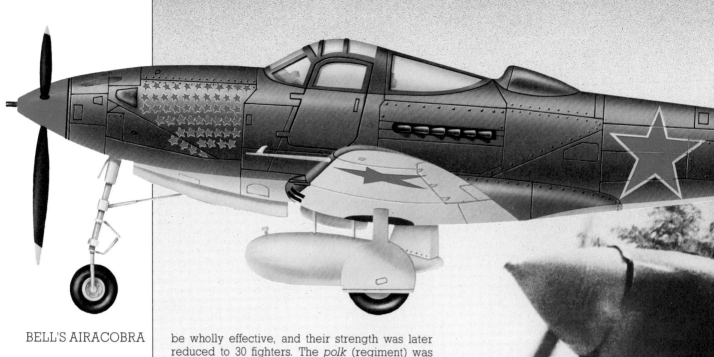

BELL'S AIRACOBRA

In 1935, after viewing an impressive display of the American Armament Corporation's T9 37mm gun, senior members of the Bell aircraft company asked their designers to come up with the blueprints for a fighter that could carry the cannon, fired through the propeller, and two 12.7mm machine guns synchronised to fire through the blades. The decision to house the T9 in the forward fuselage forced the designers to place the aircraft's engine to the rear of the cockpit, and the subsequent problems of balance meant that a tricycle-type landing gear had to be fitted to the front of the aircraft.

Given the go-ahead by the US Army Air Corps, Bell produced a series of successful prototypes and full-scale manufacture of the fighter, known as the P-39 Airacobra, began in August 1939, with the first large batch of fighters being delivered in early 1941. Although more than a dozen versions of the Airacobra were produced, the basic design remained remarkably unaltered. The P-39M, typical of the series, had a maximum speed of 621km/h and a range of over 1000km. Armament comprised the T9 cannon, two 12.7mm machine guns in the front fuselage and four 7.62mm machine guns mounted in the wings. The final production versions, the P-39N and P-39Q, were mainly supplied to the Russians.

be wholly effective, and their strength was later reduced to 30 fighters. The *polk* (regiment) was made up of three *eskadrilya* (squadrons), which were sub-divided into *zvena* (flights) of three, or later four aircraft. The strength of a regiment was some 200 officers and men – 34 of whom were pilots, 130 mechanics, and the remainder administrative and support troops.

Pokryshkin's first combat on 22 June 1941 provided an ironic illustration of the Soviet High Command's lack of preparedness for war. Encountering a formation of unfamiliar light bombers over Moldavia, Pokryshkin dived into the attack. His first burst of fire was accurate, but on breaking away he saw to his consternation that his victim was marked with red stars. In fact, he had attacked a formation of Soviet Sukhoi Su-2s, that was based at Kotovsk, near his own airfield at Mayaki. As he later bitterly commented, 'any peasant women on their way to market could have seen them there', but the Su-2s' existence had been kept secret from the pilots of the 55th.

However, on the following day there was no mistake. In the vicinity of the German airfield at Jassy, Pokryshkin surprised a formation of Messerschmitt Bf 109Es and succeeded in shooting one down before he was himself attacked from behind: 'White ribbons of his tracers shot by and then my plane shuddered – its port wing had been torn by bullets. I dived to zero feet and hedge-hopped all the way home.' On 20 July Pokryshkin was less fortunate: his MiG-3 was hit by flak during a reconnaissance mission over the Beltsy area and he had to come down behind enemy lines. Joining up with Soviet troops cut off by the German advance, he fought his way through to Soviet territory and was able to rejoin his regiment a week later.

On 7 March 1942 the combat record of the 55th Fighter Regiment was recognised by the award of the coveted 'Guards' title and the unit became the 16th Guards Fighter Regiment. This honour had been first instituted in the Soviet Air Force during December 1941, to coincide with the Red Army's counter-offensive in the Moscow area. In an elaborate ceremony, the retitled unit was presented with new colours and all members took the following oath:

'In the terrible years of the Great Patriotic War, I swear to you my country and to you my party to fight to the last drop of blood and my last breath –

and to conquer. Such is the Guards' creed. Forward to victory! Glory to the party of Lenin!'

The Guards aviation units were a true elite; each member's uniform was distinguished by a special badge and this emblem was often painted on their aircraft. They were also given priority in the supply of replacement aircraft and in re-equipping with new types as they became available. Yet these distinctions were not lightly earned, as the regiments were expected to spearhead Soviet air operations and to set an example to other units by their courage and tactical skill in fighting the Luftwaffe.

After participating in the defensive air battles over the Caucasus in 1942, the 16th Guards Fighter

Above left: Pokryshkin's Airacobra with his victories marked on the fuselage. **Above:** Chocks away! – a Soviet fighter begins a sortie. **Right:** Armourers check over machine-gun belts and bombs before a mission.

Regiment's first chance of offensive action came in the spring of 1943, during the fierce combats for air superiority over the German Kuban bridgehead. The loss of Kuban would threaten German forces in the Crimea, and provide the Soviets with bases within range of the Romanian oilfields. By this time, the unit's unsatisfactory MiG-3s had been replaced by Bell P-39 Airacobras. These American aircraft had been supplied under the Lend-Lease programme and ferried from Iran to the Caucasus front by their Soviet pilots. Nicknamed the *britchik* (little shaver), the P-39 was popular in Soviet service and pilots particularly valued its nose-mounted 37mm cannon. However, the fighter had its faults, recovery from a flat spin being especially difficult.

When the fighting over Kuban began, the 16th Guards Fighter Regiment was commanded by Lieutenant-Colonel I. M. Dzusov and Pokryshkin was one of his squadron commanders. The latter was by then, in the words of the Soviet official history, 'an

HERO OF THE SOVIET UNION

Pilot Alexsander I. Pokryshkin (below), destined to become the Soviet Air Force's foremost fighter tactician and its second-ranking ace, was born in 1913 at Novosibirsk in Siberia and worked as a labourer and factory hand before being called up for military service in 1932. Initially, Pokryshkin trained as an aviation mechanic, but in 1939 he began learning the skills of a fighter pilot.

However, he was no stranger to aircraft: in the years before the war, Pokryshkin, like many other of the Soviet Union's future aces, was a member of the Volunteer Defence Society, a paramilitary body that taught flying skills and aircraft maintenance. After qualifying as a fighter pilot, he was posted to the 55th Fighter Regiment, and was flying with this unit when the Germans launched Operation Barbarossa on 22 June 1941. Pokryshkin flew with the regiment until 1944, reaching the rank of squadron commander by the time of the fighting around Kuban in early 1943. A pilot with a wealth of active service, Pokryshkin developed the sophisticated combat tactics that helped the Soviet Air Force gain air superiority over the Luftwaffe in the closing years of the war. By the summer of 1943, he was placed in charge of the regiment, notching up further kills. However, Pokryshkin was destined for greater things, and in the following year he was given command of the 9th Guards Fighter Division.

experienced, mature commander and a remarkable fighter pilot, who had completed more than 350 sorties and shot down nearly 20 enemy aircraft.'

Pokryshkin's influence on Soviet fighter tactics was to be far-reaching, for as he wrote:

'the offensive spirit was now the keynote of our activity. It was over Kuban that the pilots of our regiment arrived at the formula for aggressive air combat. It consisted of four elements: altitude, speed, manoeuvre, fire.'

Hitherto, Soviet fighter pilots had tended to fight only in the horizontal plane, flying in inflexible three-aircraft formations and forming defensive circles as soon as they were attacked. Their new-found confidence and willingness to seize the initiative was shown by the adoption of the Luftwaffe's two-aircraft element of leader and wingman, known in Russian as the *para*. This enabled more fluid combat tactics, with manoeuvre in both the horizontal and vertical planes. Superior altitude and speed, Pokryshkin stressed, gave Soviet pilots the initiative and freedom of manoeuvre. Once an advantageous position had been gained behind an enemy aircraft, the fighter pilot would close to minimum range in order that his fire would have the maximum effect.

The Kuban battles were a severe test of individual endurance as the Soviet fighter pilots flew from dawn to dusk, sometimes carrying out as many as seven sorties in a day. Massive air battles involving up to 100 aircraft were commonplace, and 16th Guards Fighter Regiment pilot Grigory Golubev, who often flew as Pokryshkin's wingman, has described the confusion of such fights, 'the flash of tracer, the rattle of machine-gun fire, flak bursts and the wild intermingling of aircraft at various altitudes.' Yet, whenever possible, the Soviet fighters were controlled by the air division or regimental commander from his ground control post. For example, on 29 April General A.V. Borman, the 216th Fighter Division's commander, directed Pokryshkin's P-39s to intercept a formation of 12 Luftwaffe fighters over the battlefield. Borman's instructions enabled the Soviet fighters to surprise the enemy formation and eight of them were claimed as destroyed. Pokryshkin himself recalls.

'As far as I was concerned the Kuban battle began one spring morning when I led a flight of aircraft to the patrol area. We were flying fast machines and in this sortie we had the opportunity of putting into practice all the elements of our air combat formula: altitude, speed, manoeuvre and fire.

'We approached the front line at high altitude and great speed. I espied three Soviet LaGG-3s below us desperately keeping at bay 10 Messerschmitts. The LaGGs were having a hard time of it. They were maintaining a circling defence. Our patrol already had the advantage over the Germans of altitude and speed. It now remained to bring the third element of our formula into play: manoeuvre. I ordered the patrol to attack.

'We swooped down upon the swarm of Messerschmitts. It was a "falcon's strike" accompanied by accurate fire from short range. The pilot I attacked reacted with the delay of a split second, but this was enough to undo him. A single burst, fired point-blank, set his aircraft on fire.'

Pokryshkin's achievements were recognised by the award of the Hero of the Soviet Union

The record of air victories gained by the pilots of the 16th Guards Fighter Regiment over the Kuban bears eloquent testimony to the rejuvenation of the Soviet fighter force. Pokryshkin himself was credited with 20 victories during the campaign and his achievements were recognised by the award of the Hero of the Soviet Union on 24 May 1943. Senior-Lieutenant Grigory A. Rechkalov received the same decoration at that time in recognition of his 11 victories. He ended the war as the fourth highest-scoring Soviet air ace, with a total of 56 victories gained in 609 combat missions. Fifteen of N. Ye Lavitskiy's 26 victories were gained with the 16th Guards Fighter Regiment over the Kuban and he too received the highest Soviet award on 24 August 1943. One of the most promising of Pokryshkin's pilots was A.F. Klubov, in whom his commander saw 'the true seed of the born fighter – the ability to impose one's will upon one's adversary.' This confidence was fully justified, for at the time of his death in a flying accident in November 1944, Captain Klubov had gained a total of 50 air victories.

Fine leadership and careful training had brought the pilots of the 16th Guards Fighter Regiment to a peak of efficiency. Pokryshkin had realised that courage alone was no substitute for skilled tactics, and the performance of his regiment showed the way forward for the rest of the Soviet fighter force, in the finest traditions of the Guards units. Pokryshkin continued to serve with the Soviet Air Force after the war, but his finest achievement was without doubt during the spring of 1943 when he did so much to give substance to the Soviet fighter pilot's motto: 'Seek out Your Enemy'.

THE AUTHOR Anthony Robinson was formerly on the staff of the RAF Museum, Hendon and is now a freelance military aviation writer. He has edited the books *Aerial Warfare* and the *Dictionary of Aviation*.

Above: Its wings riddled with machine-gun bullets, a German fighter trails smoke as it dives to destruction. With mounting confidence in their own deadly skills, the hard-pressed pilots of the Soviet Air Force were gradually able to wrest control of the skies away from the Luftwaffe. Losses on both sides were very high, but the Russians, with help from their British and US allies were more able to supply their frontline units with much-needed replacements.

NIGHT WITCHES

When women's air regiments were incorporated into the Soviet Air Force in 1941, the old guard was sceptical. However, the tenacious female pilots dispelled all doubts as they fought to prove their prowess in combat

**Lieutenant Valeria Khomyakova,
Red Air Force, January 1943**

One of the most outstanding pilots with the 586th Fighter Air Regiment, a unit equipped with Yak fighters, Khomyakova wears standard issue clothing. A khaki tunic with lieutenant's collar patches is just visible beneath her black flying overalls. The remainder of her kit comprises a fur-lined leather flying helmet, a parachute harness, leather belt and boots.

IT WAS IN the dark days of October 1941, with victorious German armies advancing on Moscow, that the Soviet Air Force (VVS, or Voenno-vozdushnye sili) conceived the unprecedented idea of forming women's air regiments for combat duty. The Soviet air losses during the early months of the Great Patriotic War had been immense, with some 7500 aircraft destroyed in action by September 1941 and a correspondingly high level of losses amongst trained aircrew. Under such circumstances it was not surprising that the authorities decided to recruit trained women pilots, many of whom had gained considerable experience in the Osoaviakhim (Society for the Support of Defence and of Aviation) sports flying programme before the war. Nonetheless, the decision was regarded with deep suspicion by many traditionally-minded officers of the Soviet Air Force and the women's units were very much on trial until they had proved themselves in combat.

A leading part in the recruitment of women aircrew was taken by the well-known pre-war pilot Marina Raskova. She and two companions had established a long-distance record in 1938, with a flight from Moscow to Komsomolsk-on-Amur, and had been made Heroes of the Soviet Union in recognition of their achievement. An appeal for women volunteers was broadcast by Radio Moscow and resulted in a flood of applications. Raskova interviewed the hopeful candidates in Moscow and those she selected as suitable material were despatched to an airfield at Engels on the Volga for operational training, under the 122nd Composite Air Division. Not only were women recruited as pilots and for other aircrew duties, but they also worked as mechanics and carried out the other necessary support jobs. There were to be three women's regiments, each with a strength of some 400 personnel and, apart from the day-bomber regiment which had some male members, they were entirely 'manned' by women.

The regiments' organisation followed the standard Soviet pattern, each comprising three squadrons, with three regiments making up an air division. The nominal strength of the fighter and night-bomber regiments was 40 aircraft, while the day-bomber regiment was slightly smaller with 32 aircraft. Although initially the women's regiments were grouped together within the 122nd Composite Air Division, when they were ready for action they split up and were assigned to different divisions. The first to enter combat was the 586th Fighter Air Regiment (IAP, or Istrebitelnyy aviatsionnyy polk), under the command of Major Tamara Kazarinova, which had trained on Yak-1 single-seat fighters and later progressed to the improved Yak-7B. It ended the war flying the long-range Yak-9, one of the most successful of the Soviet wartime fighter aircraft. The 587th Bomber Air Regiment (BAP, or Bombardirovochnyy aviatsionnyy polk), initially commanded by Major Marina Raskova herself, was the last of the three regiments to become operational. This was because it flew the twin-engined Petlyakov Pe-2 day-bomber, which was one of the more modern and

Many of the women selected to join the Soviet Air Force had gained their wings in civilian flying schools, where they mastered aircraft maintenance (above left) and parachuting (left centre). Far left: The commander of the 586th Fighter Air Regiment, Lieutenant Valeria Khomyakova, confers with three pilots including Lieutenant Tamara Pamyatnika (second from left). Left: Preparing for a sortie. Page 13 : Major Yevdokia Bershanskaya, commander of the 588th Night Bomber Air Regiment.

WOMEN PILOTS

During the 1930s the opportunities for women in the Soviet Union to learn to fly gliders and powered aircraft increased considerably. The first Russian woman pilot, Lydia Vissarionova Zvereva, had been granted her aviator's certificate as early as 1911. However, it was not until the expansion of Osoaviakhim (a quasi-military organisation responsible for preliminary training for the Soviet Air Force, as well as for generally stimulating public interest in aviation) that many women learned to fly. By 1932 this organisation had more than doubled its membership to a figure of about 11 million, gliding was a mass popular pastime and numerous flying clubs were established for part-time sports pilots.

As in the West, women began to establish themselves in the aviation field. The glider pilot Olga Klepikova set up a distance record in 1939 that was not bettered until 1951, and the three long-distance women pilots Valentina Grizodubov, Palina Osipenko and Marina Raskova became household names. Yet apart from a few women professional pilots in the Civil Air Fleet (GVF or Grazhdanski vozdushny flot), most pre-war flying by women was for recreation.

On the outbreak of war in June 1941, the Civil Air Fleet was absorbed by the Soviet Air Force and the Osoaviakhim schools concentrated on turning out pilots and parachutists for military service. Women were, therefore, involved in non-combat flying with the Soviet Air Force from the outset. Since the work of women in such activities as the army medical service and the air defence force's gun and searchlight crews often brought them into the firing line, it was a logical step to recruit already-trained women for combat, especially since the Soviet Air Force was desperately short of pilots during the early months of the war.

The Eastern Front
1942 – 1944

FINLAND
Helsinki

Leningrad

Volga

EAST
PRUSSIA

SOVIET

• Moscow

Minsk• Smolensk

POLAND

UNION

Bryansk

•Kursk

Zhitomir   • Kiev   • Voronezh

HUNGARY   Dniestr   Vinnitsa   Kharkov   Don

Krivoy Rog,   Dniepr   Stalingrad.

Odessa

RUMANIA   Sea of   • Rostov
           Azov

CRIMEA

Key   BLACK SEA

········ Front line, Nov 1942
— · — Front line, July 1943   **Key**
— ·· — Front line, Nov 1943   German occupation,
— ··· — Front line, April 1944   Nov. 1942
———— Front line, Aug 1944   Soviet control, Nov. 1942

relatively complex aircraft in Soviet service during the early war years. By contrast, the equipment of the 588th Night Bomber Air Regiment (NBAP, or Nochnoy bombardirovochnyy aviatsionnyy polk), commanded by Major Yevdokia Bershanskaya, was the epitome of rugged simplicity – the Polikarpov Po-2 biplane. This in its U-2 version was the standard Soviet training aircraft, but it was also widely used for night-harassing raids.

There were many difficulties to be overcome before the women's regiments were considered ready for combat. Major Bershanskaya recalled that:

'the girls seemed little more than children in many ways. Training was a very difficult time for all of us. Although most of them were good basic raw material, with a certain standard in their various skills, they had an awful lot to learn.'

None of the women took kindly to military discipline, which traditionally was particularly harsh in the Soviet armed forces. They were concerned with preserving their individuality and distinctions of rank were largely ignored by them. None of this helped to remove the doubts of the military traditionalists as to the effectiveness of women's regiments. Nonetheless, the regiments soon developed

into cohesive fighting units and Lieutenant Marina Chichnova of the 588th NBAP recalled that: 'there was so much mutual respect that people just tended to get on with the job without having to be ordered.'

In May 1942 the 586th IAP was deployed to Saratov, a city which lay in the path of the German advance towards the Caucasus and the Caspian oilfields. Its task was to provide air defence cover for the region, both by day and by night. The regiment's first confirmed victory was not gained until September. The successful pilot was Lieutenant Valeria Khomyakova, who sent a Ju 88 bomber down in flames – the first enemy aircraft in the history of air warfare to be shot down by a woman pilot. She later recorded:

'I drew very close to the enemy bomber and squeezed the buttons on the stick to fire my guns. The enemy fired back furiously. Then I watched him go into a steep dive and explode near the railway bridge that was his target. The crew were all killed. The pilot was thrown out. He proved to be a veteran bomber pilot, decorated for bombing towns in Poland, France, the Netherlands and England.'

Khomyakova's background was in many ways typical of that of the Soviet women pilots. The daughter of a chemist, she graduated from the Moscow Institute of Chemical Technology in 1937. By that time she was a qualified glider pilot, and in the following year she

Above: Their engine cowlings bedecked with the insignia of a Guards unit and the Order of the Red Banner, four Yak-9 fighters scour the skies for enemy aircraft. Below: The Yak-9 had a top speed of 371 mph at 13,123ft and was equipped with a single 20mm cannon and one or two 12.7mm machine guns. This agile single-seat fighter was flown by the 586th Fighter Air Regiment. Below, far left: Lieutenant Natalia Meklina, a pilot of the 588th Night Bomber Air Regiment and a Hero of the Soviet Union. Below left: Lieutenant Klavia Fumicheva, a Pe-2 pilot in the 587th Bomber Air Regiment. Far left: Dressed against the biting cold, five Polikarpov Po-2 pilots return from a combat mission.

learned to fly powered aircraft and then became a flying instructor. In the autumn of 1942 she was appointed as an assistant squadron commander, but shortly afterwards she was killed during an interception mission.

The 586th IAP moved to the vicinity of Voronezh in the autumn of 1942 and flew patrols to cover the important road and rail bridges over the Don. The regiment was also called upon to fly strafing missions in support of Soviet armies. With the approach of winter, low temperatures became a problem and the regiment's mechanics had to work through the night to prevent the fighters' engines from freezing solid. Food was also in short supply and pilots and ground-crew alike frequently went hungry. It was at this time that the regiment lost two of its most promising pilots, when Lieutenants Lydia Litvak and Ekaterina Budanova were transferred to the hitherto all-male 73rd Fighter Regiment. This unit was in action over Stalingrad, and, in the fierce battles of that winter and the following year, both women showed outstanding courage and skill. Both died in action during the summer of 1943. Budanova's final score of 11 victories was second only to that of Litvak, who with 12 kills was the leading woman fighter pilot. In the words of a fellow pilot: 'Lydia Litvak was the greatest of all our women pilots. She was unrivalled among Soviet women fighter pilots during the Great Patriotic War. Her achievements were previously thought to have been impossible.'

During their first pass two enemy bombers were sent down in flames

The 586th IAP's greatest test was to come in the summer of 1943 during the Battle of Kursk, when it was heavily engaged in the massive air battles which swirled above the ground fighting. Lieutenant Galia Boordina remembered that: 'the sky was so full of aircraft in such a small area of airspace that it was terrifying.' Two of her fellow pilots, Lieutenants Tamara Pamyatnika and Raissa Surnachevskaya, fought a notable air combat at this time. Flying together, they encountered a formation of more than 40 German bombers. They dived into the attack and during their first pass sent two of the enemy aircraft down in flames. Pamyatnika, who ended the war as a squadron commander with four victories to her credit, described the next moves in the combat:

'This time we attacked from behind and both sides. The enemy retaliated with concentrated

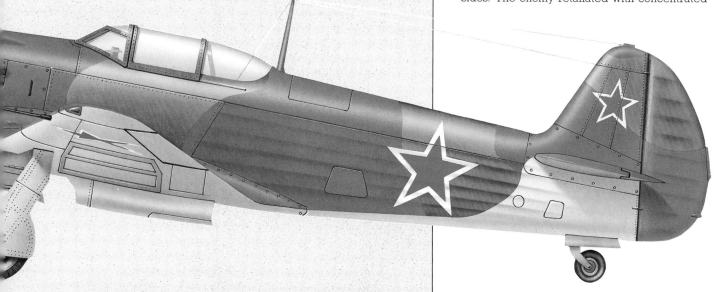

fire. We came up so near to them that I could see the gunner of the rearmost aircraft and even make out his features. I pressed the firing button and saw flames bursting from the Junkers' right wing. Then suddenly my own aircraft jerked, turned over and spun down towards the ground. I tried to slide the cockpit hood open and release my safety straps, but found myself pressed hard back into my seat, while the ground came nearer by the second. Finally, the air pressure tore off the hood; I managed to unfasten the straps and bale out. I felt a jerk as the parachute opened and the next instant I touched the ground. The wreck of my fighter lay burning nearby.'

Flying skill and the cover of darkness were the crews' only protection

The work of the 588th NBAP, while very different in character from that of the fighters, was every bit as hazardous. The night-bombers first saw action in the Voroshilovgrad region in June 1942, becoming part of the Fourth Air Army's 218th Night Bomber Division. A nightly routine of operations was soon established, with relays of Po-2 biplanes flying over the German positions to drop their loads of bombs. They would usually maintain a separation of between five and 15 miles between aircraft, operating at heights of up to 5000ft. Since the Po-2's bomb load was only some 135lb, these raids were primarily of nuisance value, although on occasions significant material damage was inflicted on the enemy. However, the psychological impact of these nightly operations on exhausted troops denied a proper period of sleep was considerable. Operating from rough airstrips near to the front, the Po-2s were so close to their targets that they could fly several sorties in a single night – sometimes as many as 10. Such an effort imposed a tremendous strain on the night-bombers' crews, or 'Night Witches' as they were nicknamed. Night-flying aids were extremely primitive, since the only airstrip lighting was provided by hooded paraffin flares. There was no radio communication with the ground and navigation had to be by dead reckoning or map reading. Flying at a speed of little more than 60 miles per hour, the biplanes were extremely vulnerable to German flak guided by searchlights. Flying skill and the cover of darkness were their crews' only protection. However, the pilots of the 588th NBAP soon became adept at evasive manoeuvres. Sometimes the Po-2s would operate in pairs, with one aircraft acting as a decoy to attract the attention of the flak and searchlights, while the other slipped in unnoticed to deliver its attack. These tactics were found to be especially effective if the Po-2s' targets were the flak batteries themselves.

In January 1943, when the 588th NBAP was operating in the northern Caucasus, the unit was honoured by being awarded the title of Guards Regiment. This was an especially significant distinction, since it acknowledged that the women had fully proved their worth in combat. At a special ceremony the regiment received its Guards' banner and all members took the special oath. Henceforth, they would wear the distinctive Guards' badge on their uniforms and the regiment was retitled the 46th Guards Night Bomber Regiment (46th Guards NBAP). For the greater part of 1943, the unit operated in the Kuban region, where German forces were struggling to maintain a bridgehead in the northern Caucasus in

the aftermath of their defeat at Stalingrad. Their defensive positions, known as the Blue Line, were a frequent target for the Po-2 night-bombers. It was during this campaign that the regiment suffered its most serious casualties of the war: four Po-2s lost in a single night to German night-fighters operating in conjunction with searchlights over the Blue Line. Lieutenant Nadia Popova was piloting the leading aircraft on that night and has vivid memories of being caught in the German searchlights:

'The terror for us of being caught in that light was almost indescribable... I couldn't see the instruments. I couldn't see anything at all. My only chance was a violent manoeuvre. I screwed my eyes tight against the glare, rolled the aircraft upside down and pulled the stick back into my stomach, diving off in the opposite direction. I kept diving and stuck my head down into the cockpit to try to orientate myself. All was pitch blackness again. I'd shaken off the searchlights.'

Popova's skilful flying saved her and her navigator from the German night-fighters, but eight of her comrades had died. The combats took place so near to the front that they were visible from the regiment's airfield. It was a severe blow to the unit and the women felt these losses deeply.

After the German evacuation of the Crimea, the 46th Guards NBAP transferred to the Belorussian Front in the summer of 1944. They then followed the swiftly advancing Soviet armies into Poland, making frequent changes of airfield in order to keep up with the ground fighting. The regiment then began to operate by day on reconnaissance missions, searching for groups of Germans who had been overrun by the Soviet advance and were hiding in the forests. Such bands of desperate men often threatened the Soviet airstrips and on at least one occasion the women had to fight off a night attack. The regiment took part in the operations to occupy Warsaw, Gdynia and Gdansk and it was operating from an airfield just to the northwest of Berlin when Soviet forces occupied the German capital in May 1945.

'I saw one Messerschmitt drop like a stone with a trail of black smoke behind it'

Its sister unit, the 587th BAP, by that time retitled the 125th Guards Regiment, also ended the war supporting the advance on Berlin. The last of the women's units to enter combat, it had received its baptism of fire over Stalingrad in December 1942. Day after day, in the bitter winter weather, it flew bombing missions in support of the troops. Sometimes the bombers had to fight their way through enemy fighters in order to reach their targets. One such combat was described by Lieutenant Klavia Fumicheva, a Hero

of the Soviet Union. Nine Pe-2s, whose fighter escort had been drawn off by German fighters, were attacked by eight Messerschmitt Bf 109s:

'The whole Fascist pack swooped down on our squadron. They wanted to hit the leader, break up the formation and knock us out one by one with impunity. The navigators and radio operator/gunners opened concentrated fire on them with their machine guns. The Nazis turned away, but only to counter-attack us in ones or twos from all directions. The squadron commander slowed down a little to keep the group together in compact formation. As she looked back, she saw everybody in her place, as if nailed down, and tracer bullets from machine guns rising in streams like the spikes of a porcupine... I saw one Messerschmitt drop like a stone with a trail of black smoke behind it.'

Yet it was the weather, rather than enemy action, which caused the regiment its most grievous loss. On 4 January 1943 Major Marina Raskova's bomber crashed while flying through a snowstorm, and she and her crew were killed. She was mourned not only as a much-loved commanding officer, who was known personally by everyone in the three women's regiments, but also as the pioneer aviator whose pre-war exploits had inspired many of the women to take up flying. Her successor, Major Valentine Markov, was a stern and unbending officer of the old

school, who perhaps realised that he could never hope to inspire the same affection as had his predecessor. The regiment transferred to the Caucasus and by the autumn of 1943 had moved again to the Smolensk area. Thereafter, it took part in the campaigns to liberate Belorussia and the Baltic, before finishing the war on the outskirts of Berlin.

The three women's regiments had convincingly vindicated the trust placed in them by the Soviet High Command. The 586th IAP ended the war at Budapest with a total of 38 enemy aircraft destroyed, credited to them in the course of 4419 combat sorties and 125 air battles. The Po-2 bombers of the 125th Guards BAP had delivered a total of 980 tons of bombs onto enemy targets in the course of 1134 combat sorties, and the regiment had been awarded the Order of Suvorov and the Order of Kutuzov in recognition of its wartime service. Yet perhaps the greatest achievement of all was that of the 46th Guards NBAP. Its members had carried out no fewer than 24,000 night sorties and won 23 of the 30 awards of Hero of the Soviet Union made to women aircrew during the Great Patriotic War. Named the 'Taman Regiment' in honour of its operations on the Kuban Front in 1943, the unit was awarded the Order of the Red Banner and the Order of Suvorov for its courage, valour and heroism in action.

THE AUTHOR Anthony Robinson was formerly on the staff of the RAF Museum, Hendon, and is now a freelance military aviation writer. His books include *American Air Power* and *Aerial Warfare*.

LYDIA LITVAK

The most successful woman fighter pilot of the Great Patriotic War and probably the most famous of the Soviet women military pilots, Lydia Litvak was born in Moscow in 1921. At the age of 16 she graduated from the Kherson Flying School and then became a flying instructor. In October 1941 she responded to Marina Raskova's appeal for volunteers and joined the Soviet Air Force. Her great natural ability as a pilot resulted in her assignment as a fighter pilot to the 586th Fighter Air Regiment and she first saw action with this unit in the defence of Saratov in the spring of 1942.

In September 1942 Litvak and Ekaterina Budanova, the most talented of the women fighter pilots, were transferred to a male unit, the 73rd Fighter Regiment, which was operating on the Stalingrad front. Initially they were regarded with considerable distrust by their new commander, but soon demonstrated their abilities as combat pilots. By the end of the year Lydia Litvak had gained six combat victories over Stalingrad, three of them being German fighters. She had adopted the white rose as an emblem, which was painted on her Yak fighter, and her victories were recorded in miniature white roses painted beneath the cockpit (Soviet pilots never used German emblems to record their kills). In March 1943 Litvak claimed her ninth success, shooting down an He 111 bomber, but was herself wounded in the leg. After a brief convalescence, she returned to the 73rd Regiment, which was by then based at Rostov-on-Don, and was promoted to flight commander.

Her brilliant career ended on 1 August 1943, when she was shot down and killed in combat with German fighters. During a period of barely a year, she had claimed 12 enemy fighters destroyed.

ACES OF THE WINTER WAR

THE FINNISH AIR FORCE

In the face of vastly superior Soviet forces, the pilots of the Finnish Air Force fought a heroic struggle in defence of their country

The Finnish Air Force originated in 1918 and consisted initially of a motley collection of imported aircraft. In 1919 a French military mission undertook its reorganisation, but by 1924 the task had fallen to Britain, on whose air force it was modelled, with many instructors and some aircraft supplied by the RAF. The US Navy supplied The Brewster B-239 Buffalo, though by now the Finns were becoming less dependent on imports, and began manufacturing the Fokker D.XXI under licence.

The air force was organised into three regiments, the First (ground support, dive bombing, reconnaissance) made up of four squadrons, each with three flights of four aircraft; the Second (fighter defence) with two squadrons, each of three flights; and the Third (bombing and long-range reconnaissance) with two squadrons, each of three flights. In addition there were two squadrons for naval reconnaissance, three Operational Training Regiments and an Air Combat School. Fighter strength comprised only the two squadrons of Lieutenant-Colonel Riku Lorentz's Flying Regiment 2 (Lentorykmentti 2), and they were responsible not only for the air defence of Finnish cities and towns, but also for providing air cover over the frontline troops. At the beginning of the war, the Finnish Air Force was severely below establishment strength, but they fought hard and inflicted heavy losses on the Red Air Force, claiming 208 victories. Above: The Finnish Air Force pilot qualification badge.

Botton left: Crack fighter pilot Eino Luukkanen, just after his promotion to captain. Altogether he logged 620 hours of combat flying during 440 missions and gained a total of 54 kills. Bottom right: Fighter Group L, at Värtsilä, in 1940. Luukkanen is fifth from the right. Seventh from the right is his deputy, Tatu Huhanantti. An inspired pilot and an excellent marksman, Huhanantti was shot down shortly after this picture was taken. Badly wounded during a fierce conflict, he still managed to ram and bring down one of his Russian opponents during his last moments. Below: A Soviet Yak-7A, brought down on the shore of Lake Laatokka in 1943.

ON 6 OCTOBER 1939 a telegram was delivered to Lieutenant Eino Luukkanen of the Finnish Air Force: 'Leave cancelled. Report to unit immediately!' He packed quickly and within the hour was aboard a train heading for Utti and his squadron, his mind racing with speculation. He reached the base early the following morning to discover that, as a result of continual Soviet demands for Finnish soil, Finland had begun to mobilise. Luukkanen's squadron had received instructions to transfer immediately to the Immola airfield near the vital Imatra power stations, and attain full combat readiness with speed.

The Winter War between the Soviet Union and Finland opened on 30 November 1939 with an all-out Soviet ground offensive across the Finnish border and heavy bomber raids on Helsinki and other towns in southern Finland. With 19 divisions, five armoured brigades and 800 tanks, the Soviets poured in. The Finns, with only nine divisions, 100 tanks and one quarter the manpower fought back valiantly using highly mobile guerrilla tactics. It was nothing less than a sheer David-and-Goliath struggle.

In the air, the odds were even more daunting. Fighter pilots were pitted against overwhelming superiority of airpower: the Finnish Air Force could muster only 114 operational aircraft to meet an initial attack by some 900 Soviet planes. Finland was a tiny nation standing alone. However, if the Soviet commanders anticipated an easy victory, they were soon to be disillusioned. The Finns, fighting for the independence of their homeland, in atrocious weather conditions and over territory that they knew well,

proved to be formidable enemies.

On the day of the first Russian offensive, the Finnish Flying Squadron 24 (Lentolaivue 24) was equipped with Fokker D.XXI monoplanes, while its sister unit, Flying Squadron 26, was in the process of converting from elderly Bristol Bulldog Mk IVA biplanes to the newer fighters. It was decided that the two flights of Flying Squadron 26 equipped with D.XXIs would be transferred to Flying Squadron 24,

THE WINTER WAR

During the winter of 1939-40, after the fall of Poland and before the German invasion of Norway, only in a corner of Finland was there decisive fighting. In 1938 Russia had requested permission to build air and naval bases on Finnish soil. Requests turned to demands, and relations became increasingly strained until, in the autumn of 1939, the Finnish government ordered mobilisation in response to the Soviet occupation of Estonia, Latvia and Lithuania.

Then came the infamous Mainila Incident. The Russians claimed that Finnish border guards had fired across the border, killing a Russian NCO and several troops. As a direct result, on 30 November 1939, Russia launched an all-out attack on Finland which became known as the Winter War.

Facing 19 Soviet divisions and five armoured brigades, Marshal Carl von Mannerheim, the Finnish commander, had only nine divisions, and only 100 tanks with which to confront 800 Soviet machines. But, familiar with low temperatures, well disciplined and imaginatively led, the Finnish troops became known to their enemy as the 'white death' after their white camouflage smocks for winter operations.

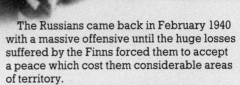

The Russians came back in February 1940 with a massive offensive until the huge losses suffered by the Finns forced them to accept a peace which cost them considerable areas of territory.

From March 1940 until June 1941 the country enjoyed peace. Russia, however, again began attacking Finland over rights of passage granted to German supplies, and Finland's agreement with Germany to mount attacks in the Lake Ladoga area to coincide with Operation Barbarossa. The War of Continuation commenced. The final onslaught came in June 1944, when the Russians unleashed tremendous forces, and the Finnish government was forced to yield.

thus bringing its strength up to five flights. A single flight of 10 Bulldogs remained with Squadron 26, and despite being hopelessly outclassed by the majority of Soviet aircraft, the Bulldogs succeeded in gaining four victories before they were replaced by more modern Gloster Gladiators and Fiat G.50s in January and February 1940. Initially, however, the 35 Fokker D.XXIs of Flying Squadron 24, based at Immola, were forced to bear the brunt of the air fighting.

The commander of Squadron 24 was Captain Gustaf Erik Magnusson, who was himself to gain four air victories during the Winter War and to receive Finland's highest decoration, the Mannerheim Cross, in 1944. The 1st Flight was commanded by Captain E. Carlsson; the 2nd Flight, which was detached to the airfield at Suur-Merijoki, by Lieutenant Vuorela; and the 3rd Flight by Lieutenant Eino Luukkanen. All had six fighters on strength. The 4th Flight, led by Magnusson himself, had seven D.XXIs. Lieutenant L. Ahola's 5th Flight was the strongest, with 10 fighters. Each flight was able to operate as an independent unit away from the squadron. In addition to its pilots, both commissioned and non-commissioned officers, the flights were assigned some 30 groundcrew. The work of these technicians had to be carried out in sub-zero temperatures, in the open air and often under poor light conditions.

On 30 November 1939, the first day of the Winter War, Flying Squadron 24 had little success. A flight of

Fokker D.XXIs was scrambled to intercept a Russian bomber raid on Viipuri, but missed the enemy aircraft. Icy winds and intermittent snowstorms added to the defenders' difficulties, often making flying impossible. The following day, Lieutenant Luukkanen and his wingman, Flight Master Viktor Pyotsia, were on patrol in the Imatra area, when they spotted a pair of Soviet bombers, and gave immediate pursuit. Luukkanen recalled:

'Quite rapidly the nearest bomber grew in my

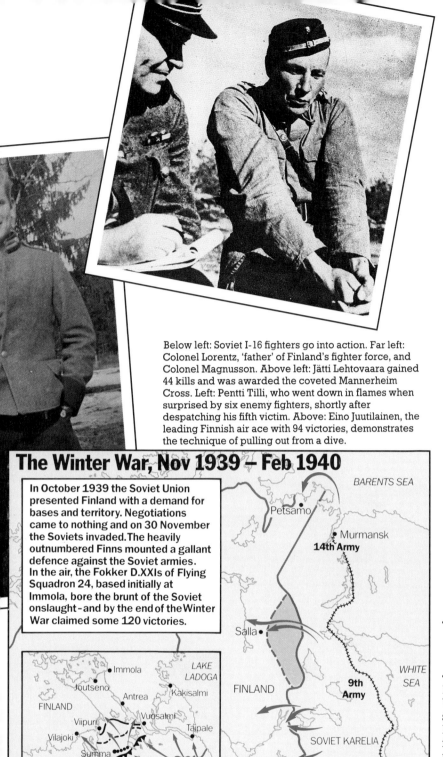

Below left: Soviet I-16 fighters go into action. Far left: Colonel Lorentz, 'father' of Finland's fighter force, and Colonel Magnusson. Above left: Jätti Lehtovaara gained 44 kills and was awarded the coveted Mannerheim Cross. Left: Pentti Tilli, who went down in flames when surprised by six enemy fighters, shortly after despatching his fifth victim. Above: Eino Juutilainen, the leading Finnish air ace with 94 victories, demonstrates the technique of pulling out from a dive.

The Winter War, Nov 1939 – Feb 1940

In October 1939 the Soviet Union presented Finland with a demand for bases and territory. Negotiations came to nothing and on 30 November the Soviets invaded. The heavily outnumbered Finns mounted a gallant defence against the Soviet armies. In the air, the Fokker D.XXIs of Flying Squadron 24, based initially at Immola, bore the brunt of the Soviet onslaught – and by the end of the Winter War claimed some 120 victories.

Key

Ceded to Soviet Union in 1940

→ Soviet offensives, Nov 1939 – Jan 1940

Mannerheim Line
—— Rear position
– – – Intermediate position
•••••• Summa position
vvvvv Forward position

BARENTS SEA
Petsamo
Murmansk
14th Army
Salla
LAKE LADOGA
Immola
Joutseno
Antrea
Kakisalmi
FINLAND
Viipuri
Vuosalmi
Vilajoki
Taipale
Summa
GULF OF FINLAND
SOVIET UNION
WHITE SEA
9th Army
SOVIET KARELIA
Kuhmo
SOVIET UNION
Värtsilä
8th Army
KARELIA
Tampere
Joutseno
Immola
LAKE LADOGA
Viipuri
SWEDEN
Turku
Helsinki
GULF OF FINLAND
13th Army
ESTONIA
7th Army

sights. Four hundred, three hundred, two hundred, one hundred yards. Never had my feet been planted more firmly on the rudder pedals, my hands gripped the control column so tightly, or my eyes been glued so closely to the gunsight as at that moment. I depressed the firing trigger and saw my tracers curve in towards the bomber. Simultaneously, brilliant orange flashes danced in front of my windscreen. The dorsal gunner was pumping away at me for all he was worth! The target now completely filled my sight, and I was forced to break sharply to starboard to avoid a collision. Pulling the Fokker around, I again lined up the bomber in my sight. The dorsal gunner was still blazing away at me – his tracers winking all around my fighter. But in the excitement of the moment I felt no sense of danger. I edged in to make absolutely sure of my opponent.

'Our altitude was down to 500ft by this time, and suddenly several large objects tumbled away from the bomber. The pilot had decided to jettison his bombload to lighten the aircraft, and the blast from the bombs tossed my little Fokker around like a piece of straw in a high wind. Once again I positioned myself on the bomber's tail. A little more throttle and he was squarely in my sight. Now I could not possibly miss!

'I depressed the firing trigger, but just as my burst began raking along the rear fuselage, the pilot of the bomber lowered his undercarriage which, acting as an air brake, slowed the aircraft immediately, forcing me to pull up the nose of the Fokker to avoid ramming the Russian amidships. This pilot evidently knew his stuff. I had no intention of being caught a second time, however, and I swung in to the attack once more, throttling back to match my speed with that of the bomber. I loosed a long burst into the starboard engine from a distance of no more than 50yds, and dirty grey smoke belched back from the cowling. The airscrew windmilled momentarily, came to a standstill, and the bomber nosed down, just cleared a clump of trees and pancaked in a small field.'

The tail gunner was blazing away at me but in the excitement of the moment I felt no danger

It was the first Finnish fighter victory of the Winter War. Pyotsia had carried out two firing passes at the second bomber, but it then escaped into the clouds. However, the warrant officer pilot was to have further opportunities for combat during the following months, and he ended the Winter War as the second highest-scoring Finnish ace with 7½ victories. By the end of the day, Flying Squadron 24 had claimed a further nine Soviet bombers for the loss of only one Fokker D.XXI, the commanding officer, Captain Magnusson, being one of the successful pilots.

The weather worsened on 2 December, and heavy snowstorms put an end to all flying. On the ground, the Finnish soldiers repulsed all assaults on the Mannerheim Line, which defended the Karelian isthmus, and north of Lake Ladoga mobile troops claimed humiliating defeats on much stronger Soviet columns. The Finns swooped in on skis to pick off Russian units, and snipers inflicted heavy casualties on badly organised Russian soldiers. The snowstorms ceased on 18 December, and a freeze set in, allowing air operations to resume once the Fokker D.XXIs' wheeled undercarriages had been replaced by skis. During a patrol on that same morning,

however, one of the precious fighters was lost. Lieutenant Luukkanen's plane was hit by friendly groundfire:

'My fuel was all but gone. The engine coughed once more and then died completely. I approached a ploughed field in a steep glide, but my calculations were thrown out by some telephone lines which suddenly popped up in front, forcing me to jam down the nose of the Fokker to scrape beneath them. The skis hit the ground with a tremendous thwack, shaking every bone in my body, my straps cutting into my shoulders.

'The aircraft bounded 100ft into the air, then dropped back onto the skis with a second jarring crash. I had about as much control as I would have had over an unbroken horse. The rudder no longer had any effect, and the nose plunged into a deep drainage ditch. Everything was suddenly eerily still. The Fokker's wings straddled the ditch, its tail pointing skywards, and I hung from my safety belt about 10ft from the ground.'

His 3rd Flight was thus reduced to five planes, until a replacement arrived on 23 December. The air war was intensifying.

The pilot was shocked by the sight of a Russian airman impaled on one of his wing guns

Two days after Luukkanen's crash landing, on 19 December, Flying Squadron 24 intercepted a bomber formation escorted by Polikarpov I-16 fighters, and accounted for 11 of the bombers and two of the escort, at no loss to themselves. The 3rd Flight, led by Luukkanen's deputy, Lieutenant Tatu Huhanantti, claimed five of these victories. One of the successful pilots was Sergeant Eino 'Illu' Juutilainen, who shot down an Ilyushin DB-3 for his first victory. When the Continuation War ended in September 1944, he had become Finland's top scoring fighter pilot with a total of 94 victories. Another pilot of the 3rd Flight who claimed a bomber shot down in this combat was Sergeant Pentti Tilli. He had just completed his attack when a violent blow on the wing slewed his aircraft to the right. Looking out of his cockpit, Tilli was shocked by the gruesome sight of a Russian airman impaled on one of his wing guns.

He had great difficulty in dislodging this unwelcome burden, and control was extremely difficult with the Russian's parachute streaming back from the wing. Gradually, the parachute disintegrated, and the body finally dropped clear, leaving Tilli to

bring his fighter back to base with only a tear in the wing fabric. On the following day, Lieutenant Huhanantti claimed his first victory when Flying Squadron 24's base at Immola came under attack. All six pilots of the 3rd Flight had then at least one enemy aircraft to their credit.

The squadron was airborne in force on 23 December, when 18 Fokker D.XXIs covered a Finnish withdrawal on the Summa front: 11 Soviet planes were shot down for the loss of one D.XXI. Two days later the 3rd Flight, reinforced by two pilots and their fighters from the 1st Flight, was ordered to Värtsilä in order to provide cover for the troops of IV Corps fighting north of Lake Ladoga. This detachment was known as Fighter Group L (Osasto L), taking the initial letter of its commander Luukkanen's surname as its designation. On 28 December 1939, Flying Squadron 24's headquarters transferred from Immola to Joutseno on the border. During a number of engagements, the D.XXIs regularly found themselves in brief, but furious, free-for-alls with the nimble Russian I-15 fighters. But despite the vastly superior manoeuvrability of these little biplanes, the Finnish pilots' sharper eyes and skilful flying easily redressed the balance.

By the end of the year, Flying Squadron 24 was credited with 10 Soviet fighters destroyed out of its total victory claims of 50 enemy aircraft. Luukkanen describes a wild dogfight with I-16s:

'Finnish and Russian pilots alike firing quick bursts every time an opponent flashed fleetingly across their sights. One moment I had a Russian fighter squarely in my sights and the next I was frenziedly endeavouring to avoid their fire. Time and again the tables were turned in that whirling conflict, but the bursts were short as aiming was difficult under such conditions, the fight actually taking place amongst the treetops.'

One of the most remarkable combats of the war was fought on 6 January 1940, when two D.XXIs intercepted a formation of seven Ilyushin DB-3s and shot all of them down. Six of the bombers fell to the guns of Lieutenant Jorma Sarvanto of the 4th Flight, who disregarded return fire from the enemy gunners, and consequently returned to base with his fighter riddled with bullet holes. It was only after Sarvanto had run out of ammunition that Lieutenant Per Erik Sovelius finished off the surviving bomber in the formation for his second victory of the day. Sarvanto ended the Winter War with 12 victories plus two shared kills, and was the top scoring Finnish pilot of the conflict.

Above: Brewster B-239 Buffaloes carrying the famous Lynx emblem, still used by Fighter Squadron 31. Far right: One of Squadron 24's Fokker D.XXIs, after landing with a ski damaged by Russian fire. Right: A Gloster Gladiator II, newly arrived from England, in 1940. Below: Luukkanen's own D.XXI. The Finns produced a total of 93 D.XXIs under licence. Other aircraft came from France, Italy and Germany. In fact, it was said that Japan was virtually the only aircraft manufacturer not represented – including Russia!

Flying Squadron 24 did not achieve its remarkable successes without loss, however. The unit's first serious casualty came on 20 January, a day on which eight Soviet bombers were shot down. One of the victors was Sergeant Tilli, who had just accounted for a Tupolev SB-2, and was attacking a second, when he was bounced by six enemy fighters. His Fokker D.XXI crashed in flames and Tilli was killed. The 22-year-old pilot had five victories to his credit.

January was a period of severe winter weather, even by Finnish standards. It was 40 below. The Soviet army took advantage of a lull in the fighting to strengthen and reorganise their forces, and during the same period, the air forces were boosted to a strength of some 1500 aircraft. Reinforcements were also reaching the Finnish Air Force, though on a much more modest scale. Fiat G.50

THE FOKKER D.XXI

Although it was the most modern fighter in Finnish service, the Fokker D.XXI was not a particularly advanced design by world standards. It was, however, a complete breakaway from previous Fokker biplane and high-wing monoplane designs. A low-wing monoplane with a fixed undercarriage, the D.XXI was powered by an 830hp Bristol Mercury VIII single-radial engine, which gave it a top speed of 460km/h and a range of 950km. Armament comprised four 7.92mm machine guns, with 300 rounds per gun.

The prototype had first flown in the Netherlands on 27 March 1936, and Finland acquired seven aircraft the following year. Licenced production then began at the Finnish State Aircraft Factory in Tampere. Finnish D.XXIs had all four guns mounted in the wings instead of two in the upper cowling and two in the wings, and most were fitted with 'snow shoe' landing gear during the winter. The Finnish pilots found the fighter to be a steady gun platform. However, it was not without its faults, for example, it was prone to high-speed stalls with little or no warning to its pilot. Yet, once in combat, the Finns found that the sturdy Dutch fighter could absorb considerable battle damage.

Left: Nils 'Hard Luck' Katajainen, with his first scoreboard. His nickname was ironic; with 'more lives than a cat', he survived the war and made 36 kills.

and Morane Saulnier M.S.406 fighters arrived from Western Europe. Britain sent 30 Gloster Gladiator IIs, but despite their extreme agility, these were found too slow, lacking in firepower, and tended to burn easily.

Foreign volunteers also turned up, including a complete Swedish squadron equipped with Gladiators and Hawker Harts. Among the first foreign pilots to arrive was a group of Danes, several of whom served with Flying Squadron 24. One of the Danes, Lieutenant E. Frijs, was credited with one and a half victories when flying Fokker D.XXIs. Yet, welcome as this additional strength was, it could not fully compensate for the increased aggressiveness of the vastly more numerous Soviet air forces.

In early February 1940, the Soviet army launched a massive assault on the Mannerheim Line, which it threatened to breach by sheer weight of numbers. Fighter Group L was quickly redeployed from Värtsilä to Ruokolahti, where it operated from the frozen Lake Saimaa over the Karelian isthmus front. 'Enemy fighters had begun to range over our bases,' recalled Luukkanen, 'and the Russians had learned so much during the conflict that we seemed to be fighting an entirely different enemy.' In the middle of the month, Luukkanen was promoted to captain, and his unit was reinforced by a flight of Gladiators from Flying Squadron 26, remaining detached from the rest of Flying Squadron 24 at Joutseno. On 29 February, Fighter Group L's D.XXIs and Gladiators were surprised just after take-off by some 40 Soviet I-153 and I-16 fighters. Caught thus at a serious disadvantage, the Finnish pilots suffered their most serious defeat of the Winter War. Five Gladiators were shot down, and only two of their pilots managed to parachute to safety. Lieutenant Tatu Huhanantti was killed when, after being badly wounded, he crashed his Fokker D.XXI into one of his opponents. He had previously gained six aerial victories.

As the Soviet armies advanced towards Viipuri, Flying Squadron 24 was forced to pull back to Lemi on 1 March, where it was joined by Fighter Group L. By that time it was clear that the Fokker D.XXI was less able to deal with the Soviet fighters than the newer Fiat G.50s and M.S.406s. Accordingly, for the last two weeks of the Winter War, Flying Squadron 24 switched its operations to ground strafing and escorts to the Bristol Blenheim bombers. 'These strafing sorties were undoubtedly the toughest missions we had been assigned,' thought Luukkanen, 'and we feared them.' On 13 March, Finland recognised the hopelessness of its position, and concluded an armistice with the Soviet Union.

The country's gallant resistance in the face of impossible odds had captured the imagination of the world. Flying Squadron 24 had borne the brunt of the fighter combat for most of the war, and was credited with some 120 air victories for the loss of only 11 Fokker D.XXIs. This fine fighting record was maintained by the squadron during the Continuation War of 1941-44, when it gained a further 781 victories.

THE AUTHOR Anthony Robinson was formerly on the staff of the RAF Museum, Hendon, and is now a freelance military aviation writer. he has edited the books *Aerial Warfare* and the *Dictionary of Aviation*.

Fighter pilot, Finnish Air Force 1939-40

This pilot wears the blue Finnish Air Force service dress and black riding boots. His cap bears the Finnish Air Force emblem – winged propeller over a gold Finnish lion – and the stripes on his sleeve denote the rank of captain.

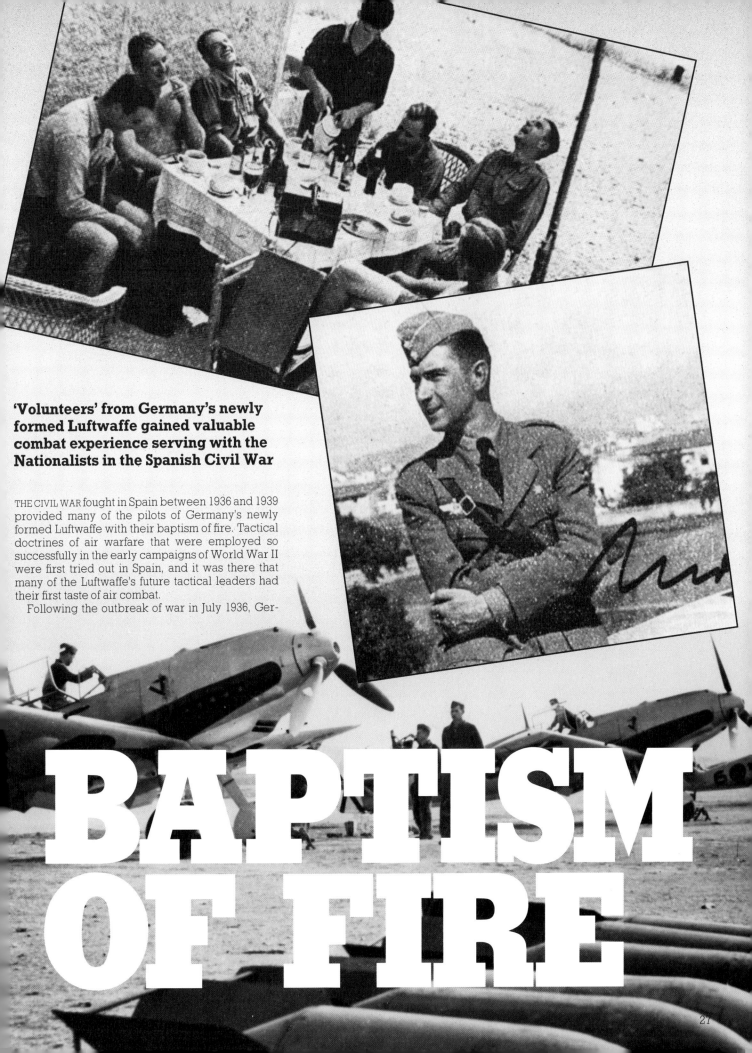

'Volunteers' from Germany's newly formed Luftwaffe gained valuable combat experience serving with the Nationalists in the Spanish Civil War

THE CIVIL WAR fought in Spain between 1936 and 1939 provided many of the pilots of Germany's newly formed Luftwaffe with their baptism of fire. Tactical doctrines of air warfare that were employed so successfully in the early campaigns of World War II were first tried out in Spain, and it was there that many of the Luftwaffe's future tactical leaders had their first taste of air combat.

Following the outbreak of war in July 1936, Ger-

BAPTISM
OF FIRE

many was quick to offer help to Franco's Nationalist forces. Initially, 20 Junkers Ju 52/3m transport aircraft ferried Nationalist troops from Morocco to the Spanish mainland. A number of these aircraft then switched to the bomber role, carrying out an attack on the Republican battleship *Jaime I* in Málaga harbour on 14 August. In the same month, six Heinkel He 51

fighters, together with pilot instructors and groundcrew, were shipped to Cádiz. It was intended that they should equip and train a Nationalist fighter unit, but as Spanish pilots had difficulty in mastering the German biplanes, they were operated instead by the Luftwaffe. This unit, known after its commander as Jagdstaffel (Fighter Squadron) Eberhard, had gained six aerial victories by the end of the month.

German aid to the Nationalist cause was stepped up with the arrival of reinforcements in September. Two months later it was increased further with the formation of the Condor Legion, and soon afterwards Jagdstaffel Eberhard was absorbed by the Legion's fighter wing, Jagdgruppe 88.

Considerable secrecy surrounded the deployment of German airmen to Spain. Friends and relatives could only write to them care of 'Max Winkler, Berlin SW 68', a cover address for the Air Ministry's Special Branch W, which dealt with Condor Legion personnel matters. On arrival in Spain, the 'volunteers' were issued with a Spanish-style uniform and assumed a temporary rank one grade higher than

Page 27 : The Condor Legion encompassed all the German air units operating in Spain. A group of German pilots (top) relax between missions. Until the Legion received Bf 109s (bottom), German fighter pilots had to cut their teeth in combat with He 51s against superior Soviet I-16s. Top-scoring ace of the Legion was Werner Mölders (centre).

that which they held in the Luftwaffe. Even their comrades in Germany knew little of what was happening in Spain. Oberleutnant (Lieutenant) Adolf Galland, who was himself to join the Condor Legion in May 1937, recalled that:

'One or other of our comrades vanished suddenly into thin air without our having heard anything about his transfer orders and after about six months he returned, sunburnt and in high spirits. He bought himself a new car and in the greatest secrecy told his closest friends the most remarkable stories about Spain, where World War II was being rehearsed on a small scale.'

Until the appearance of Soviet Polikarpov I-15 biplanes and I-16 monoplanes in Republican service during November 1936, the He 51 had been well able to hold its own in air combat. Its opponents had been for the most part French-supplied fighters, such as the Nieuport-Delage NiD 52, Dewoitine D.372 and Spad S.510 flown by Spanish Republicans or foreign volunteers – the latter often ill-disciplined mercenaries attracted by high rates of pay. One of the original Jagdstaffel Eberhard pilots, Oberleutnant Knüppel, had gained five victories by November and Leutnants (2nd Lieutenants) Trautloft, Henrici and von Howald all had four victories at that time. However, on 6 November the Jagdstaffel was surprised by a superior force of I-15s and I-16s. In the ensuing combat, Oberleutnant Eberhard was killed when his He 51 collided with an I-15, and Leutnant Henrici received wounds from which he later died. It was clear that the agile and well-armed enemy fighters, flown by experienced and disciplined

Right: Strict secrecy surrounded the deployment of German airmen to Spain, who normally travelled in the guise of tourists. Here, newly arrived pilots, still in civilian clothes, are greeted by their comrades.

Above: A Condor Legion Messerschmitt Bf 109 fighter makes a low-level attack on Republican positions. Below right: German pilots confer over a map before setting out on a mission.

The Condor Legion was formed in November 1936, some four months after the outbreak of the Spanish Civil War, and quickly absorbed existing German air units operating in support of the Nationalist cause. The Legion's first commander was General-major Hugo Sperrle, and his force was made up of fighter, bomber and reconnaissance Gruppen (wings), with additional coastal reconnaissance floatplanes and associated flak, signals and other support units.

Each unit was identified by the number '88', the bomber element being Kampfgruppe 88, the fighters Jagdgruppe 88, and the reconnaissance unit Aufklarungsgruppe 88. The Condor Legion's fighter force, Jagdgruppe 88, was made up initially of three Staffeln, each of which had an established strength of twelve He 51 fighter aircraft.

Jagdgruppe 88's Gruppenkommandeur was Hauptmann von Merhart, with Oberleutnant Harro Harder commanding the 1st Staffel, Oberleutnant Lehmann commanding the 2nd Staffel, and Oberleutnant Douglas Pitcairn – a German officer of Scottish descent – commanding the 3rd Staffel. The Legion's fighter wing was soon increased in strength to four Staffeln when Jagdstaffel Eberhard, a fighter unit that was already operating in Spain with He 51s, was absorbed by Jagdgruppe 88.

Above: The cuff title worn by Luftwaffe personnel who saw service in the Condor Legion.

Soviet 'volunteers', were in every respect superior to the German He 51s. Consequently, their replacement became a matter of extreme urgency.

On 9 December Leutnant Hannes Trautloft was ordered to report to Tablada airfield near Seville, where he was to carry out an evaluation of the new

The Spanish Civil War
July 1936 – Mar 1939

Key
Republican, July 1936
Nationalist, July 1936

The Spanish Civil War broke out in July 1936. At the start of the war, the country was evenly divided, with the Nationalists strong in north and southwest Spain, and the Republicans holding the Basque country in the far north, Catalonia, and central and southern Spain. Germany's military aid to the Nationalists included the Luftwaffe's Condor Legion which saw action from November 1936 until the war ended with a Nationalist victory in March 1939.

enable the Condor Legion to regain air superiority over the Republicans. Trautloft's tour of duty ended in February 1937, and on his return to Germany he was able to report his views to Hitler in person.

Priority was given to the supply of sufficient Bf 109s for the Condor Legion to allow a single Staffel of Jagdgruppe 88 to be re-equipped. Sixteen Bf 109Bs from the first production batch arrived in Spain during March 1937. The Gruppe's 2nd Staffel re-equipped and was operational by the following month. Surplus He 51s were passed on to the Nationalist air force, and after that the remaining German biplanes were used primarily for ground attack missions, leaving air combat to the high-performance Bf 109s. At the same time a new Staffel-kapitän (Squadron Leader) was appointed to command Jagdgruppe 88's 2nd Staffel: Oberleutnant Günther 'Franzl' Lützow, a tall, haughty-looking man

Messerschmitt Bf 109 fighter. Three prototypes had been shipped to Spain and the Condor Legion's chief of staff, Oberstleutnant (Lieutenant-Colonel) Freiherr Wolfram von Richthofen, a cousin of the World War I ace, was anxious to establish whether the type could provide an adequate replacement for the He 51s. Trautloft was well qualified to carry out the trials. One of the original instructor pilots who arrived in Spain in August 1936, he had acquired considerable combat experience. Trautloft held the dubious honour of being the first Luftwaffe pilot to be shot down in the Civil War. That mission, on 13 August, had started well with a successful attack on a Republican Potez 540 bomber. However, Trautloft had been so intent on his victim that he did not see an enemy Dewoitine D.370 closing in on him. The Republican fighter's first burst of fire was effective and Trautloft had to bale out of his crippled He 51.

For a pilot of Trautloft's considerable bulk, the cockpit of the Bf 109 was extremely cramped, but he was greatly impressed with the fighter's overall performance and became convinced that it would

Below: The wreck of a Republican Polikarpov I-16 fighter, destroyed during a Condor Legion attack on an enemy airfield at Villajuiga in Catalonia. Right: The personal Bf 109 of Gruppenkommandeur Hauptmann Gotthardt Handrick, commander of Jagdgruppe 88, the Condor Legion's fighter wing, from July 1937 onwards.

Bottom left: Three of the Condor Legion's distinguished pilots. From left to right are Wolfgang Schellmann, Harro Harder, and Werner Mölders. Bottom right: A flight of Condor Legion Heinkel He 51s. The He 51 biplane was the Condor Legion's workhorse fighter. Inferior in every respect to the enemy's Soviet-built Polikarpov I-15 and I-16 fighters, it was gradually superseded by the Bf 109.

who was remembered by a fellow fighter pilot as 'a real gentleman with a fine sense of humour'. Lützow claimed the Bf 109's first victory in Spain on 14 April, when he shot down an I-15 over the Northern Front. However, it was not until July, with the fierce fighting around Brunete, that the Bf 109 became heavily engaged in air battles with the Republicans.

During the battle of Brunete, the Bf 109Bs were required to fly three or four missions daily, and these usually resulted in combat with enemy aircraft. Generally, the Bf 109s provided high-level escorts for bomber and reconnaissance aircraft at altitudes of around 20,000ft. The German fighter had a better ceiling than its Soviet opponents, and it was faster both at higher altitudes and in a dive than the I-16. Conversely, the Soviet fighters were considerably more manoeuvrable, and the I-16 had a better rate of climb. Armament of both the Bf 109B and the I-16 Type 5 comprised twin machine guns mounted above the engines, but the Soviet 7.62mm ShKAS weapon had a higher muzzle velocity and higher rate of fire than the German 7.9mm MG 17. The Luftwaffe pilots accordingly sought to exploit the good qualities of their fighters by engaging the Republican formations from superior altitude in diving attacks. Using these tactics, they could often pick off inex-

perienced opponents before the rest of the enemy formation had a chance to react. Among the most successful German pilots at this time were Leutnant Rolf Pingel, who scored four victories in Spain, and Feldwebel (Sergeant) Wilhelm-Peter Boddem, who gained a total score of nine victories.

Republican bombers frequently attacked the 2nd Staffel's airfield at Avila and during one such raid on 23 July the Bf 109Bs scrambled to intercept. Such was their success that not a single bomb fell on the airfield and Feldwebel Boddem succeeded in shooting down one of the bombers. In addition to the strain of flying numerous escort missions and airfield defence sorties, the pilots had to endure intense heat, with daytime temperatures sometimes rising as high as 46 degrees Centigrade. Oberleutnant Adolf Galland, who became Staffelkapitän of the He 51-equipped 3rd Staffel in the summer of 1937, remembered that 'on hot days we flew in bathing trunks and on returning from a sortie looked like coalminers, dripping with sweat, smeared with oil and blackened by powder smoke'. The work of the groundcrews, refuelling and re-arming the fighters in such heat, was equally arduous. By the following December, the crews had to contend with extreme cold, and when night-time temperatures fell to minus 20 degrees Centigrade they had to run the fighters' engines periodically throughout the night to prevent the oil from freezing.

The German policy of rotating pilots through the Condor Legion brought about numerous command

The Spanish Civil War provided a highly effective training ground for the Luftwaffe fighter leaders of World War II. Werner Mölders, on his return to Germany, was especially influential in training the Luftwaffe fighter units in radical new tactics based on the four-aircraft Schwarme which gave German airmen considerable advantages in the early campaigns of World War II.

Mölders fought in the Battle of Britain as Kommodore of Jagdgeschwader 51 and was the first pilot of any nationality to shoot down more than 100 enemy aircraft – his final score was 115. At the age of 28, Mölders was appointed General of Fighters, but in November 1941 he died in an air crash. Mölders' successor was Adolf Galland who had continued to develop the Luftwaffe's tactics of close air support on his return from Spain and commanded a ground attack unit during the Polish campaign of September 1939.

Galland never abandoned his hope of returning to air combat and, once he achieved this ambition, his rise was meteoric. In August 1940 he became Kommodore of Jagdgeschwader 26. After his dismissal as General of Fighters in January 1945, Galland formed and led the jet-equipped Jagdverband 44, ending the war with 103 victories.

Günther Lützow and Hannes Trautloft, like Mölders, played an important part in training the Luftwaffe's young fighter pilots for the coming war, and both later served as colonels on Galland's staff. Many other Condor Legion veterans rose to the command of Gruppen (wings) or Geschwadern (squadrons) during World War II, including Balthasar, von Bonin, Oesau, Pingel, Schellmann and Schlichting.

changes within Jagdgruppe 88 during the latter half of 1937. In July, Hauptmann (Captain) Gotthardt Handrick, a Gold Medal Winner at the 1936 Berlin Olympics, became Gruppenkommandeur (Wing Commander). The spinner of his personal Bf 109 was decorated with the Olympic five rings symbol. Later in the year the veteran Staffelkapitän of Jagdgruppe 88's 1st Staffel, Oberleutnant Harro Harder, returned to Germany. At that time his 10 victories represented the highest score of a German pilot in Spain and only two of his comrades were to better it. His place was filled by transferring Lützow from the 2nd Staffel, as the 1st Staffel was by then converting to Bf 109Bs and an experienced commander was needed. Lützow's replacement, Oberleutnant Joachim Schlichting, returned to Germany in November 1937 and command

Pilot, Condor Legion, Spain 1939

This pilot wears a German RAD uniform, re-tailored for the Condor Legion, and German officers' boots. On his right breast pocket is a German 'Spanish Cross' and above, a Spanish Air Force pilot's brevet.

of the 2nd Staffel then passed to Oberleutnant Wolfgang Schellmann. Schellmann was to end his tour of duty in Spain with 12 victories.

While their comrades exploited the Bf 109's high performance, the pilots of Adolf Galland's 3rd Staffel soldiered on with He 51s in the ground-attack role – a state of affairs that Galland saw as 'most regrettable, since air combat after all gives the best proof of a fighter pilot's ability and skill'. Nonetheless, Galland's work in Spain was to gain him a high reputation in the development of the Luftwaffe's close air support tactics.

In January 1938 Jagdgruppe 88 recorded its 100th air victory, a fitting opening to a year of hard fighter combat which firmly established the ascendancy of the Condor Legion's fighter force over the Republicans. During the closing stages of the battle of Teruél, the Legion's Bf 109Bs fought one of their most successful actions of the war. On 7 February Hauptmann Handrick was leading the 1st and 2nd Staffeln on a bomber escort mission, when they encountered a large formation of some 20 Republican Tupolev SB-2 bombers. As there was no sign of a fighter escort, the Bf 109s tore into the enemy bombers. Several SB-2s fell burning to earth after the first firing pass. Then, belatedly, three squadrons of the Republican I-16 fighters intervened in a futile attempt to prevent the carnage. A confused mêlée developed as the Bf 109s switched their attention to the agile I-16s. Yet the Republican pilots had little inclination to stay and fight and after a few minutes they broke off combat. Two I-16s and 10 of the SB-2 bombers had fallen to the German fighter pilots, for no loss to themselves. On the same day Leutnant Wilhelm Balthasar succeeded in shooting down four enemy aircraft in a single sortie, when he intercepted an escorted bomber raid on Jagdgruppe 88's airfield at Calamocha. This tremendous feat of arms was unequalled by any other Condor Legion pilot and Balthasar ended the war with seven victories.

The long-awaited re-equipping of the 3rd Staffel with the Bf 109 came in June 1938, its He 51s being passed on to the re-formed 4th Staffel. The new fighters were Bf 109C models, armed with four rather than two MG 17 machine guns in order to match the capabilities of the four-gun I-16 Type 10s then being

Below: A Condor Legion Bf 109E – the up-gunned and improved variant that arrived in Spain too late to see active service. Right top: Freiherr von Richthofen (left), the Condor Legion's chief of staff, receives a medal at a parade held to celebrate the Nationalist victory of March 1939. Right: At a Condor Legion parade in Berlin during June 1939, Hitler and Goering (left) march alongside Legion officers Hugo Sperrle and Freiherr von Richthofen.

supplied to the Republicans. By that time, Galland had returned to Germany and handed over his command to Oberleutnant Werner Mölders. A reserved and serious-minded young officer, Mölders became the top-scoring ace of the Condor Legion and Germany's leading fighter tactician. On 15 July he led six of his fighters in the Bf 109C's first combat. Over 40 I-15s were engaged and the Germans shot down three of them for no loss. Among the successful pilots was Mölders himself, and the stocky and aggressive Leutnant Walter Oesau. Four days later the Staffel was in combat with I-16s, shooting four of them down. By the time that Mölders relinquished command of the 3rd Staffel in late November, he had increased his personal score to 14 victories, all of them against fighter aircraft.

'We suffered only slight losses due to the inadequate training and erratic leadership of our opponents'

A further increase in Jagdgruppe 88's fighting capabilities was projected early in 1939, with deliveries of the much-improved Bf 109E. However, the 2nd Staffel, the first to re-equip with the new variant, did not complete its conversion training before hostilities ended in March. The Condor Legion's last victory was scored on 5 March by Oberleutnant Hubertus von Bonin.

Jagdgruppe 88's fighter pilots had claimed a total of 313 kills in Spain for the loss of only 42 of their own aircraft to enemy action. Although there had been occasions when the Republican fighters had threatened to overwhelm all opposition, especially before the arrival of the Bf 109, Jagdgruppe 88's pilots had gained the upper hand. Indeed it was confidently asserted that Condor Legion aircrew were more likely to be killed on the Spanish roads than to die in air combat. Oberleutnant Lützow later claimed that 'the fact that we suffered only slight losses is due to the inadequate training and erratic leadership of our opponent's airmen and to the greater speed of our own fighter aircraft'. Nevertheless, thanks to the experience gained in Spain, the Luftwaffe fighter pilots entered World War II confident of the excellence of their aircraft and tactics.

THE AUTHOR Anthony Robinson was formerly on the staff of the RAF Museum, Hendon, and is now a freelance military aviation writer. He has edited the books *Aerial Warfare* and the *Dictionary of Aviation*.

49TH FIGHTER GROUP

The 49th Pursuit Group (it was not redesignated as the 49th Fighter Group until May 1942) was activated on 15 January 1941 at Selfridge Field, Michigan. Its three component squadrons, the 7th, 8th and 9th, were equipped with Seversky P-35 fighters. One year later, the unit's personnel were despatched by sea to Australia, where they were re-equipped with P-40E Warhawk fighters. Originally tasked to defend Australia's northern coast from Japanese bombers and their fighter escorts, the 7th Squadron was based on Horn Island while the 8th and 9th flew from the Darwin area. As the Allied offensive in the Pacific gained momentum, the group provided air support for the ground forces, and undertook bomber-escort and ground-strafing missions from consecutive bases at Port Moresby, Dobodura, Leyte and finally Okinawa. In September 1945 the group moved to Japan as part of the occupation forces. The unit flew Mustangs and Shooting Stars during the early stages of the Korean War, before being redesignated the 49th Fighter-Bomber Wing in September 1951 and converting to the F-84 Thunderjet.

From 1957 to 1967 the wing served in France and West Germany as part of the United States Air Forces in Europe.

In 1967 the 49th returned to the US, and has remained there, apart from a six-month deployment to Thailand in the aftermath of the Spring Invasion of Vietnam in 1972.

Today, the 49th Wing operates McDonnell-Douglas F-15 Eagles from Holloman Air Force Base, New Mexico.

Above: The badge of the US Fifth Army Air Force.

PACIFIC LIGHTNING

In the vanguard of the Pacific air war, the pilots of the US 49th Fighter Group despatched the enemy with speed and efficiency

'WE DELIVERED a head-on diving attack. The Zeros were completely surprised and attempted to climb, I shot down one bomber and one Zero. The escort, along with the bombers, never took any fighting position due to the fact that they were caught unawares.'

The pilot was Captain Andrew Reynolds, leading ace of the 49th Fighter Group with 10 kills; the date was 4 April 1942. Reynolds had been leading a force of 14 Curtiss P-40Es when enemy aircraft were spotted below. Their opponent was a formation of seven Japanese bombers, escorted by six Mitsubishi A6M Zero fighters, heading for Australia's northern coast. In a furious attack, all of the bombers and two of the Zeros were despatched for the loss of only two American aircraft.

The 49th Fighter Group of the USAAF had arrived on station one month earlier; the lightning Japanese advance through the Pacific had brought enemy bombers within range of Australia's Northern Territory, and fighters were urgently needed to provide air defence over Darwin. Since the attack on Pearl Harbor in December 1941, the Japanese sphere of occupation had expanded with frightening speed.

Emperor Hirohito's forces were now firmly entrenched in the Pacific, and controlled an area bordered by Singapore to the west, Timor to the south and the Solomons to the southeast. For the 49th, seeking to stem the tide of invasion, the situation was bleak. However, the enemy had overstretched and, as the Allies launched their counter-offensive, the roles

were gradually reversed. Moving base four times as the Allies pushed up from New Guinea into the Philippines and on to Okinawa, the 49th Fighter Group was continually at the forefront of battle. By August 1945 the group had claimed 678 enemy aircraft destroyed, and had been awarded three Distinguished Unit Citations.

The group's first operation was launched on 14 March 1942 from Horn Island off the northeast tip of Australia. Although the unit's personnel were badly in need of training – 89 out of 102 pilots possessed no combat experience – this was a luxury that could not be afforded given the close proximity of the enemy. On this first operation, the first action by USAAF fighters in the Southwest Pacific area, nine P-40E fighters intercepted a force of Japanese bombers and their escorts. The dogfight that followed resulted in five enemy aircraft being downed for the loss of only one American fighter. The most remarkable of these victories was that gained by Lieutenant

A. T. House. Flying as wingman to Captain Robert Morrissey, House saw his leader come under attack. He loosed off a burst of machine-gun fire at the marauding Zeros, but at a critical moment during the engagement his guns jammed. Undeterred, House closed in and sliced the leading edge of his aircraft's wing into the lightly constructed fuselage of one of the Zeros. It plummeted in a ball of flame, while House – his P-40 barely controllable – managed to limp back to base and make an emergency landing.

The P-40E was far from being the most likely candidate to wrest air superiority from the Imperial Navy's agile Zero fighters. As one of the group's pilots, Lieutenant Clay Tice, later commented: 'The Zero could outclimb us, out-turn us and outrun us at altitude. We could outdive and outrun on the deck only.' Yet, for all its shortcomings, the P-40 had one significant advantage over the Zero. In Tice's words: 'We could take punishment. He couldn't.'

The combat record of the 49th Fighter Group over

The 'fork-tailed devil' in action (main picture). Although less manoeuvrable than other Allied fighters such as the Mustang and Thunderbolt, the P-38 Lightning was a formidable opponent. Twin-engine operation and a streamlined design afforded a top speed envied by the Japanese pilots. Its devastating armament was capable of virtually disintegrating the skin-stressed fuselage of the Zero. Left: An appointment with destiny for one of the Imperial Navy's A6M Zero fighters. As flames pour from one of its wings, the enemy begins his inexorable descent following a surprise attack from above. Below: Striding into the record books, four pilots of the indefatigable 49th Fighter Group exchange their fighters for a little light refreshment, during one of the rare breaks from combat duty. Left to right: Lieutenants Landers, Donaldson and Sauber, and Captain Reynolds.

Darwin reflects how quickly the American pilots learned how to exploit their opponents' weaknesses by carrying out fast diving attacks from superior altitude. Between March and August 1942, the newly blooded pilots of the 49th accounted for over 60 enemy aircraft destroyed – earning the first of their Distinguished Unit Citations. The work of the commanding officer, Lieutenant-Colonel Paul Wurtsmith, in moulding the group into an effective fighting unit was duly recognised in November 1942. Wurtsmith was promoted to full colonel, and given command of the Fifth Army Air Force's Fighter Command.

During late September and October 1942, the 49th Fighter Group moved forward from Darwin to Port Moresby on the southeast coast of New Guinea. Here, as part of the Fifth Army Air Force, it was to play a significant role in blocking the Japanese advance from the north. The 7th Fighter Squadron was the first to arrive, and started operations almost immediately as the Allies strived to maintain local air superiority. Had it not been for the air force, providing support for the beleaguered ground forces, the troops of the Japanese Eighteenth Army might well have reached Port Moresby. The 8th and 9th Squadrons deployed to New Guinea during October,

having relinquished the air defence of Darwin to a Spitfire wing newly arrived from Britain.

When the group arrived at Port Moresby, its operational commitments included not only air defence, but also bomber-escort and ground-attack missions, frequently in the face of large numbers of enemy aircraft. Living conditions for the pilots were extremely harsh, with only the bare minimum of facilities. Not only did they have to contend with a variety of tropical diseases, including malaria, but their hastily constructed airstrips were at the mercy of the highly unpredictable weather. In dry conditions, clouds of dust would fill the air, while after the rains the runways degenerated into a sea of mud. Yet air combat continued regardless of these problems and, on 1 November, a group of P-40s, during a bomber escort mission to Lae, engaged a formation of Zeros. In the mêleè that followed, two enemy aircraft were destroyed for the loss of one US fighter.

The 49th Fighter Group gained its 100th victory on 26 December, during a dogfight over Dobodura, north of Port Moresby. Twelve P-40s of the 9th Squadron, led by Lieutenant John D. Landers, engaged 20 Zeros. Landers shot down two of the enemy before falling prey to the surprise attack of a third. Forced to take to his parachute, Landers came down

USAAF Pilot, Pacific 1942-45

The P-38 Lightning had a maximum ceiling of 40,000ft, and in order that they could perform effectively in the thin atmosphere, pilots were issued with M-10 oxygen masks. In addition, this pilot wears a lightweight cloth flying helmet and the standard light-khaki USAAF uniform. The seat-type parachute pack and inflatable life-vest were also standard issue to the P-38 pilots flying in the Pacific theatre.

in the heart of the inhospitable Owen Stanley mountain range of New Guinea. It took him five whole days, tormented by blisters and leeches, before he reached the Allied lines. Meanwhile, the battle had continued overhead and, with a magnificent display of combat skills, the American fighters claimed seven victories, including the group's 100th – which had fallen to Landers before he was shot down. With six more kills to his credit, Landers was assigned to the Eighth Army Air Force in Britain, and ended the war with 28½ kills.

On 10 January 1943, the group's strength was augmented by the arrival of Lieutenant Richard Bong, assigned to the 9th Fighter Squadron. Bong was already an ace, having destroyed five enemy aircraft while attached to the 35th Fighter Group during the previous three months. This remarkable marksman was to become the top-scoring American pilot of World War II, with a total of 40 kills.

By early 1943, the Japanese advance on Port Moresby had been halted and the Allied counter-offensive had begun in earnest. With ground forces starting to make inroads into enemy positions on New Guinea, in February the 49th Fighter Group once again moved up into the thick of battle, operating from an advance base at Dobodura. The

makeshift airstrip at Dobodura was, at that time, only temporary, and the group continued to fly from both Port Moresby and Dobodura, using the forward base to inflict damage on Japanese positions to the north. Communications between the two bases were so poor that serious problems were encountered by the groundcrews at Dobodura, particularly in relation to spare parts and fuel supplies for the aircraft.

There was no let-up in the action, however, and from March onwards the group became embroiled in an intense period of air fighting. Lieutenant Bong's first success with the group came on 3 March, during a bomber-escort mission to Lae, on the northeast coast of New Guinea. As Bong later recalled:

'While on cover flight for our bombers, our flight was intercepted by seven Oscar-type Zeros [Nakajama Ki-43 Oscars]. In the ensuing engagement I made a forty-five degree deflection shot from above and behind and he started smoking. I made another pass at him just before he hit the water and crashed. While pulling up, I saw another smoking Zero hit the water about a mile to my right. I made two more passes at another Zero and started his gas tank leaking, but he kept going.'

The forward base at Dobodura enabled the 49th

Action stations on New Guinea (main picture). No time to lose as a truck delivers the P-38 pilots to their aircraft immediately prior to a combat mission against the advancing Japanese forces. Below (left to right): A Curtiss P-40E Warhawk equipped with drop-tank for long-range operations; Lieutenant A. Watkins and a vengeful-looking Donald, complete with parachute; the indomitable Lieutenant John Landers, photographed beside his mascot – a red-blooded Texas steer.

Fighter Group to provide air support for the Allied forces advancing northwards from Port Moresby, up through New Guinea. In the opinion of Fighter Command, this far outweighed the disadvantages of the airstrip and, in April, the entire group was placed on permanent station at Dobodura. Undaunted by the task expected of them, the pilots of the 49th responded with devastating efficiency – between March and May the group claimed 160 enemy aircraft destroyed for the loss of only seven pilots.

The 9th Fighter Squadron was, by this time, equipped with Lockheed P-38 Lightnings, while the other two squadrons had to wait until September 1943 before they could replace their Curtiss fighters with the twin-engined P-38s. In the meantime, the 9th took full advantage of their versatile new charges. On 26 July the Lightnings of the 9th Fighter Squadron were on patrol over the Markham Valley, northwest of Lae, when they spotted a formation of 20 Japanese fighters, A6M Zeros and Kawasaki Ki-61 Tonys, approaching them head-on. In a fast and furious combat, Bong accounted for four of the enemy aircraft and his score was equalled by Captain James A. Watkins, who was to end the war as the 49th Fighter Group's fourth-ranking ace, with 12 victories.

'I fired a long burst into him while he was hanging from his prop and he went straight into the sea'

Two days later, both of these pilots were again in action, when Japanese fighters intercepted a formation of North American B-25s which they were escorting. Watkins later recalled:

'We were at 6000ft when we sighted twelve to eighteen enemy fighters 3000ft above us off Cape Raoult at 0815 hours. We dropped belly tanks and the flight turned ninety degrees into the attack. I fired at the attacking leader and missed. I climbed to 8000ft out to sea and made a head-on pass at one of two Oscars attacking Lieutenant Bong. This plane burst into flames about 75 to 100yds in front of me.

'I turned to find Lieutenant Bong and made a head-on attack on one of three Oscars coming down on me. This plane burst into flames and pieces barely missed me as he passed under. The other two didn't bother me. I went back towards the fight in a steep dive. At 4000ft I levelled out to meet a head-on attack of two Oscars. Neither one would meet me. The lead ship of the attackers pulled straight up into a stall at about 6000ft. I fired a long two- or three-second burst into him while he was hanging on his prop and he went straight into the sea, exploding as he hit. I got in several more short bursts at others but was chased off.'

Meanwhile, Bong had shot down an Oscar before coming under attack from two more. However, he was able to escape the enemy simply by applying full power to his Lightning – and outrunning them.

During the next four months, Allied landings on the Huon peninsula were threatening to encircle the Japanese bases and to the east, the island of Bougainville was under siege from the US 3rd Marine Division. The New Guinea campaign was proceeding as planned, and gradually the fighter units' operations shifted from air combat to ground-attack missions. In November 1943 the 9th Fighter Squadron relinquished its Lightnings in favour of Republic P-47D

Above: Sweltering in the hot, humid environment of Darwin, northern Australia, groundcrew tune a P-40's engine up to combat performance. Below: The P-38 Lightning – much prized by the pilots of the 49th Fighter Group for its high-altitude capabilities. Far right: Fighter pilot, Major Richard Bong. A keen marksman and hunter from childhood, Bong exhibited an extraordinary aptitude for aerial gunnery.

Thunderbolts, but it flew these for six months only before reverting to P-38s in April 1944. One of the 9th Fighter Squadron's pilots at this time was Captain Ralph Wandrey, who ended the war with six aerial victories. On 23 May, the squadron was tasked with a ground-strafing mission in northern New Guinea. Spotting four powered barges off the island of Biak, Wandrey led his flight of Lightnings down to attack them:

'I lined up the two lead barges and opened fire. What looked like a boatload of coconuts suddenly became helmets of Jap soldiers, who were jammed into the barge. As my bullets and cannon shells exploded in those packed quarters, the Japs poured overside like bees from a disturbed hive. I flashed past the first barge and concentrated my fire on the second. Some brave character climbed atop the engine room, where a 20mm cannon was mounted and aimed it in my direction. I raked him and the cannon overboard with one burst, setting fire to the engine room also.'

By July 1944, the Japanese army on New Guinea had been isolated and neutralised following superb co-operation between Allied land, sea and air forces,

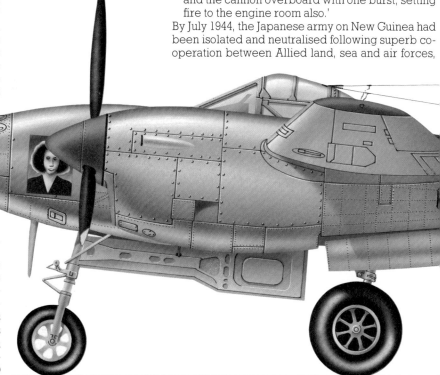

A LEGEND IN HIS LIFETIME

One of the most remarkable fighter pilots in the annals of air force history, Richard Bong was born at Superior, Wisconsin, in September 1920. Growing up on a farm, he graduated in 1938 and began training as a teacher. However, deciding to fulfil his boyhood ambition to be a pilot, Bong enlisted

in the US Army Air Force as a cadet in 1941.

On 9 January 1942, he received his pilot's wings and a commission as second lieutenant. However, Bong's hoped-for posting to a fighter unit did not materialise, and instead he found himself transferred to Luke Field in Arizona as an instructor.

In September 1942 Lieutenant Bong escaped from his training assignment and was sent overseas to join the Fifth Army Air Force in the Southwest Pacific theatre. Serving with the 39th Squadron of the 35th Fighter Group for three months, Bong gained the five victories he required in order to qualify as an ace. In January 1943 the newly blooded lieutenant reported for duty to the 49th Fighter Group's 9th Squadron. His victory streak continued, and, by the end of his first combat tour in November 1943, Bong had destroyed 21 enemy aircraft. (Above: The nose of Bong's P-38 Lightning, pictured here one kill short of his eventual total.)

Lieutenant Bong returned to combat in February 1944, and on 12 April he registered his 27th kill, exceeding the total scored by

World War I ace Eddie Rickenbacker. One of Bong's most deadly skills was his deflection

shooting, which required perfect timing and an uncanny degree of accuracy.

On 17 December 1944, Bong, now promoted to major, gained his 40th and final victory, and was ordered back to the United States. Tragically, however, Major Richard Bong was killed in a flying accident while piloting a P-80 Shooting Star jet fighter in August 1945.

and the Solomon Islands had also been secured. To the north lay the next objective. The American invasion of the Philippines provoked a further period of bitter air fighting. On 27 October 1944, a week after the landings on Leyte, the 49th Fighter Group – by then completely equipped with P-38 Lightnings – landed on the recently captured airstrip at Tacloban. Within hours of arrival, the group was in action. Colonel Robert Morrissey, a veteran of the defence of Darwin, shot down one Ki-43 Oscar, Bong claimed another, and Major Gerald Johnson, who was to become the group's second-ranking ace with 22 victories, accounted for an Oscar and an Aichi D3A Val dive-bomber. On the following day, Bong gained a further two victories before teaming up with Morrissey and the 49th Fighter Group's commanding officer, Colonel George Walker, to break up a formation of 17 bomb-carrying Oscars. Although no victories were claimed, the three pilots succeeded in turning back this fighter-bomber raid with no damage to the ground forces on the beach-head.

The period from October to December 1944 saw

FORK-TAILED DEVIL

Developed as a high altitude interceptor, the Lockheed P-38 Lightning served on every battlefront of World War II. Extremely versatile, the P-38 could perform a number of roles, from hard-hitting long-range fighter to torpedo bomber.

Used primarily for escort and ground-attack duties, the aircraft's twin-boom design meant that armament was unhampered by synchronising gear, allowing the pilot to unleash parallel streams of fire that retained their accuracy up to 1000yds. These booms also provided for the mounting of turbo-super-chargers in addition to the P-38's two 1600hp Allison engines.

Maximum range, depending on the fuel-to-armament ratio, was 2600 miles, though a combat range of 500 miles was normal. A superbly effective bomber-destroyer, the P-38 had a maximum speed of 414mph at 25,000ft and a speed of ascent that could rarely be matched in combat. Armament consisted of one 20mm and four 12.7mm guns, plus up to two 726kg bombs and ten 127mm rocket projectiles carried under the wings. Altogether, nine variants were produced, including the F-4 in which all armament was replaced by four K-17 cameras for use in photo-reconnaissance operations. In Europe, the Lightning was largely outclassed by the more manoeuvrable Fw 190 and Bf 109.

In the Pacific, however, the P-38 was instrumental in securing air superiority. During the island-hopping campaign of 1942-45, the Lightning claimed more Japanese aircraft destroyed than any other fighter. Unarmed conversions carried either a bombardier or 'Mickey' BTO (Bombing Through Overcast) radar, and served as lead ships for P-38 bomber formations. By the end of the war, total P-38 production had almost exceeded 10,000. It was fitting that the Lightning should cap a distinguished career by becoming the first USAAF aircraft to land in Japan following VJ-day.

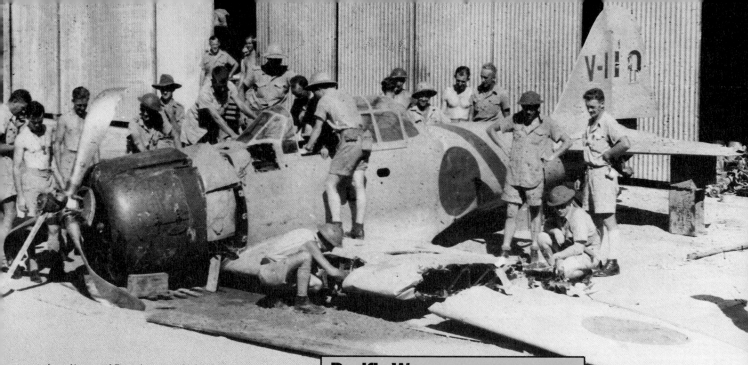

the climax of Bong's remarkable career. He was to receive the Medal of Honor for conspicuous gallantry in action between 10 October and 11 November, during which he gained eight air victories. In December he added a further four kills to his score, bringing his total up to 40. The achievements of the 49th Fighter Group during this crucial phase of the Philippine campaign were recognised by the award of its third Distinguished Unit Citation.

From their bases on the Philippines the USAAF

Pacific War
1942 – 1945

By July 1942 the lightning Japanese advance south and east across the Pacific was halted. But the Japanese were within striking distance of Australia, and pushing them back was to prove a hard and costly task.

The Japanese attempt to capture Port Moresby, and effectively complete the conquest of New Guinea, was frustrated in May 1942 by the Allied naval victory in the Battle of the Coral Sea. Further Japanese advances overland towards Port Moresby were held, and throughout 1943, US and Australian forces on New Guinea mounted a series of offensives, securing Lae by September and pushing north and west during the first months of 1944. By July 1944, Japanese resistance in New Guinea was effectively over. Throughout the New Guinea campaign, the 49th Fighter Group had distinguished itself in action against the enemy. With the Allies victorious in New Guinea, and in the Solomons, Marshalls and Marianas, the war moved on to the Philippines. The 49th Fighter Group was deployed on Leyte a week after the first landings there in October 1944, moving finally to Okinawa in August 1945.

Following the Zero's decimation of Allied aircraft at Pearl Harbor, this well-armed fighter became a symbol of Japanese invincibility. For the next seven months, it stunned the Allies with its long-range capability and combat performance. However, when one of the Imperial Navy's Zeros was captured intact near Port Moresby in April 1942, the aircraft was dissected (above) and the myth of its invulnerability was dispelled. Modern Allied fighters, such as the P-38 Lightning, were developed which totally outclassed the Zero in both speed and armament. The once-feared Zero gradually lost air superiority and, by late 1944, Japanese pilots were using them on kamikaze missions.

Key
+ Airfields used by 49th Fighter Group
▮ Maximum extent of Japanese empire, July 1942
→ Allied forces

fighters could range as far afield as Formosa and the Chinese mainland. On 22 January 1945, Lightnings of the 49th Fighter Group and 8th Fighter Group escorted the first daylight raid by heavy bombers on Formosa. The 49th Fighter Group also accompanied the bombers to Hong Kong and carried out bombing and napalm attacks on targets in Formosa. Then, in August 1945, the group moved forward to the island of Okinawa in preparation for the final assault on Japan. In the event, the Japanese surrender came before the Lightnings could see further action, and the 49th Fighter Group ended the war with the second highest total of any fighter unit in the Pacific theatre – 678 kills. Within the group, the 9th Fighter Squadron had contributed the greatest number of victories, with 276 to its credit.

THE AUTHOR Anthony Robinson was formerly on the staff of the RAF Museum, Hendon, and is now a freelance military aviation writer.

CACTUS

An impromptu formation of Marine Aviation units, the Cactus Air Force fought tooth and nail to keep Guadalcanal in American hands

ON 7 AUGUST 1942 Major-General Alexander Vandegrift's 1st Marine Division launched the first American offensive of World War II – the landings on Guadalcanal, codenamed Cactus. Although the initial assault was unopposed, the Japanese reaction was not long in coming. That afternoon, two air raids were launched against the Marines and, on the night of the 8/9th, a Japanese cruiser force came down 'the Slot' (New Georgia Sound) and destroyed the Allied screening force in the Battle of Savo Island. In the face of the strong enemy naval threat, the remains of the US invasion fleet sailed away, taking much of the Marines' supplies and equipment with them. Vandegrift was now left with 11,000 men on the Canal.

The Marines' first objective was to capture an airfield that the Japs had been building. This was accomplished on the afternoon of the 8th and, using the heavy equipment left behind by its previous owners, the Marines completed the construction work, naming the strip Henderson Field in honour of Major Lofton R. Henderson, a US Marine pilot who had been killed at the Battle of Midway back in June. Twelve days later, on 20 August, the first two Marine Squadrons flew into Henderson: VMF-223, an F4F Wildcat fighter squadron under Major John L. Smith, and VMSB-232, an SBD Dauntless squadron commanded by Lieutenant-Colonel Dick Mangrum. The Cactus Air Force had arrived.

Throughout the rest of August and September, with some navy and marine air reinforcement, the Marines on the 'Canal were subjected to concerted Japanese efforts to retake the island, but the stubborn defences of the men on the ground, and the determination of the pilots of the Cactus Air Force in the skies above, kept the enemy at bay. By the end of September, it was clear that the Japs had put a hold on their plan for an assault on New Guinea in favour of repossessing the 'Canal. They wanted to push the Marines back into the Solomon Sea once and for all, but Vandegrift and General Roy Geiger, commander of the First Marine Aircraft Wing, plus admirals Turner and McCain, were not about to buy that idea.

For the big push, US intelligence pegged the Japs as having two main objectives: to land further troops and heavy artillery, and to destroy American air power. By 10 October the enemy had twice the bomber strength of Cactus, and three times the number of fighters. What they did not have was a way to convince the likes of Vandegrift, Geiger and company that they should throw in the towel.

On the eve of the enemy thrust, VMF-121, com-

MARINE AVIATION ON THE 'CANAL

The original units of the First Marine Aircraft Wing (I MAW, whose badge is shown above) to fly to Guadalcanal and lay the foundations of the Cactus Air Force arrived on 20 August 1942 with Marine Air Group 23 (MAG-23). They were VMF-223, an F4F Wildcat squadron, and VMSB-232, an SBD Dauntless squadron. On 22 August they were joined by the P-400 (a version of the Bell P-39 Cobra) aircraft of the 67th Pursuit Squadron. The first of the valuable Navy carrier detachments arrived from USS *Enterprise* on 24 August, and on the 30th the rest of MAG-23 landed in the form of VMF-224 and VMSB-231.

In September, October and early November, many units served with the Cactus Air Force for periods varying from three days to more than six weeks. These detachments from Navy carrier groups include VS-3, VF-5, VT-8, VMSB-141, MAG-14, VS-71, VMF-121, VB-6, VMF-212, VMSB-132, VMF-112, VMSB-131, VMSB-142, VF-10, VB-10, VS-10 and VT-10. Altogether, this ad hoc air force did a superb job at Guadalcanal.

AIR FORCE

'Cactus' Air Force
August 1942 – February 1943

The construction of an airfield by the Japanese on the island of Guadalcanal (codenamed 'Cactus' by the Allies) in early July 1942 alerted Allied commanders to a new threat posed to the sea routes between Australia and the United States. Once intelligence of this move reached Vice-Admiral Robert Ghormley's South Pacific Area headquarters in New Zealand, he took immediate countermeasures. An initial landing by US Marines took place on 7 August. The first aircraft arrived at Henderson Field on 12 August and further aircraft reinforcements arrived throughout the rest of 1942. They soon gained the appelation of 'Cactus Air Force'.

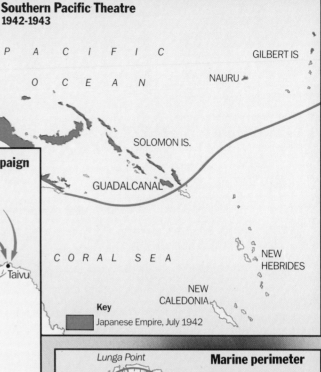

Southern Pacific Theatre
1942-1943

PACIFIC OCEAN

GILBERT IS

NAURU

SOLOMON IS.

GUADALCANAL

CORAL SEA

NEW HEBRIDES

NEW CALEDONIA

Key
Japanese Empire, July 1942

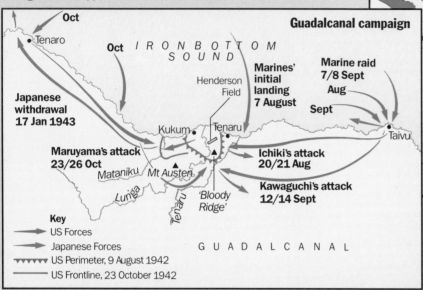

Guadalcanal campaign

Oct
Tenaro

IRONBOTTOM SOUND

Oct

Marines' initial landing 7 August

Marine raid 7/8 Sept

Aug

Sept

Henderson Field

Japanese withdrawal 17 Jan 1943

Kukum

Tenaru

Taivu

Maruyama's attack 23/26 Oct

Mataniku

Mt Austen

Luniga

Tenaru

'Bloody Ridge'

Ichiki's attack 20/21 Aug

Kawaguchi's attack 12/14 Sept

GUADALCANAL

Key
→ US Forces
→ Japanese Forces
▽▽▽▽▽ US Perimeter, 9 August 1942
— US Frontline, 23 October 1942

manded by Major 'Duke' Davis with Captain Joe Foss as his executive officer, flew in from a transport carrier with 20 Wildcats. Two days later, John Smith and Marion Carl, two of the great Cactus fighter pilots who had become legends during the early days of the battle for the 'Canal, were evacuated with the last of the surviving VMF-223 pilots. The fighting in the air had been heavy and, during early September, a grim contest had been shaping up between Carl and Smith, when Carl was shot down. Fortunately, he was picked up by friendly natives. Carl got back to Henderson after an absence of some five days and was greeted by General Geiger who told him that Smith was now six or seven Japs ahead, and the 'Old Man' wanted to know what he was going to do about it. Carl, who was much quieter than the ebullient Smith, paused awhile and then said, 'Well, Goddamit General! Ground Smitty for five days and we'll see how it comes out.'

On 11 October, the Japanese plan went into top gear, leaving no doubt in anyone's mind that a truly critical period for Cactus had arrived. In addition to the expected heavy raids on the fields, search planes picked up a surface force of Japanese transports, accompanied by destroyers and three heavy cruisers, late in the afternoon. The latter could mean only one thing – a heavy bombardment of the fields

Previous page: The wreck of a Japanese Zero fighter lies on a Guadalcanal beach, while (inset) Lieutenant-Colonel 'Indian Joe' Bauer demonstrates combat tactics. Below right: A Japanese fuel dump burns on Tanambogo Island, victim of an American air strike prior to the landings by the 1st Marine Division on 7 August 1942. Below: Shark-mouthed Bell P-400 Airacobras line up at Henderson Field.

Marine perimeter

Lunga Point

IRONBOTTOM SOUND

Kukum

Lunga Lagoon

Lunga

Henderson Field

Ilu

Tenaru

Key
— US Defensive Line
◯ US Bivouac Areas

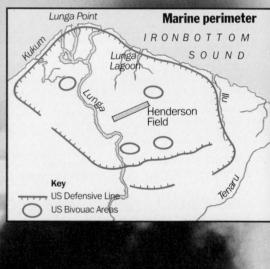

Above: Captain Joe Foss of VMF-121 gained most of his 26 air combat kills at Guadalcanal. Above right: VMF-212, commanded by 'Indian Joe' Bauer, is photographed with a Grumman F4F Wildcat at Efate in the New Hebrides. Bottom right: Groundcrew go over a Grumman TBF Avenger torpedo bomber before arming it for another mission. The Avenger was nicknamed 'The Turkey' by US aircrews.

that night while the transports unloaded at Tassafaronga. But this one turned out to be a bit different. The Jap force was met on the surface by Admiral Norman Scott, with two heavy and two light cruisers. He surprised them just before midnight and his force succeeded in sinking a cruiser and a destroyer, while heavily damaging a third ship, for the loss of one US destroyer. But, during the course of the sea battle, the two big Jap transports landed their heavy artillery and other reinforcements unopposed.

At first light on the 12th, all available SBDs, F4Fs and P-39s were off in search of any cripples from the night engagement. They were led by Colonel Al Cooley, whose MAG-14 had just relieved MAG-23, and Lieutenant-Commander John Eldridge, commanding VS-71, one of those great Navy detachments that contributed so much to the saving of the 'Canal. The attack group found the survivors north of the Russell Islands, and during the day repeated attacks put away two more destroyers and heavily damaged the remaining ships before nightfall.

With the events of the 12th, things were looking up for the beleaguered troops on the island. On the morning of the 13th, they looked even better, as Admiral Turner arrived with the amphibious shipping to unload the 164th US Army Infantry. But the rosier outlook did not last long. Around noon, a raid by 27 bombers and 18 fighters was not detected early enough for the F4Fs to climb to meet them. From about 30,000ft, the Japs bombed with extreme accuracy, putting 13 craters in the runway and igniting at least 5000 gallons of aviation fuel. There was only minor interception contact, and the 42 F4Fs were still climbing when the Japs gave it 'bombs away'. Two hours later, 18 more escorted bombers were

on their way in, with most of the F4Fs were still back on the ground being refuelled. Joe Foss led 14 VMF-121 fighters in an intercept attempt, but was surprised by the Jap escorts and his flight was scattered, with Foss himself almost finished in a wild and bouncing, dead-stick, high-speed landing, which he managed, fortunately without injury. Again the bombers were unopposed in their drop on the field, but luckily the damage was nowhere near what it could have been. The day ended with a feeling of foreboding that ran deeper than usual. it was not misplaced.

Just after 0130 on the 14th, a 'Washing Machine Charlie' seaplane clanked over the field and dropped three flares: a red one at the west end, a white over the middle, and a green at the east end. Then, with an ear-splitting roar, 16 14in guns salvoed from the two Jap battleships, *Kongo* and *Haruna*, lying close to the Guadalcanal shoreline. For more than an hour, they generated a nightmare of rocketing and roaring shells, concussions that shook the earth like a giant quake, deadly steel splinters that ricocheted for hundreds of yards, huge fires everywhere, and as a grotesque accompaniment to it all, hideous and nerve-shattering noise. Fourteen-inch guns make a barrage of proportions seldom seen in normal ground artillery employment. After an hour, flames were rising hundreds of feet into the air from gasoline dumps, planes were blazing everywhere, and a fireworks 'spectacular' was signalling the demise of an ammo and bomb dump. Marines knew it henceforth not by the date, but only by the name – 'the bombardment'. Nine hundred and eighteen 14in shells were fired into the beachhead, most of them landing on the field and in the coconut grove at

THE BATTLE FOR GUADALCANAL

Taken by surprise by the invasion of 7 August 1942 by Major-General Alexander Vandegrift's 1st Marine Division, the Japanese on Guadalcanal fled into the jungle and offered little opposition. On the night of the 8th, however, the Japanese Navy defeated the Marines' naval screening force, compelling it to abandon the 11,145 Marines on the island with only the supplies they had thus far managed to bring ashore. The task of reconquering Guadalcanal was given to Lieutenant-General Harukichi Hyakutake and a force of 50,000 men. On the night of 20 August, a detachment led by Colonel Kiyono Ichiki was thrown against the Marines on the western bank of the Ilu River. Vandegrift succeeded in enveloping the force and only a few of the Japanese escaped the subsequent air attacks. Ichiki chose to commit hara-kiri.

On 8 September it was learnt that Major-General Kiyotake Kawaguchi's reinforced 35th Brigade was poised for an attack on Henderson Field. The Marines were able to prepare their defences and, in the Battle of Bloody Ridge of 12/13 September, they succeeded in wiping out 1200 of Kawaguchi's men. Both the Americans and the Japanese then received reinforcements, and by mid-October Vandegrift had 23,000 men on the island. The Japanese launched repeated attacks on the western side of the US perimeter on 23 October, but 3500 of their number lay dead when they withdrew on the 25th. Vandegrift was then able to go onto the offensive, and in November he widened the perimeter and sent Carlson's Raiders (the 2nd Raider Battalion) to harass the Japanese over a wide area. Two of his battlions fought a two-day battle which began on 19 November; Hyakutaki was forced to withdraw with heavy losses.

From early December, American reinforcements poured onto the island. Hyakutake finally evacuated 13,000 men under fire from Cape Esperance in February, leaving Guadalcanal securely in American hands.

Top left: A squadron of Douglas SBD Dauntless dive-bombers warms up on Henderson Field. Visible on the right is a PBY Catalina. Above: Members of a Black Cat squadron on the 'Canal. These men flew black-painted PBYs against the Japanese at night. Top right: A Japanese Mitsubishi A6M Zero-Sen 'Zeke' carrier-borne fighter. Left: A Japanese heavy cruiser frantically manoeuvres to evade aerial attack. Below: A Wildcat smokes into life, watched by an appreciative audience of 1st Division Marines. Bottom: An F4F Wildcat in Cactus Air Force markings.

the northeastern side of the strip where the pilots and crews were billeted. Miraculously, only 41 officers and men were killed.

Few people have the mental make-up to see the lighter side of things in such circumstances, but there are invariably some. Major Duke Davis of VMF-121 was one of these. Possessed of a delightful and ever-present sense of humour, Duke and Joe Foss were huddled together in a foxhole at the height of the bombardment. During a brief lull in the infernal noise, Foss was idly drumming his fingers on Davis' steel helmet, when Duke came out with, 'Dammit, Joe. Knock off that bloody noise!'

The work of the battleships created a scene of total chaos. Apart from the casualties, the radio station was completely demolished and word of the attack could not be sent out to SoPac and AirPac headquarters for several hours. The striking power, so carefully nursed by General Geiger, was practically wiped out. All the fuel was gone and much of the ordnance. Of the 38 SBDs that had been oper-

ational the day before, only seven were now flyable. Six P-39s were still in commission, but all the torpedo planes had been either destroyed or put out of action. Henderson Field was pockmarked with craters and strewn with wrecked and burned-out aircraft. But, by some miracle, the fighter strip was relatively untouched and 29 of the 42 F4Fs were still in flyable shape.

At 0930 on the 14th, the available fighters were scrambled on receipt of a Coastwatcher's report of a major raid coming in. The F4Fs were airborne for an hour, but no raid materialised so they were landed to refuel. They were still on the ground when the first attack of the day arrived at noon. Twenty-six bombers hit the field unopposed. All operational aircraft were on the fighter strip but, as luck would have it, the Japs went for Henderson Field next door, and the fighters survived unscathed. The second attack came an hour later and was met by every fighter on hand. Nine bombers and three fighters were downed, with the loss of only one plane from VMF-121. In spite of these good results, the day took on an ominous look when the morning searches reported two groups of ships bound for the island. One force consisted of six transports, escorted by eight destroyers, while the other was made up of two heavy cruisers and two destroyers.

With the third flare, all hell broke loose again as a 16-gun salvo of 14in shells bore in

Admiral 'Jake' Fitch, who had relieved Admiral John McCain as Commander Air Forces South Pacific a short time before, had jumped into action on the 14th to provide Cactus with some striking power. All the remaining SBDs at Espiritu Santo, including nine spares, were alerted to move to the 'Canal immediately, with the pilots for the spares to come from Lieutenant-Colonel Joe Bauer's VMF-212, based on Efate. Bauer was to move his squadron from Efate to a stand-by status at Espiritu, and thence to Guadalcanal as soon as Geiger had room for his 20 F4Fs. Fitch also took emergency steps for the delivery of drummed fuel. Things were on the move but the situation was still critical. Efforts during the day against the Japanese air attacks had used up all the available fuel by nightfall, and as far as strike aircraft were concerned, there were only five SBDs left. It was a grim outlook.

At 0200 on the morning of the 15th, the drama of the previous night opened for its second performance with the same clanking entry of the seaplane with its coloured flares. With the third flare, all hell broke loose again as a 16-gun salvo of 14in shells bore in. For the next 35 minutes, these blasts poured into the airfield at 45-second intervals. As before, there was heavy damage, but this second performance of the 'big stuff' did not create the tremendous emotional impact and shock effect of the previous night. Powerless to do anything about it, the Marines simply had to live with the thought that the Jap transports were unloading at Tassafaronga, unopposed, and over 4000 fresh troops, complete with heavy equipment, were coming ashore for the final assault. It was not a good night.

The following morning brought the abject humiliation of seeing these anchored transports, less than 10 miles up the coast, and the frustration of not being able to do anything about it. There they were, using lighters and small boats to complete their unloading, with fighters and seaplanes flying cover

'INDIAN JOE' BAUER

Born in 1908, Harold William Bauer entered the US Naval Academy in 1926 and graduated in 1930. He was appointed a second lieutenant in the US Marine Corps, and, after entering flight training in late 1934 at Pensacola, Florida, he qualified as a naval aviator in 1936. During the period preceding US involvement in World War II he did much to develop and modernise fighter tactics and fighter gunnery in the Marine Corps. Possessed of great drive and humour, he was universally liked by his associates and the men serving under him. Lieutenant-Colonel 'Indian Joe' Bauer was given command of VMF-212 in the spring of 1942, and he took his largely untrained second lieutenants to Efate in the New Hebrides, where he gave them a practical course in operating an airbase from the jungle. Several of his men joined VMFs 223 and 224 when those units went into action at Guadalcanal, and in the crises of September and October 1942 he and some of his pilots went into action over the island.

In mid-October, VMF-212 was ordered to Guadalcanal to join the Cactus Air Force. One month later, during the last Japanese attempts to retake Guadalcanal, he was shot down at dusk near the Russell Islands by a Japanese seaplane fighter. Although his combat total of 11 victories was exceeded by other pilots in the Solomons, in Bauer the US Marine Corps lost its greatest all-round ace in the Pacific theatre.

Below: Bauer (right) and Major-General Roy Geiger hold a captured flag at Henderson Field.

over them. Obviously, the Japs thought they had finished off the Cactus Air Force, but they were in for a few surprises.

Before daylight, Major Joe Renner, Geiger's 'right hand' operations officer, was guiding the three remaining SBDs to a take-off position that avoided most of the holes in the fighter strip. In the dark, one ran into a huge crater near the taxiway, but the second made it into position and gave it the gun. The pilot, Lieutenant Robert Patterson, ran about 300yds, dropped one wheel into a shell hole, and rolled the plane up into a ball. Miraculously, neither Patterson nor his gunner was injured. Patterson begged to be permitted to take the third plane and, as dawn broke, succeeded in getting it off the ground, only to discover that, due to a hydraulic leak, he could neither retract his landing gear nor open his dive flaps. He decided to make his run on the transports regardless, got a hit with his bomb, and returned safely to the strip.

At 0600, using fuel drained from wrecks, five F4Fs took off, led by Duke Davis, to strafe the transports. As the morning progressed, every SBD that Major Bill Woodruff, the MAG-14 maintenance officer, and his exhausted crews could resurrect was wheeled out, bombed up and sent off to make a run on the transports. Some of these small attacks were escorted, some were not. Geiger soon put an end to this piecemeal approach by waiting for enough resurrections to put on some kind of a co-ordinated attack. It was to take a most unusual form.

The day before, Major Jack Cram, General Geiger's aide, had flown in to the fighter strip from Espiritu with the general's PBY Catalina amphibian. Hanging from the wings of the big, lumbering plane were two torpedoes. Since all the TBF Avenger torpedo bombers had been destroyed in the bombardment the previous night, Cram and Renner cooked up a plan to rig releases on the PBY and use it as a torpedo plane. With General Geiger's approval, co-ordination was achieved with the SBDs and available fighters and the attack was launched around noon.

With 12 SBDs bombing from the west and eight fighters engaging the Jap cover, Cram came in from the east in a glide from 6000ft, faster than any PBY

was ever meant to go, and jerked the jury-rigged releases at about 200ft. One torpedo 'porpoised', but the other hit one of the transports amidships and blew. Cram wheeled the big bird left and headed for the field with fighters all over him, but he made it back with the help of a landing F4F, who shot the last of the Japs off his tail, without bothering to pull up his gear. It was probably the most remarkable torpedo attack ever delivered. The Catalina had 175 holes, end to end, but it got back safely.

In the afternoon of the 15th, two more attacks were

46

Below: A Japanese troop transport lies wedged against the Guadalcanal shoreline, one of the many victims of Cactus Air Force bomb and torpedo strikes. Bottom left: While an American supply ship burns after a hit, essential supplies are ferried away to Guadalcanal aboard landing craft. Bottom centre: A Marine Aviation unit displays one of its trophies gained in the battle with Japan for the island. Bottom right: The author of this article, John P. Condon (photographed during the Korean War) served as a major in the air war over Guadalcanal.

made on the transport group, getting three hits, and six Jap fighters were shot down. But the efforts against the transports were costly: three SBDs, one F4F and two P-39s were lost. One piece of good news, however, was that several small caches of drummed aviation fuel that had been revetted in the first days of the operation, and almost forgotten, had been found, all of a sudden giving the dried-out Cactus Air Force more than two full days of fuel.

Just after midnight on the 16th, the now familiar drama was again on stage. Between 0030 and 0130, 1500 rounds came into the beachhead, but, fortunately, the Jap fire-control people could not seem to find the fighter strip. In the morning, there were 10 SBDs and seven P-39s available. In addition, Admiral Fitch had directed Task Force 17 towards the area and the air group of USS *Hornet* was overhead and in the immediate vicinity for the day. Seven attack missions were flown against the supplies the Japs had landed at Kokumbona near Tassafaronga

Point. It was a case of getting off, bombing and strafing the dumps, landing to refuel and rearm, and going off again. The Jap air force was preoccupied for most of the 16th with attempting to find the *Hornet* task force, but it was by no means an easy day for the Cactus pilots.

Late in the afternoon of the 16th, the Marines witnessed an action typical of the tenacity of the Cactus Air Force. A flight of nine Jap dive-bombers attacked the old 'four-piper' destroyer USS *McFarland* while she was unloading fuel to a barge alongside, having arrived recently from Espiritu. The bombers hit both the ship and the barge, turning the latter into a blazing inferno, and killing 27 of the destroyer's crew. As this was going on, VMF-212 was landing at the fighter strip after a flight from Espiritu. Joe Bauer, circling the field to make sure that his boys were putting down at the right spot, saw the attack. Without any hesitation, and in spite of the fact that he was very low on fuel after the long flight from Espiritu, he went after the Japs single-handed. With his men applauding on the ground, as was the whole beachhead, in less than one minute Bauer had knocked down four of the bombers and was on his way in to land. For this, and numerous other feats, he was awarded the Congressional Medal of Honor.

There were many more 'crisis-to-crisis' operations to come after the turning point in October on Guadalcanal, but it was steadily uphill from there. The Marines successfully repulsed a three-day assault by the Japanese on Henderson Field in mid-November and in January 1943, having sustained massive casualties in their attempt to reconquer the island, the Japanese withdrew. The psychological effect of the seizure and heroic defence of Guadalcanal by the US Marines was incalculable, but there is not a man who had any part in the battle for the 'Canal who does not have a special spot in his heart for the Cactus Air Force.

THE AUTHOR Major General John P. Condon, as a major, was the Fighter Command Operations officer for ComAirSols during the Solomons campaign. During the Korean War he commanded both MAG-12 and MAG-33, a rare distinction in US Marine Aviation.

Below: Pilots of No. 71 (Eagle) Squadron line up beside one of the Hurricane Mk1s with which the squadron became operational in February 1941. New recruits spent a short period training in the Miles Master (top right). Colonel Charles Sweeney (top far right) was made an honorary group captain for his part in the squadron's creation.

The Americans who volunteered to join No. 71 (Eagle) Squadron in 1940 soon proved themselves to be more than a match for the Luftwaffe

ON 19 SEPTEMBER 1940 the first Eagle Squadron of American volunteers was formed at RAF Church Fenton, Yorkshire. The idea of creating an all-American fighter unit in the Royal Air Force, along the lines of the famous American Escadrille Lafayette of France's Aviation Militaire in World War I, came not from the Air Ministry but from a wealthy American family named Sweeney. Charles Sweeney, a businessman living in London, wrote to the authorities in June 1940 to propose that volunteers with flying experience be recruited in the United States at his family's expense and formed into an 'American Air Defence Corps' within the RAF. A similar scheme had been operating to provide pilots for the Armée de l'Air before the collapse of France, and the American aviation artist (and former Royal Flying Corps pilot) Clayton Knight was already recruiting American citizens for the Royal Canadian Air Force. All this activity, incidentally, was in flagrant breach of the United States' neutrality laws. Charles

Sweeney proposed that his volunteer unit be placed under the command of his uncle, Colonel Charles Sweeney, who had enjoyed an amazing career as a military adventurer in many parts of the world, as well as serving with the French Foreign Legion and American Expeditionary Force during World War I. By then in his late fifties, Colonel Sweeney was too old for active command, but was given the honorary rank of group captain in the RAF in recognition of the Sweeney family's work in founding the Eagle Squadron.

Designated No.71 Squadron, the unit's first commanding officer was, in fact, an Englishman, Squadron Leader Walter Churchill, DSO, DFC, a distant relative of the Prime Minister who had led No.605 Squadron during the Battle of Britain. Churchill was to be understudied by an American officer, Squadron Leader W.E.G. Taylor. Taylor had served as a pilot with the US Navy and the Fleet Air Arm, before transferring to the RAF. This system of dual command had been instituted for Fighter Command's Czechoslovakian and Polish squadrons, the idea being that an experienced RAF leader would initiate pilots who already had considerable military experience into the ways of the RAF. However, in the case of the Eagle Squadron the situation was rather different, and the system led to some friction. Many of the

AMERICAN EAGLES

THE EAGLE SQUADRONS

Following the creation of the first Eagle Squadron, No.71 Squadron, in September 1940, sufficient American volunteers became available for the formation of two more such units in 1941. The second Eagle Squadron, No.121 Squadron, came into being on 14 May 1941 at Kirton-in-Lindsey, Lincolnshire. Its British commanding officer, Squadron Leader R.P.R. Powell, was a veteran of the Battle of Britain and the Battle of France and his two flight commanders were also experienced RAF fighter pilots. They immediately implemented a rigorous training programme for the inexperienced American volunteers, and within two months of its formation No.121 Squadron was declared operational. It was initially equipped with the Hurricane, but in October 1941 the squadron converted onto Spitfires. In the following February it took part in the Channel Dash operation, covering bombers attacking the German battle-cruisers *Scharnhorst* and *Gneisenau*.

No.133 Squadron formed at Coltishall in Norfolk on 29 July 1941. Its first CO, Squadron Leader George Brown, had been one of No.71 Squadron's British flight commanders. Within two months the third Eagle Squadron was operational on Hurricanes, but it saw little action until the spring of 1942, when it joined the Biggin Hill Wing, flying Spitfire Mk VBs. Like No.71 Squadron, No.133 Squadron was heavily engaged during the Dieppe Raid.

Right: Squadron Leader Taylor briefs his pilots before they are scrambled for a sortie (below).

49

THE AMERICAN VOLUNTEERS

The pilots of the first Eagle Squadron, No.71, were a diverse group with little in common except a restless spirit of adventure. Three of the original Eagles, Flying Officer E.Q. 'Gene' Tobin, Flying Officer Andy B. Mamedoff and Pilot Officer V.C. 'Shorty' Keough, had all served together in No.609 Squadron, RAF, during the Battle of Britain. Tobin and Mamedoff, the latter a White Russian by extraction, had originally volunteered to fight with the Finnish Air Force during the Winter War.

Flying Officer William Dunn, who joined the Eagle Squadron in the spring of 1941, had come to Britain as an NCO in a Canadian Army infantry unit. Ironically, Chesley Peterson had begun training with the US Army Air Corps in 1939, but had been rejected for lack of basic flying ability. He then worked for the Douglas Aircraft Company in California, before he was recruited by Colonel Charles Sweeney for service in the RAF.

Few of the volunteers had any strong commitment to oppose Nazi aggression, but an exception was Pilot Officer S.M. 'Mike' Kolendorski, an American of Polish origin. Tragically, he was to become the first Eagle to be killed by enemy action. A number of Americans enlisted in the Royal Canadian Air Force (RCAF) on their own initiative and later found their way to the Eagle Squadrons. Richard L. 'Dixie' Alexander, who had been rejected for pilot training by the US Army Air Corps for lack of educational qualifications, learned to fly with the RCAF. Donald Blakeslee also joined the RCAF and flew his first operations with No.401 Squadron RCAF in Britain, before transferring to No.133 'Eagle' Squadron.

American volunteers were impatient with the RAF's insistence that they receive a thorough training in procedures and tactics before being committed to combat. Moreover, the more experienced American pilots who had joined the RAF before the formation of the Eagle Squadron were often dismayed to be posted to this inexperienced unit. Several of these pilots had fought in the Battle of Britain with RAF fighter units and wanted to stay with them, rather than being posted to an all-American squadron.

No.71 Squadron's incipient morale problems were compounded by an early and unplanned change in leaders. Squadron Leader Churchill was suffering from sinus trouble, and eventually he had to be taken off flying. Unfortunately Taylor was generally disliked by the Eagle Squadron pilots. Luckily, the situation was restored by the appointment of Squadron Leader Henry 'Paddy' Woodhouse as the next British commanding officer. His calm and masterful leadership, combined with an insistence on the highest standards of airmanship and flying discipline, soon shaped the disparate group of American adventurers into an effective fighting unit. Nevertheless, while still under Taylor, their initiation into combat in the spring of 1941 was a gentle one. Operating from Martlesham Heath in Suffolk, the squadron's Hurricanes flew convoy patrols and maintained a flight 'at readiness' for defensive interceptions. Their first skirmish with the enemy came on 17 April, when Pilot Officer G.A. 'Gus' Daymond attacked a Dornier Do 17, apparently without effect.

The Eagles' first confirmed victory did not come until 2 July, by which time No.71 Squadron was operating as part of the North Weald Wing. The successful pilot was Pilot Officer William R. Dunn, who was flying as Squadron Leader Woodhouse's No.2 during an escort mission over France. Dunn saw a Messerschmitt Bf 109F diving through the bomber formation and, jamming open his throttle, he attacked it from the port quarter. He was later to recall:

'At about 50yds range (the Hun kite filled my whole windscreen) I could see my machine-gun bullets striking all over the German's fuselage and wing-root. Then he began to smoke. I continued my attack down to 3500ft, again firing at point blank range. Now the 109 began burning furiously, dived straight down to the ground, where it crashed with a hell of an explosion near a crossroad.'

Background: Two Hurricanes beat up the airfield in a daredevil display of flying. The Eagles' aces included Pilot Officer William Dunn (right) who chalked up their first kill and (top far right) Flight Lieutenant Gus Daymond (in cockpit), seen with Squadron Leader Chesley Peterson.

Dunn went on to become the first Eagle Squadron ace – and, indeed, the first American ace of World War II. His fourth and fifth victories were gained on 27 August, but Dunn was wounded in this action and on his recovery he was posted away from No. 71 Squadron. Unaccountably, he never received the publicity that was his due for these achievements, although they have been fully authenticated by postwar research into the official records.

It was in August 1941 that No. 71 Squadron converted from the Hurricane onto the Spitfire, with which it continued to fly bomber escort missions, fighter sweeps and 'Rhubarbs' (low-level forays over enemy territory by small formations of fighters, seeking out targets of opportunity). In November 1941 one of the squadron's outstanding American pilots, Chesley G. Peterson, was promoted to squadron leader and took command of the unit. He proved to be a brave and skilful leader, and when the three RAF Eagle Squadrons were absorbed into the USAAF as the 4th Fighter Group, Peterson was promoted to colonel and became the group's commander at the age of 23 years. The most successful of No. 71 Squadron's pilots in terms of enemy aircraft destroyed, however, was Gus Daymond, who shot down a Focke Wulf Fw 190 on 1 June 1942 for his sixth victory. The winter of 1941-42 had been a quiet period for Fighter Command's squadrons, but with the return of better weather in the spring the air fighting became more hectic, culminating in the great fighter battles over the Dieppe landings on 19 August 1942.

No. 71 Squadron flew four missions over Dieppe as

Below left: Three of the first recruits to the squadron were (left to right) Pilot Officers Tobin, Keough and Mamedoff, here displaying their new badge. Another early volunteer was Michel Kolendorski (below right). Harold Strickland (above left) was, at 38, one of the oldest recruits. He is in an aircraft donated by Manchester Corporation.

part of the Debden Wing, led by Wing Commander Myles Duke-Woolley. The first of these departed from Gravesend, which the squadron was using as a forward base, at 0450 hours. One of the pilots recalled:

'When we started the Merlin engines of our

Eagle Squadrons
1940-1942

GREAT
BRITAIN

NORTH SEA

Amsterdam

Rotterdam

NETHERLANDS

Debden

Martlesham
Heath

North Weald

London

Manston

Lympne

Gravesend

Dover

Antwerp

BELGIUM

Exeter

Southampton

Biggin Hill

Beachy Head

New Romney

Plymouth

ENGLISH CHANNEL

Dieppe

Le Havre

Seine

FRANCE

Paris

Key
Route of Morlaix raid,
26 Sept 1942

Eagle Squadron bases

Site of Eagle Squadron engagement

Brest   Morlaix

Spitfires, some cloud patches had piled up in the east, making it very dark. We pointed our Spits into the breeze in tight formation of fours and took off into the night, then we quickly shifted to line astern. We flew low over Kent on our way out and, still flying almost on the deck, we arrived at our departure point on the English coast. Then we set our course for Dieppe, flying very low and close to the sea. Each of us watched his instruments carefully, for in the dark there was no horizon and the sea was flat.'

The squadron's patrol was generally uneventful. However, Pilot Officer Harold Strickland, who had become separated from the formation when he throttled back to stay in contact with his lagging wingman, did have a brush with a German fighter. His No.2's undercarriage had failed to retract properly, and, after sending that aircraft back to Gravesend, Strickland attempted to regain the squadron formation. In the half-light before dawn this proved to be impossible. But to the west of Dieppe, Strickland found a formation of four Fw 190s. He carried out a high-speed attack on the rearmost, which was straggling. He saw his cannon shells hit and the German fighter dive away. Strickland then pulled up into a steep, climbing turn to evade the remaining Fw 190s. He saw nothing more of the fighter he fired at and so could only claim it as damaged.

Dawn had just broken as No.71 Squadron returned from its first patrol. It was airborne once more at 1045 hours and on arriving over Dieppe the pilots could see many air combats in progress. Numerous fires were burning in the town and two ships were on fire in the harbour. A lone Junkers Ju 88 that had slipped past the high-cover Spitfires was pounced upon. Squadron Leader Peterson got into a firing position and saw hits on the German bomber. It was last seen 'hell-bent for Berlin, black smoke streaming from its engines and some 15 Spitfires on its tail, each of them trying to get into position to make the kill.' Peterson was credited with the Ju 88 damaged, the only squadron claim during this combat. Blue Section's Spitfires had fenced with a formation of Fw 190s, but the German pilots were reluctant to get into a fight and instead attempted to draw the RAF fighters away from the landing ships that they were covering.

At about 1300 hours cloud began building up over Dieppe and as No.71 Squadron began its third patrol of the day it became increasingly difficult to cover the shipping. By that time the withdrawal from the beaches was almost complete. Fighter cover at this critical stage was provided by the Polish Wing (No 302, 303, 308 and 317 Squadrons) and two of the

Biggin Hill units (No.222 and 611 Squadrons), as well as the Eagles. No.71 Squadron, patrolling at 4500ft, was more fortunate in finding enemy aircraft than the squadrons flying at higher altitudes. Squadron Leader Peterson spotted three Ju 88s, flying 2000ft above them and about to start a bombing run on the shipping. He attacked, forcing them to break away and dive for safety. Singling out one of the bombers, Peterson opened fire from 300yds astern. His cannon shells hit its starboard wing and the engine began to smoke. As Peterson closed in to 200yds, return fire from the bomber hit his Spitfire. He nonetheless pressed home his attack to 150yds range. Then his cockpit filled with smoke and fumes and, with his Spitfire's engine burning, Peterson was forced to resort to his parachute. He could not see what became of his target, but Wing Commander Duke-Woolley confirmed that it crashed into the sea. Peterson was lucky enough to be picked out of the water by a British MTB within 15 minutes of coming down, but then the boat was strafed by an Fw 190 and another pilot who had been rescued was killed by Peterson's side.

He opened fire at 400yds and closed in to 200yds, exhausting his ammunition in the process

Pilot Officer Stanley M. Anderson and Pilot Officer Richard D. McMinn attacked another of the Ju 88s. Anderson opened fire at 400yds above and astern of the German bomber and then closed in to 200yds range, before breaking away. He believed that he hit the rear gunner, as return fire suddenly stopped. Flight Lieutenant Oscar H. Coen, leading Blue Section, used emergency boost to catch up with the third Ju 88. He opened fire at 400yds and closed in to 200yds, exhausting his ammunition in the process. He saw the bomber's port engine belch black smoke and fragments break away from the engine and wing. His attack was followed up by his wingman, Flying Officer M.G. 'Wee Michael' McPharlin. McPharlin had pulled up slightly above Coen, so that he could fire past his leader without risk of hitting him. Concentrating his aim on the bomber's fuselage, he fired a long burst of cannon and machine-gun fire. The smoke from the Ju 88 thickened and flames appeared from the port wing-root. At this point, McPharlin spotted two Fw 190s about to engage him, and so was forced to break away from the German bomber and pull around to face their attack. He last saw the Ju 88 going down towards the sea in a shallow dive. It was assessed as probably destroyed. McPharlin evaded the Fw 190s in cloud, but his compass had been hit by enemy fire and so he had difficulty in setting a course for home. Obtaining a rough orientation from a glimpse of the sun, he flew out to sea. However, the skirmish with the German fighters had used up most of his fuel and his tanks ran dry before reaching the English coast. McPharlin

Background: Pilots relax in the dispersal hut beneath a model dogfight before going out to engage in the real thing. Centre left: Pilot Officer Luke Allen poses on the wing of his Hurricane. Bottom left: King George VI inspects the squadron.

Two pilots, mission completed, walk away from their aircraft. The squadron received its first consignment of Hurricane Mk 1s in November 1940 to replace the unsatisfactory Brewster F2A Buffalo with which it was first equipped. This aircraft, developed originally for the US Navy, was unsuitable for land-based operations and the particular models assigned to No.71 Squadron proved unreliable. Squadron Leader Churchill ensured their replacement by ordering his pilots to land their aircraft with tail wheel locked, a manoeuvre which he knew would cause them to crash land. The squadron operated with Hurricanes until August 1941, when it converted to Spitfires.

had no alternative but to bale out. He paddled the remaining seven miles to the shore in his dinghy, after obtaining some stimulation from the Benzedrine tablets in his emergency kit.

The Eagles' fourth sortie of the day met the Dieppe convoy in mid-Channel, heading back to port. The weather had worsened by 1700 hours, with low cloud and rain showers providing cover for the bombers and Fw 190s attempting to harass the raiders. Wing Commander Duke-Woolley was leading his Debden Wing, comprising No.71, 124 and 232 Squadrons. No.71 Squadron, with Peterson not yet returned, was led by Flight Lieutenant Gus Daymond. A formation of Fw 190s appeared and Daymond positioned the Eagle Squadron for an attack from above, with the sun behind them. However, the German pilots would not accept the challenge and retreated at speed towards Le Touquet. As evening approached, the last of the convoy was within sight of Beachy Head, and so the squadron flew back to Gravesend to land. The groundcrews, anticipating a further patrol, quickly refuelled and rearmed the Spitfires, but the day's fighting was by then over.

'We could not ask for better companions with whom to see this fight through to the finish'

By the summer of 1942 the USAAF was beginning to build up its formations in Britain. Boeing B-17 Flying Fortresses of the Eighth Air Force carried out their first bombing mission over France on 17 August. On 21 August No.71 Squadron was to have formed part of the fighter escort for a formation of 12 B-17s which was despatched to bomb shipyards at Rotterdam. Unfortunately, there was a complete mix-up over the orders, with the result that the Spitfires never met the bombers. The B-17s came under heavy fighter attack and were forced to abort their mission. However, over the following weeks, as the USAAF's airmen gained in experience, the co-operation between the Eighth Air Force's bombers and their RAF escort fighters gradually improved. On 5 September, No.71 Squadron escorted 31 B-17s to Rouen, the largest raid flown by the American bombers up to that time. All the bombers returned to base safely. But not all the escort missions

were to go so smoothly. On 26 September the third Eagle Squadron (No.133 Squadron) accompanied the B-17s to Morlaix in Brittany. Poor weather and high winds played havoc with the bombers' navigation, and eventually their escorts found themselves over Brest with insufficient fuel to reach the English coast. The RAF lost 10 of its new Spitfire Mk IXs as a result of this fiasco.

It had been decided that the RAF's three Eagle Squadrons should be incorporated into the USAAF's Eighth Air Force and the changeover took place on 29 September 1942. At a formal ceremony the Commander-in-Chief of Fighter Command, Air Marshal Sir William Sholto Douglas, paid tribute to the American volunteer airmen:

'We of Fighter Command deeply regret this parting. In the course of the past 18 months we have seen the stuff of which you are made. We could not ask for better companions with whom to see this fight through to the finish.'

The victory claims of the three squadrons totalled 73 and a half. The half represented a Dornier shared with a British squadron, 'a symbol of Anglo-American co-operation'.

Well over half of the enemy aircraft destroyed had been credited to the first Eagle Squadron, No.71 Squadron's score then standing at 41 victories. As the 334th Fighter Squadron of the 4th Fighter Group, the unit was to end the war as the highest-scoring squadron of the most successful USAAF fighter group. Many of the pilots who had learned their skills with the RAF went on to gain great distinction in American units. Gus Daymond became the 334th Fighter Squadron's first commander, as he had been No.71 (Eagle) Squadron's last CO. He was the top-scoring Eagle Squadron pilot with seven victories to his credit. Chesley Peterson was only a short way behind him with six victories. However, their achievements were ultimately to be overtaken by those of Duane W. Beeson, a 20-year old pilot officer at the time of the Eagle Squadron's transfer to the USAAF, who finished the war with 24 victories to his credit.

THE AUTHOR Anthony Robinson was formerly on the staff of the RAF Museum, Hendon, and is now a freelance military aviation writer. His books include *American Air Power* and *Aerial Warfare*.

JOLLY
GREEN GIANTS

HELICOPTER HEROES

Formed in early 1968, the 3rd Aerospace Rescue and Recovery Group (3rd ARRG) was based at Tan Son Nhut near Saigon and was responsible for all rescue operations in Southeast Asia during America's involvement in the Vietnam War. Initially, the group's headquarters had control of the 37th Aerospace Rescue and Recovery Squadron (37th ARRS) based at Da Nang and the 38th ARRS flying out of Tan Son Nhut. These units were later reinforced by the 39th ARRS, equipped with HC-130 Hercules aircraft, and the 40th ARRS – both of which formed at Udorn in Thailand. As numerous other recovery outfits were created, the Joint Search and Rescue Centre was established to co-ordinate the efforts of the various airborne rescue services. The 3rd ARRG reached its peak strength during the summer of 1969, with a total of 71 aircraft serving with its four squadrons. The 37th ARRS at Da Nang and the 40th at Udorn flew recovery missions over Laos, North and South Vietnam while local rescues were the responsibility of the 38th ARRS at Tan Son Nhut. The 39th ARRS, stationed at Tuy Hoa, worked with HC-130 tankers and command post aircraft.
In the period between 1966 and 1970, the 3rd ARRG was credited with saving the lives of 2039 persons. The group was finally deactivated on 31 January 1976. In some eight years, the 3rd ARRG had saved 3883 lives for the loss of 71 men killed and 45 aircraft destroyed. Their sacrifice had been made in the true spirit of the ARRG's motto: 'That Others May Live.'
Above: The shoulder badge of the ARRS.

Helicopter crews of the 3rd Rescue and Recovery Group fought a heroic campaign in Vietnam to save downed pilots from the clutches of the enemy

THE HAZARDS faced by the helicopter crews of the United States Air Force Aerospace Rescue and Recovery Service (ARRS) during the Vietnam War were considerable. They were often required to fly into heavily defended areas to pick up shot-down aircrew, and the North Vietnamese Army (NVA) and

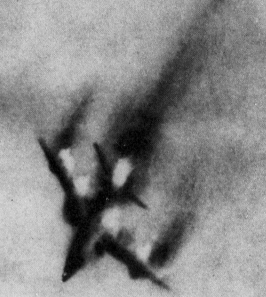

Viet Cong became adept at setting flak traps for the American helicopters in places where they knew a downed airman was hiding. In addition to the dangers of enemy action, the rescue crews had to cope with difficulties of terrain and climate: operating over thick jungles or mountainous areas in a region which was subject to fierce and unpredictable tropical storms. The early rescue helicopters were often forced to operate at the limits of their range and in 'hot-and-high' conditions in which these relatively low-powered aircraft performed badly. All these risks were accepted by the ARRS crews in order to save fellow airmen from capture by an implacable enemy, from whom they could expect harsh treatment, torture and even summary execution.

The first search-and-rescue missions of the war were carried out on an ad hoc basis by troop-carrying helicopters diverted from their normal missions. However, in 1964 specialised rescue aircraft, Kaman HH-43B Husky helicopters and Grumman HU-16 Albatross amphibious flying boats were deployed to the combat theatre. The latter could, of course, only be used to rescue airmen who had come down into the sea and so their usefulness was limited. Nonetheless, they carried out many worthwhile

missions over the Gulf of Tonkin and some of their most hazardous rescues were made under fire from North Vietnamese coastal batteries. The HH-43B helicopters, which had been designed for local rescue duties, lacked the range and loitering capability needed for operations into enemy territory, but they were the only specialised rescue helicopters available in Southeast Asia until late 1965 and had to undertake as many of these dangerous missions as was practicable.

Modifications to the basic HH-43B to improve its combat performance included the fitting of a larger capacity self-sealing fuel tank, a more powerful engine and titanium armour for the crew positions and powerplant. Perhaps the most important modification of all was the jungle penetrator fitted to a 250ft cable, which allowed survivors to be winched up safely through the jungle canopy and was fitted to all later rescue helicopters. However, even the improved Huskies (designated HH-43Fs) could only operate effectively by using forward bases. Typical of these were Lima Site 98 at Long Tieng, HQ of the Meo guerrilla leader Vang Pao, and Lima Site 36 at Na Khang, both in Laos. The latter was described as 'a strongpoint perched on the top of a mountain. It included a short dirt runway, a few sand-bagged shacks and trenchworks. Laotian troops defended it from the Pathet Lao and from the North Vietnamese who often held the surrounding countryside. Even when the improved HH-3E Jolly Green Giants entered combat from late 1965 onwards, forward bases were still needed and it was only after the introduction of helicopter in-flight refuelling that they could be dispensed with finally.

In January 1968 the crucial importance of the rescue mission was recognised with the organization of the 3rd Aerospace Rescue and Recovery Group (ARRG), under the command of Colonel Arthur W. Beale. The unit's work was described by Lieutenant-Colonel Marrion L. Costello, operations officer of the 39th ARRS. Following the ejection of an airman over enemy territory:

'The first action is to obtain an exact position and pass it on to the Rescue Control Centre [and] then secure the area in which the downed pilot is

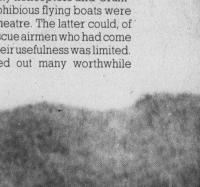

Page 55 : Unsung heroes of the Vietnam War, the pararescue-jumpers ('PJs') and chopper pilots of the 3rd Aerospace Rescue and Recovery Group fought against a tough enemy to save the lives of US Air Force personnel shot down by enemy ground fire. Air gunners (left) would cover the PJs as they were winched down to pluck crew members out of the jungle. Often flying in the face of intense fire, the group suffered heavy losses so that, in the words of its motto, 'Others may live.'
Left: Testament to the ferocity of the air battle over Vietnam, the pilot of an F-105D Thunderchief floats to earth as his aircraft plunges down, a victim of enemy AA fire.

located. Other aircraft in the area usually hear the emergency signals, and almost immediately, we are controlling rescue helicopters and escort aircraft which may be needed to protect the downed pilots.'

The basic elements of the rescue mission remained unaltered throughout the war, although tactics could be infinitely varied. Colonel William M. Harris, commander of the 37th ARRS during 1971-72, wrote: 'Rescue efforts have called upon every conceivable military resource as well as... Air America, special ground teams, clandestine operations, frogmen, aircraft carriers, tanks and so on. There is no limitation on tactics or concepts to be employed to effect a rescue.'

Once in position, the first necessity for the helicopter crew was to find out if the downed airman was injured and then discover what enemy forces were in his vicinity. If a rescue attempt was then deemed feasible, the rescue helicopters, which usually operated in pairs, were scrambled from their forward base. They would be escorted by a flight of slow-flying, piston-engined Douglas A-1 Skyraiders (which invariably used the call-sign 'Sandy'), armed with cannon, rockets and bombs to deal with any groundfire. Later in the war, the A-1s were armed with smoke munitions, so that they could lay down a smokescreen between the rescue helicopter and enemy forces, and they could also carry riot-control chemicals in cluster-bomb units.

Helicopters often had to run the gauntlet of intense groundfire to effect their pick-ups

It was the job of the A-1 flight leader to assess the situation on the ground and to direct his aircraft into attacks on enemy troops who might interfere with the rescue. If necessary, he could call on assistance from any other attack aircraft, which would be diverted from their primary mission for this purpose. Where there was a risk of North Vietnamese interceptors intervening, the rescue task force would be covered by a MiG CAP (combat air patrol) of fighter aircraft. On some occasions, rescue attempts required hundreds of sorties by relays of helicopters, A-1 escorts, attack and fighter aircraft. The job of co-ordinating these forces could be very complex, necessitating the use of an airborne command post to supplement the efforts of the ground control centres and also to act as a communications link. Initially, this task was carried out by obsolescent HU-16s and Douglas SC-54s, but in 1966 these gave way to specially-modified HC-130 Hercules. Once the A-1 escort leader had satisfied himself that the pick-up zone had been cleared of enemy forces, he would call in the rescue helicopter. However, this was often the signal for well-concealed enemy gun positions to come into action and the helicopters often had to run the gauntlet of intense groundfire to effect their pick-ups.

The hazardous rescue flights into enemy territory became the primary duty of the Sikorsky HH-3E Jolly Green Giants after their arrival in Southeast Asia during November 1965. Thereafter, the Huskies were relegated to the local rescue missions for which they were best suited. The HH-3E was both faster and further-ranging than its predecessor, carried more armour plating and was fitted with a single 7.62mm machine gun to provide some defensive firepower. Yet for all its fine qualities, the HH-3E lacked the performance, protection and defensive firepower needed to penetrate the most heavily defended areas of Laos and North Vietnam. A major improvement in the Jolly Green Giant's capabilities came in 1967 with the introduction of in-flight refuelling equipment. Operating in concert with HC-130P tanker/command post aircraft, the HH-3Es could remain airborne for long periods (an eight-hour patrol over the Gulf of Tonkin was soon demonstrated). This meant that instead of scrambling from forward bases when a rescue call came through, the helicopters would be already in the air flying a holding pattern and so could react to the emergency much more quickly.

One of the most famous Jolly Green Giant rescue missions was flown into the southern panhandle of Laos to extract the survivors of an army reconnaissance team from an enemy ambush. Two helicopters had already been shot down in the attempt, when a pair of HH-3Es moved into the area shortly after midnight, accompanied by a C-130 flare-dropper and three US Army gunship helicopters. The first Jolly Green Giant managed to pick up three of the survivors before it was riddled with enemy fire and, streaming fuel and hydraulic fluid, was forced to pull out. The back-up HH-3E, piloted by Captain Gerald O. Young, then attempted to recover the two wounded Americans left on the ground. With his co-pilot, Captain Ralph Brower, directing the fire of the escorting gunships, Young brought his helicopter down onto a hillside in the ghostly light of the flares. While Staff Sergeant Eugene Clay attempted to suppress the enemy's fire with the helicopter's single machine gun, Sergeant Larry Maysey leapt to the ground and carried the wounded men aboard.

The Jolly Green Giant was about to lift off when enemy fire ripped into its engine compartment. This caused an explosion that flipped the aircraft onto its back and sent it tumbling down the hillside in a ball of fire. Young, his clothing aflame, fought his way out of the wreckage. Only one other crewman survived and he was unconscious. Fearing that he would be used as bait to lure further rescue helicopters into a trap, Young refused to use his survival radio to bring in help; instead, he allowed a group of the enemy to pick up his trail and led them away from his wounded comrade. Despite the increasing pain from his burns, Young evaded capture for a period of 17 hours. Then, judging that he had lost his pursuers, he finally called in a rescue helicopter. His selfless courage was recognised by the award of the Medal of Honor.

Not all of the 3rd ARRG's heroes were helicopter pilots, however. The pararescue-jumpers or 'PJs', whose job it was to recover the survivors, often took a large share of the action. They were responsible for winching able-bodied airmen aboard and, if necessary, going down to assist the wounded. On several occasions PJs elected to remain in enemy territory to allow an overloaded helicopter to carry a rescued airman to safety. All PJs were qualified parachutists, medical technicians and divers. They were experts in survival under all conditions from arctic to tropical terrains and were skilled in combat techniques.

Duane D. Hackney of the 37th ARRS was the most-decorated PJ to serve in Southeast Asia and he took part in many hazardous missions. During one rescue, on 16 February 1967, Hackney descended into a jungle area of North Vietnam to recover an injured pilot. He strapped him into a litter and the two were winched back up to the hovering HH-3E when NVA troops opened fire. The pilot pulled up, but not before the enemy gunners had found their mark.

Hackney strapped a parachute onto the wounded pilot, before climbing into one himself. Seconds later the Jolly Green Giant exploded. Hackney, whose parachute opened just above the treetops, was the only survivor.

A survivor's view of one of the 3rd ARRG's rescues was written by Captain Gene I. Basel, an F-105 pilot of the 355th Tactical Fighter Wing (TFW). His aircraft had been hit by AA fire when attacking targets on the Ho Chi Minh Trail and exploded in mid-air. Basel was thrown clear and his parachute opened. However, both of his legs had been broken and his parachute became entangled in high trees, leaving him suspended helpless 50ft above the jungle floor. Basel managed to contact the rescue forces on his survival radio, although he was very weak from his injuries and only conscious for part of the time:

'Strength pumped through me when the "whap-whap-whap" of the Jolly Green Giant filtered down through the tangled jungle growth. The chopper hovered over me, creating a small hurricane that sent branches flying around and me tumbling merrily out of the tree. The chute snagged again about 10ft from the ground. I hugged a big grey tree trunk for dear life.

'Down came a long rope with a young man dressed in striped jungle fatigues hanging on the end. We stared at each other while leaves and dirt and branches flew around. It was a sort of slow-motion, nightmare scene. He was reaching out and I was reaching out, but our hands lacked five feet of touching. He was on the rope and I was in the tree. Finally, he radioed something and the line was let down to the jungle floor.

'I know I probably looked like a madman, with flying hair, a bloody face and wild eyes. Those hanging legs were a feature that added to the overall effect. I wonder to this day if I may have scared him, just a little. His name was Joe Duffy and he was 20-years-old. I'm sure it occurred to him (as it did to me) that if we kept fooling around down here, there was a good chance that some alien people would come and kill us both.

'Joe was getting ready to scale the tree when I motioned I was coming down. I swung away from the tree trunk and pulled the emergency release. Down I went, like a giant rag doll and damn near landed on top of him. We both scrambled onto the folding jungle penetrator at the end of the rope. Then Dale Oderman, the chopper pilot, began to ease us out of the jungle slowly, up five, left three, with Joe radioing instructions. I was so weak that my pale hands would hardly grip anything. I was in danger of slipping off. Even though I was trying with all my might, gritting my teeth, my hands wouldn't grab. Joe kept a white-knuckle grip on my sleeve, as we agonised our way slowly up through the trees and vines.

'Then we were free and I heard Joe shout, "Let's get out of here!" Dale gunned the big Super Jolly and the jungle fell away. Joe and I were on the end of 200ft of swinging cable and I should have been scared and nervous about the ever-increasing height, but I just hung there and watched the jungle whirl and recede.'

In September 1967 the 37th ARRS received the first two Sikorsky HH-53Bs to arrive in Southeast Asia. These large and powerful helicopters represented as big an improvement over the HH-3E as those aircraft had over the Huskies. In addition to its normal crew of five, the HH-53 could carry up to 38 passengers or 24 stretcher patients. It was armed with three

Right: Two of the most vital elements of any rescue mission; a KC-135 tanker and a Jolly Green Giant. Working in unison, they were able to reach out and pluck downed airmen from the jaws of captivity in most areas of Vietnam. Flying at low level, however, the choppers were often sitting ducks for enemy anti-aircraft guns and missiles.

7.62mm Miniguns, each having a rate of fire of 4000 rounds per minute. The HH-53's tremendous power reserves made rescue operations in mountainous areas much less hazardous than with the earlier helicopters, but its massive size sometimes made manoeuvring in restricted spaces a problem and offered a tempting target to enemy gunners. Officially known as the Super Jolly Green Giant, the new helicopter was soon dubbed the BUFF by its crews, which stood for 'Big Ugly Fat Fellow'. Hand-in-hand with improvements made to rescue aircraft during the early 1960s were numerous advances in the design of such associated equipment as survival radios, signals and flares and helicopter protection from groundfire.

12 helicopters had been badly battle-damaged and a PJ aboard one of them killed

One of the largest-scale actions in support of a rescue mission took place over Ban Phanop in Laos during three days of December 1969. It began on 5 December, when the crew of an F-4 Phantom was forced to eject after being hit by groundfire. The two men, Captain Benjamin Danielson and his weapons-systems officer Lieutenant Woodrow Bergeron, landed in the bottom of a valley which was dominated by enemy AA guns. In spite of the fire from relays of A-1 Skyraiders, supported by F-4 Phantom, F-100 Super Sabre and F-105 Thunderchief jets, the enemy gunners maintained a withering fire against the rescue helicopters throughout the day. Nine sorties were flown by HH-3Es and HH-53s and eight battle-damaged helicopters limped back to Nakhon Phanom airbase in Thailand with no pick-up accomplished.

The next day opened with repeated tactical air strikes on the gun positions, but rescue helicopters were still unable to reach the survivors. That morning, searching North Vietnamese troops found Danielson's hiding place and shot him dead. Later in the day, the A-1s laid a smokescreen around Bergeron, but it proved to be too effective and the rescue helicopter could not find him in it. Finally, on 7 December a helicopter, closely escorted by A-1 Skyraiders, reached Bergeron's position and pulled him to safety. The operation had lasted for over 50 hours, involving a total of 336 sorties. Five A-1s had been hit by AA fire, 12 helicopters had been badly battle-damaged and a PJ aboard one of them killed. It had been a tremendous effort for the rescue of one man.

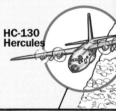

Radar Picket

An EC-121 radar picket watches out for MiG take-offs and SAM launches. Information is analysed by the 'Red Crown' warship and passed on.

HC-130 Hercules

Airborne Command Post

A specially modified HC-130 Hercules transport circles, providing a communications link and co-ordinating the rescue forces. The airborne command post works in conjunction with ground control centres and other airborne control and surveillance aircraft.

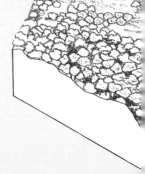

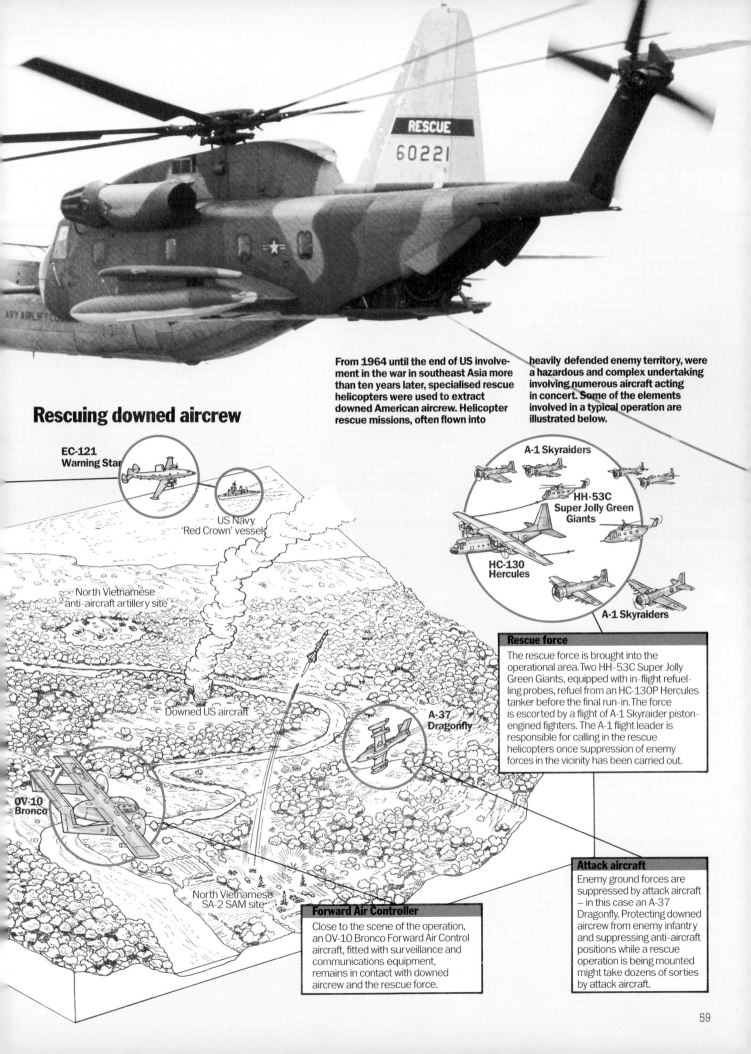

RESCUE

60221

Rescuing downed aircrew

From 1964 until the end of US involvement in the war in southeast Asia more than ten years later, specialised rescue helicopters were used to extract downed American aircrew. Helicopter rescue missions, often flown into heavily defended enemy territory, were a hazardous and complex undertaking involving numerous aircraft acting in concert. Some of the elements involved in a typical operation are illustrated below.

EC-121
Warning Star

US Navy
'Red Crown' vessel

A-1 Skyraiders

HH-53C
Super Jolly Green
Giants

HC-130
Hercules

A-1 Skyraiders

North Vietnamese
anti-aircraft artillery site

Downed US aircraft

A-37
Dragonfly

OV-10
Bronco

North Vietnamese
SA-2 SAM site

Rescue force

The rescue force is brought into the operational area. Two HH-53C Super Jolly Green Giants, equipped with in-flight refuelling probes, refuel from an HC-130P Hercules tanker before the final run-in. The force is escorted by a flight of A-1 Skyraider piston-engined fighters. The A-1 flight leader is responsible for calling in the rescue helicopters once suppression of enemy forces in the vicinity has been carried out.

Forward Air Controller

Close to the scene of the operation, an OV-10 Bronco Forward Air Control aircraft, fitted with surveillance and communications equipment, remains in contact with downed aircrew and the rescue force.

Attack aircraft

Enemy ground forces are suppressed by attack aircraft – in this case an A-37 Dragonfly. Protecting downed aircrew from enemy infantry and suppressing anti-aircraft positions while a rescue operation is being mounted might take dozens of sorties by attack aircraft.

SUPPORT MISSIONS

Widely recognised as one of the most successful post-war aircraft designs, the Douglas A-1 Skyraider enjoyed a career that lasted from the end of World War II to Vietnam, where the aircraft proved particularly successful in the ground-support role.

The brainchild of Ed Heineman, the chief engineer with Douglas, the Skyraider's prototype, known as the XBT2D-1, first flew in mid-March 1945.

Although the aircraft entered full production too late to see service in World War II, it saw action in the Korean War, where its large weapon-carrying capacity, up to 8000kg, and its endurance of 10 hours proved invaluable in support of ground forces. Production quotas of the Skyraider were fulfilled in 1957, by which time over 3000 aircraft had been built. However, the Skyraider remained in use with both the USAF and US Navy. In 1962 those aircraft still in use were redesignated A1-D to A1-J, and as American involvement in Vietnam escalated, Skyraiders flew with the USAF's 1st Air Commando Group of the Tactical Air Command and the US Navy. Affectionately known as 'Sandy' or 'The Spad', the A-1 proved invaluable in winkling out pockets of guerrillas.

The AD-7 Skyraider, redesignated as the A1-J in 1962, was powered by a Wright radial piston engine and had a top speed of 515km/h at 5640m. A wide variety of armaments, weighing up to 3600kg, could be carried on 15 hardpoints: mines, depth-charges, bombs, napalm, rockets and torpedoes. The Skyraider was also fitted with four 20mm cannon.

The rundown of American forces in South Vietnam from 1970 onwards had its effect on the 3rd ARRG, with a number of its subordinate units being disbanded while others were moved from South Vietnam to Thailand. Nonetheless, the unit's combat career was far from being over. On the night of 20 November 1970, helicopters and aircrew from the 37th ARRS and 40th ARRS took part in the raid on Son Tay prison camp, 23 miles from Hanoi. In spite of an initial mistake which led to troops being landed at a nearby sapper training camp instead of the prison compound, the helicopter operation went according to plan. However, it proved to be a fruitless effort as all the prisoners of war had been moved from Son Tay months before the raid.

During the return flight, one HH-53 came under attack from a North Vietnamese MiG-21. The chopper's pilot, Lieutenant-Colonel Royal C. Brown of the 37th ARRS, dived down to low level, where his violent manoeuvres soon shook off his pursuer. Yet, the night's excitement was not over for Brown. One of the raider's support aircraft, a Wild Weasel F-105F of the 388th TFW, had been hit by an SA-2 Missile and its crew ejected over Laos. Teaming up with a second HH-53, Brown elected to remain in the area until first light. He then went in to pick up the downed pilot, Major Donald W. Kilgus, while his partner rescued the backseater. By that time, the two HH-53s had been airborne for over nine hours, most of the time over enemy territory and at night.

The North Vietnamese spring invasion of the South in 1972 led to an upsurge in the 3rd ARRG's operations. Moreover, in addition to the usual dangers of AA fire, the rescue aircraft became increasingly at risk from enemy surface-to-air missiles (SAMs),

Pages 60 and 61 : Helicopters often needed in-flight refuelling to reach the operational area (main picture). Once in situ, enemy groundfire was neutralised, either by the use of close-support aircraft, such as the A-1 Skyraider (below left), or the 7.62mm minigun (below right). After the immediate rescue area had been saturated by fire, 'PJs' would descend to effect the recovery (below centre). Below left: A PJ drops down into the Gulf of Tonkin to recover wreckage from a downed aircraft and (above) displays his find for the camera. Below: Members of the 3rd ARRG's 37th Squadron pose for the camera inside a Jolly Green Giant at their base near Da Nang. Bottom right: The aircrew of a downed Phantom, their faces etched with the strain of a terrifying ordeal, wait for a medical check at one of the group's bases. Main picture: Nose view of a 'Giant'.

which were moved southwards with the advancing troops. On 2 April, a Douglas EB-66 electronic-warfare aircraft was hit by an SA-2 in the vicinity of the demilitarized zone. Only one crewmember, Lieutenant-Colonel Iceal E. Hambleton, survived. However, since he had come down in an area infested with North Vietnamese troops, his rescue proved to be impossible. From that day until 13 April, an average of 90 tactical strike sorties a day were flown in an attempt to silence the enemy gunners. The only HH-53 to attempt a pick-up was shattered by AA fire and crashed killing its entire crew. Eventually a US Marine Corps ground team was sent in to carry out the rescue.

Another hazardous mission fell to the 3rd ARRG on 1 May, when four HH-53s of the 37th ARRS were despatched to Quang Tri to pull out the besieged defenders of the city's citadel. More than 100 American and South Vietnamese troops had been cut off there by the advancing North Vietnamese Army. The mission had to be flown at low level, because SA-2 SAMs now covered the area, but in avoiding this threat the helicopters would put themselves within easy range of groundfire. Some A-1 Skyraiders blasted a path up to the walls of the fortress for the three leading HH-53s, while a fourth acted as back-up aircraft. As the first helicopter touched down within the citadel, enemy fire intensified. This caused panic on the ground and only 34 troops

climbed aboard before the HH-53 lifted off. Its PJ, Staff Sergeant Robert La Pinte, courageously remained behind to restore order. The following two helicopters then picked up the remaining troops. However, as they were pulling out, the reserve HH-53 picked up a frantic radio call from the ground, 'Hey, we've got more people down here'. Its commander, Captain Donald A. Sutton, swooped in to land. The message proved to be an enemy ruse and the HH-53 came under close-range attack from North Vietnamese troops. Return fire from the helicopter was devastating and allowed Sutton to make his escape, so the mission was accomplished without loss.

After the ceasefire agreement of January 1973, the 3rd ARRG moved its HQ from South Vietnam to Nakhon Phanom in Thailand. It continued to operate over Laos and Cambodia, took part in the final evacuations of Phnom Penh and Saigon and the operation to rescue the merchant ship *Mayaguez* from Cambodian forces in May 1975. The latter mission ended the group's involvement in Southeast Asia, and marked the end of a distinguished wartime career.

THE AUTHOR Anthony Robinson was formerly on the staff of the RAF Museum, Hendon, and is now a freelance military aviation writer. He has edited the books *Aerial Warfare* and the *Dictionary of Aviation*.

MOBILITY AND FIREPOWER

Helicopters gave the US 1st Cavalry Division a devastating strike capability and meant that troopers could be in action at a moment's notice – but were the slicks and gunships too fragile for the long grind of the Vietnam War?

AIR CAVALRY TACTICS

The 1st Air Cavalry Division (Airmobile) had no 'book' to go by when its units first went into action, and tactics, which varied from unit to unit, had to be evolved to meet local conditions. In general, however, the basic combat formation was the troop of four platoons, divided up into 'teams', colour-coded for easy reference and earmarked for a particular task. The 'pink' hunter-killer team was formed from the 'white' aero scouts flying OH-6 Loaches, and the 'red' section of Cobra gunships. The 'blue' team consisted of the troop's lift element – eight UH-1D Hueys and the Aero Rifle Platoon (ARP). A mission's success depended heavily on a high degree of co-ordination between these two elements.

In action, pink teams identified enemy positions, marked-out suitable landing zones (LZ), and then called up the blues to deal with the enemy on the ground. As the ARPs dismounted and set up a defensive perimeter, Loaches directed them towards an enemy target. The pink team's Cobras remained on station to provide aerial artillery support.

Combat experience in Vietnam justified the use of teams; they enabled the air cav to locate, fix and destroy the enemy before he could escape. The tactics proved that helicopter mobility and firepower could work in close harmony.

WHEN the 1st Cavalry Division (Airmobile) arrived in Vietnam in 1965 it was a formation under close scrutiny, not only from within the US Army itself, but also from the wider military fraternity around the world. Equipping a unit of divisional strength with lavish air support was a controversial decision, and both sides of the 'airmobility debate' awaited with interest the results of the 1st Cavalry's baptism of fire. Supporters of the idea believed that their faith could be justified only by the successful deployment of thousands of troops, fully supported by all the essential back-up services, into a combat zone. Their critics argued that this was a wasteful use of valuable resources, and that smaller airborne units working alongside conventional forces would perform better.

Over the next five years, however, the 1st Cavalry Division totally vindicated the faith placed in it by its supporters. From its first real test in the battle for the Ia Drang Valley in 1965, through a whole series of major engagements – Hue, Khe Sanh, A Shau Valley and Liberty Canyon, right up to the invasion of Cambodia in 1970 – the 1st Cavalry gained for itself the title of premier combat division in the US Army.

The two cornerstones of the division's success in Vietnam were, first, the quality of the men – the flying skills of the pilots, the inventiveness of the engineers, the determination of the ground troops ('grunts'), and the tactical flair of the commanders – and, second, the new weapons and equipment that were made available to them.

The weapons and equipment used by the 1st Cavalry transformed the relationship between firepower and mobility. Previously, any increase in firepower could only be made at the expense of mobility (or vice-versa), but the airmobility concept added a new dimension to the equation: firepower could now be allied to mobility – and an increase in one could enhance the effectiveness of the other.

The 1st Cavalry could muster over 400 aircraft. A few of them were fixed-wing types used for reconnaissance and surveillance purposes, but the vast majority were helicopters – the tactical lynchpin around which the division revolved. When the division arrived in Vietnam the two most important helicopter types were the UH-1 Iroquois, a highly versatile multi-mission helicopter, and the CH-47 Chinook, a twin-engined transport.

Known to the troops as the Huey, the UH-1 was the most successful helicopter to see service in Vietnam. The variety of roles it performed, including the movement of personnel, equipment and supplies,

reconnaissance, medical evacuation (medevac) and armed escort, were crucial to the success of any operation. The UH-1D was the most numerous of the Huey series, and, as the division's assault-troop transport, it was armed with two door-mounted 7.62mm M60 machine guns. It could also carry 11 or 12 fully-equipped soldiers. Besides the two gunners, one of whom acted as the crew chief, there were two pilots, seated side-by-side with dual controls, in each helicopter. Fully loaded – whether with troops or an 1810kg cargo payload – the UH-1D was capable of a maximum speed of little more than 160kph.

All the Huey variants could be up-armed, but it was the UH-1C that acted as the 1st Cavalry's main gunship. Although capable of transporting only six troopers, it was a potent weapon when armed with 2.75in rockets, 40mm grenade launchers and the 7.62mm minigun mounted within a ball-turret in the helicopter's nose.

While the Hueys performed their role as assault helicopters, equally important work was carried out by the division's CH-47 Chinooks which had been specially developed to supplement the activity of the smaller UH-3 transports. The 1st Cavalry had its own Chinook battalion in Vietnam, but, shortly after its arrival, the division received additional aid in the shape of a separate Chinook-equipped helicopter company. Besides its crew of two pilots and a machine gunner/crew chief the Chinook could carry as many as 44 men, but in Vietnam, 30 to 35 troops were a more usual load. The CH-47A was the first type in US Army service, but was soon followed by the B and C models, which had a better performance and greater capacity.

Despite its troop-carrying capabilities the Chinook was mainly used to transport artillery and heavy supplies. Whole batteries of 105mm howitzers could be flown into the steepest and most inaccessible positions and kept supplied with ammunition. Under ideal conditions the CH-47C was able to transport up to 22 tonnes on its external cargo hook, but in extremely mountainous terrain A-model Chinooks were limited to a 3175kg payload as a safety measure.

Thanks to the Chinooks, the 1st Cavalry could position a fire support base (FSB), an essential part of any successful operation, virtually at will. After the deployment of the CH-47 the siting of mutually supporting FSBs could be based on tactical needs, rather than being determined by terrain.

Ever resourceful in developing new techniques to meet changing tactical situations, the 1st Cavalry adapted several Chinooks to act as bombers during Operation Pershing early in 1967. The Viet Cong had built a maze of tunnels and underground fortifications in Binh Dinh Province and tear gas was needed to drive the enemy out into the open. Standard tear-gas drums were rolled out of the Chinook's rear door and fusing systems, attached to a static line, armed the projectiles after they had fallen clear of the helicopter. Napalm was also dropped using this system. More than two tonnes of the chemical could

be carried by a single Chinook, and used to bomb specific targets where conventional fixed-wing aircraft would not have been as effective.

Another special 1st Cavalry adaptation of the Chinook was its conversion to a gunship. Popular with the grunts – who called them Go-Go Birds – three Chinooks underwent extensive combat trials armed with twin 20mm multi-barrel cannon, 40mm grenade launchers and 0.5in heavy machine guns. While the men on the ground liked the Go-Go Bird for its impressive air-to-ground fire support, the high level of maintenance required to keep the machine in the air, combined with the demand for Chinooks as transport helicopters, brought the experiment to an end.

The Cobra could take out Viet Cong positions with almost surgical precision

Although Hueys and Chinooks were the backbone of the 1st Cavalry's air support during the first couple of years in Vietnam, other helicopters performed equally important missions. The CH-54 Tarhe Sky Crane was responsible for moving oversize loads and for the recovery of downed aircraft, and the diminutive OH-6 Cayuse acted as an economical and speedy reconnaissance helicopter.

The fighting in the Ia Drang Valley in 1965 highlighted the combat limitations of the UH-1C. It was clearly too large and too slow to be an effective gunship. Acting on their own initiative the Bell Helicopter Company developed the extraordinary AH-1 Huey Cobra. For the pilots who had been flying the old UH-1Cs the Cobra was a revelation when it arrived in Vietnam at the end of 1967. A fast, agile, and armoured gun platform, the Cobra changed everyone's thinking.

The most telling argument directed against the helicopter was its inability to survive heavy ground fire, and it was this criticism that was paramount in the minds of the Cobra's designers. The machine's 'survivability' was improved by having a high top speed (over 309kph) and a superbly designed forward profile that gave very good all-round visibility. Protection of crew members was seen as a major priority – armoured seats and personal body armour soon proved to be a cheap and simple means of ensuring their survival against enemy ground fire.

Most impressive of all was the armament used by the Cobra. Initially a single 7.62mm minigun was carried, but later the XM-28 weapons' sub-system allowed a number of options: two miniguns each with 4000 rounds, two 40mm grenade launchers each with 300 rounds or one minigun and one grenade laun-

cher. The Cobra's stub wings allowed further external armaments to be fitted, including 2.75in rocket packs and, eventually, guided missiles. In a direct-fire role, the Cobra's ability to take out Viet Cong positions with almost surgical precision was as heartening to the US ground forces as it was demoralising to the enemy.

The advantages in mobility and firepower enjoyed by the 1st Cavalry were made possible by advances in helicopter technology, but these benefits would have been worthless without the professional skills and raw courage of the helicopter pilots and their crews. In the early years of the war there was a serious shortage of pilots (rectified later by the expansion of aircrew schools in America) but, fortunately, peace-time training had produced aviators of the highest calibre. Later the prestige and glamour of the job brought a steady stream of applicants, and ensured that only the best were selected.

During the Ia Drang battle one 1st Cavalry battalion commander was sufficiently impressed by the helicopter crews supporting his men to write:

'I have the highest admiration, praise and respect for the outstanding professionalism and courage of the pilots and crews who ran a gauntlet of

Top: The Huey Cobra gunship. Above: A Chinook hovers over thick jungle, waiting to move out as part of Operation Pegasus, the relief of the Khe Sanh, 1968. The man on the right carries the M16A1 rifle. Left: A CH-54 Sky Crane, the division's heavy carrier, flies into a forward base.

M60 GPMG

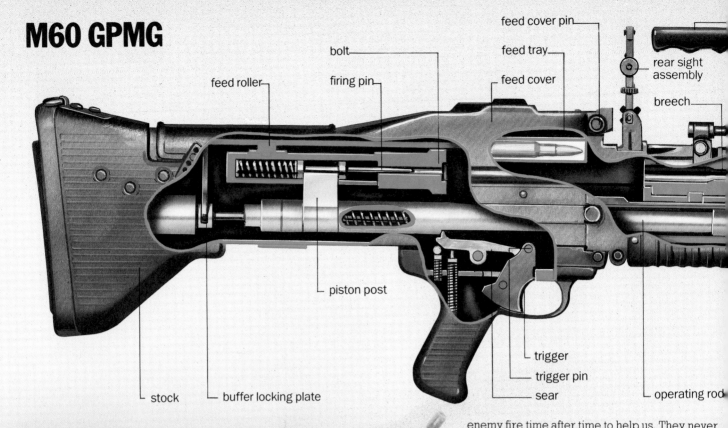

feed roller — bolt — firing pin — feed cover pin — feed tray — feed cover — rear sight assembly — breech — piston post — trigger — trigger pin — sear — operating rod — stock — buffer locking plate

enemy fire time after time to help us. They never refused to come in; they followed instructions beautifully; they were great.'

During major engagements the demands made on men and machines were particularly heavy – peacetime rules and regulations had to be sacrificed to the need for combat readiness. A senior officer working alongside the 1st Cavalry noted:

'The super performance did not stop with the pilots. The crew chiefs flew all day and worked on their birds all night. The sight around the average company maintenance detachment when the birds staggered home in the evenings was a sight to behold. The maintenance crews rolled out, turned on the lights, worked with flashlights, worked by feel, worked anyway, in the rain, in the sun, in high winds and dust storms, all night long if necessary to patch up the aircraft, pull the required inspections, correct deficiencies and get them back on the line by the next morning.'

While the helicopters were the most visible element of the 1st Cavalry, and the one that most readily distinguished it from other formations, eight infantry battalions and the divisional artillery formed the fighting core of the division. The division's aviation group was capable of airlifting three infantry battalions – around 2000 men – at any given time, while the remaining battalions acted either in an ordinary infantry role or were held in reserve for later aerial deployment.

The men of the infantry battalions were equipped and armed as other units within the US Army. The semi-automatic M14 rifle was the infantryman's basic firearm until replaced by the M16 assault rifle. The M16 was a highly effective close-quarters weapon that proved popular with the 1st Cavalry troopers because of its high rate of fire, light weight and, after a few teething troubles had been eliminated, overall reliability.

The 7.62mm M60 GPMG provided the infantry section with its own firepower. A belt-fed and gas-operated weapon, the M60 was generally popular with the troops, and, while its rate of fire was rather

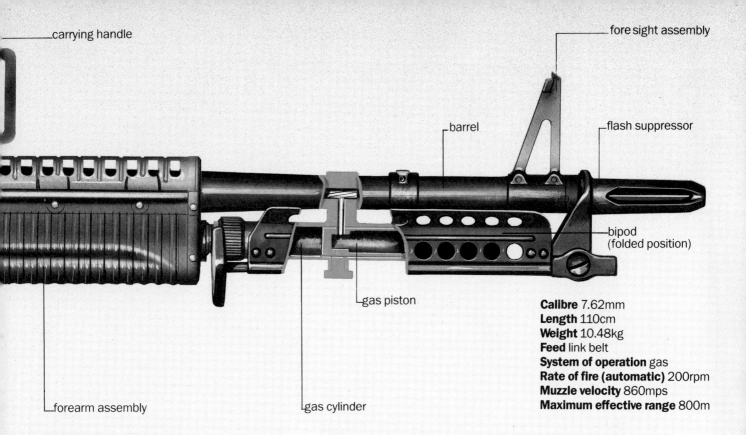

carrying handle

fore sight assembly

barrel

flash suppressor

bipod
(folded position)

gas piston

forearm assembly

gas cylinder

Calibre 7.62mm
Length 110cm
Weight 10.48kg
Feed link belt
System of operation gas
Rate of fire (automatic) 200rpm
Muzzle velocity 860mps
Maximum effective range 800m

low for sustained long-range shooting, it was a more than adequate weapon for jungle patrols.

At section level, grenade launchers proved very effective in close-quarters fighting. Two types were issued, the M79, a separate shoulder-fired weapon, and the M203, which could be attached to the underside of an M16 rifle. Capable of lobbing a grenade up to 150m they were a simple means of extending the range of the infantryman's arm.

A devastating barrage could be brought down in seconds

When the 1st Cavalry was operating along the coastal plains of the Binh Dinh region during 1967 the Viet Cong developed elaborate tunnel and bunker systems to provide protection against helicopter attack. As the Viet Cong would not leave their bunkers under any circumstances it became necessary to destroy bunker or tunnel systems in their entirety. Consequently, the 1st Cavalry requested and received a company of M48 medium tanks. Although tanks and helicopters might seem an inappropriate combination, the high-velocity 90mm guns of the M48s were able to penetrate the Viet Cong fortifications and the division's command Hueys were able to direct operations from the air. Chinooks resupplied the tanks with ammunition. In September 1967 a battalion of mechanised infantry (equipped with armoured personnel carriers) was also attached to the 1st Cavalry and, after the subsequent withdrawal of the tanks, it provided the division with a continuing armour capacity.

The weight of essential artillery pieces and ammunition seemed, at first sight, to undermine the 'lean and mean' concept of the 1st Cavalry Division's airmobility tactics, but the Chinook proved to be an early answer to the problem. The division's CH-47s could easily transport three battalions of 105mm howitzers into a battle zone. It rapidly became clear, however, that 105s lacked the range, accuracy and weight of shot of the heavier 155mm field howitzers and without these larger guns the 1st Cavalry's

Above: A quick response to a Viet Cong threat as men leap from a Bell Huey. A radio operator remains in position, ready to give covering fire.
Left: Cleaning an M16 – in Vietnam a man's best friend. This trooper's colleague is making a meal from a ration pack.
Overleaf bottom: Two troopers struggle through the jungle.

firepower would be much reduced. The CH-54 Sky Crane, capable of carrying greater loads than the Chinook, proved equal to the task and a battalion of 155mm howitzers was attached to the division.

The flexibility of the helicopter was again used to advantage in combining mobility and firepower in the formation of the aerial artillery battalion. Consisting of three batteries, each with 12 helicopters armed with packs of 2.75in aerial rockets, the batta-

Trooper, 1st Air Cavalry, Vietnam 1966

Over his olive-green fatigues this trooper wears M56 web equipment and a lightweight man-pack radio. Over the M1 steel helmet a camouflage cover is fitted, while footgear consists of US nylon and leather jungle boots. Armament comprises a fragmentation grenade and a 5.56mm M16A1 assault rifle.

lion was a fearsome sight when used *en masse* – a devastating barrage could be brought down with the greatest accuracy on specific targets in a matter of seconds. The sight of over 30 gunships racing over the jungle canopy and launching hundreds of rockets at a selected Viet Cong stronghold was a great morale booster to the men on the ground.

The tactical approach favoured by the 1st Cavalry's commanders was to deploy as much of the division as possible in the shortest time. The division was used in its entirety during the relief of Khe Sanh in 1968 and in the invasion of Cambodia in 1970. In both cases the ends justified the means, and an ideal combination of mobility and firepower caught the enemy off balance – complete units were destroyed in the open.

The US war effort in Vietnam underwent a dramatic decline after 1969. Men and material were withdrawn and the last combat troops left in 1972. The morale of the American forces, already dented by their inability to deliver a knock-out blow to the North Vietnamese, was undermined further by the obvious lack of commitment on the part of the politicians back home. To many, the war had become pointless, and, although some units, such as the 1st Cavalry Division, had displayed the utmost flair in carrying the war to the enemy, they could not hope to compensate for the inability of the US war machine to adapt to fighting an unconventional guerrilla war.

THE AUTHOR Adrian Gilbert has edited and contributed to a number of military and naval publications and is a co-author of *Vietnam: The History and the Tactics.*

Combat veterans of World War II and Korea, the pilots who flew for Air America played a major part in the undercover war for Laos. Colonel Rod Paschall, who flew with them on many of their missions, tells the story of Operation Triangle

THE SMALL, SILVER monoplane edged its way down in tight circles through the clouds. The pilot, Bill Dawson, and I had our eyes glued to the altimeter, occasionally peering through the windscreen and hoping not to see the sudden flash of a green slope. Bill Dawson's hands got a tighter grip on the controls. A few more hundred feet and we would have to pull up. There were too many damn mountains down there. It looked like I would have to go back to Vientiane, wait for visibility to improve, and then try to get to Ba Na later in the day. That didn't seem a bad proposal: the war could wait, and it sure beat sweating out the agony of looking for rocks in the clouds. Suddenly, the clouds began to thin out and we saw the ground, a comfortable 1000ft below.

There were no mountains – the ground was stretched out flat. We realised that we were in the wrong place; we had overshot our destination and were flying low – too low – over the Plain of Jars. This was territory controlled by the Pathet Lao (Laotian communists). Bill quickly banked to the left in a 180-degree turn towards the south. As he levelled the wings, we saw what we had been dreading: Pathet Lao troops running towards their 37mm anti-aircraft position. They had heard us coming and had the advantage. I was quite unprepared for what happened next. While every muscle in my body strained for our Helio Courier to go up, Bill Dawson put the aircraft in a screaming dive right onto the gun. As we roared over the crew, missing them by only a few feet, I could see sheer fright in their eyes. They hesitated, long enough for Bill to gain a few hundred yards on them. More important, we were so low that they had an impossible task in trying to line up on our weaving aircraft. I learned what Bill Dawson already knew. When you are that close to a 37mm, it's better to be right on the deck.

We darted on a zigzag route until the mountains on the southern rim of the Plain of Jars loomed ahead. Bill picked a likely ravine and, quickly gaining altitude,

we were soon flying just between the mountain tops and the low-hanging clouds. We spotted the primitive airstrip at Ba Na, and within a few minutes we were on the ground. Ba Na was the headquarters of Kong Le, commander of the Laotian Neutralist Army, and my task as army attaché was to make sure that Kong Le's force had the equipment and transport to play its role in the forthcoming Operation Triangle. Bill Dawson had other customers to deliver during that day but, in accordance with the exacting Air America schedule, I knew that he would be back. He had been informed that Captain Paschall was to be picked up at Ba Na at 1630 hours, and the airline always lived up to its motto: 'Anything, Anytime, Anywhere – Professionally'.

It was not my first trip with Air America. This, the oddest of airlines, had delivered myself and my Special Forces detachment to our first combat assignment in Vietnam some two years before. Air America had transported supplies for us and occasionally provided an air reconnaissance capability. Here in Laos, the airline was about the only asset we had going for us. Its backbone was a collection of ageing C-46 Curtiss Commandos and C-47s, the famed twin-engine logistical work-horse of World War II. These aircraft did most of the air drops to the Laotian armed forces and made scheduled runs to

Bottom: An Air America Helio Courier comes in to land on a rough airstrip in Laos. These light aircraft proved extremely useful for the ferrying of military advisors and small quantities of supplies, and were particularly suitable for operations from the primitive take-off and landing facilities available in Laos. When larger loads had to be carried, Air America used its Pilatus Porters (below).

AIR AMERICA

AIR AMERICA

When Mao Tse-Tung began to threaten the Chinese Nationalist forces of the Kuomintang in the late 1940s, US General Claire Lee Chennault, founder of the famed 'Flying Tigers' of World War II, returned to China to form Civil Air Transport (CAT), a commercial airline under Chinese licence. The role of the CAT pilots was to fly supplies to Chinese communities caught up in the war, and, following Mao's take over in 1949, the airline left China and established a new base on the island of Taiwan.

With a growing American involvement in Asia, the Central Intelligence Agency (CIA) sought out a pliable commercial airline for the transportation needs of its projects. Chennault was able to offer Washington his services, but, although the CIA began to take charge, it never gained full control of his organisation.

Air America was a 'spin-off' of CAT, a 'proprietary' of the CIA that was destined to fly in 11 different countries and grow to a workforce of 6000 employees. It was run, nevertheless, as a civilian, commercial enterprise, with most of its staff belonging to trade unions.

In the early 1960s, with no US ground forces being admitted into Laos, the CIA used the excellent pilots of Air America and their ageing aircraft to move and supply local irregular anti-communist troops, including the Neutralist Army and indigenous Meo tribesmen, against Vietnamese incursions. The war in Laos displaced numerous Meo villagers, and Air America was also employed by the US government's Agency for International Development (AID) in logistical support of their programme of education and medical aid for the Meo.

the few decent airstrips in the country. The plane that Bill Dawson and I flew in that morning was a Helio Courier. Its military designation was U-10 or L-28. With a top speed of 185mph, this amazing aircraft could stay airborne at only 35mph, permitting it to land on small patches of uneven earth. The Couriers could haul two people and about 600lb of supplies. If the load to be transported lay between the carrying capacities of the Courier and the C-47, Air America used Swiss-made Pilatus Porters. For more inaccessible sites, Air America had about 20 H-34 helicopters. Finally, the company had four C-123s, twin-engine military air transport planes that were capable of rough field landings. These were normally used for long-haul work between Thailand and Laos. Air America had everything we needed to support Operation Triangle.

This operation was not an exclusively American or Laotian idea, it was the logical way to build on an event that had recently taken place. Kong Le and his small Neutralist Army had been an ally of the North Vietnamese and the Pathet Lao for several years, as well as a favoured recipient of Soviet aid. However, when Kong Le discovered that the North Vietnamese were actually out to conquer Laos, he began to distance himself from his communist allies. When one of his favourite sergeants was murdered by the Pathet Lao, he broke from them completely and fought his way south to Ba Na.

One of Kong Le's units, unable to take its five PT-76 tanks into the mountains around Ba Na, fled to Muong Soui, on the western edge of the Plain of Jars. With his forces split and in need of supplies, Kong Le decided to throw in his lot with the Royal Lao government and the Americans. The trouble was that the young

general's land line of communications had been blocked by Pathet Lao troops along Route 13. The idea of the operation was simple: break the Pathet Lao's hold on Route 13 and consolidate Kong Le's army at Moung Soui. The government would then control the road link between the Laotian political capital of Vientiane and the royal capital of Luang Prabang. Also, by supporting its new ally on Route 7 it would be demonstrating its determination to hold the line against the communist invaders. The United States, too, by supporting the operation, would be signalling Hanoi that it was not prepared to tolerate breaches of the 1962 US-North Vietnamese agreement on the neutrality of Laos. The problem with the scheme was that all the key moves were to take place in enemy territory. That meant Air America.

Their great strength was that they knew the terrain of Laos like the backs of their hands

The success of Operation Triangle would be almost entirely dependent on the skill of Air America's pilots. These men were almost all ex-US military personnel, the pilots of the fixed-wing aircraft being former USAF members and the chopper pilots almost invariably being ex-US Marines. With a few exceptions, they were combat veterans who had fought in World War II or Korea, if not both. Their contracts with Air America usually specified a base salary of 12,000 dollars per year, but there were bonuses for the more hazardous flights. Unlike their counterparts in the US armed forces, the Air America pilots did not have to conform to a long list of safety regulations. They often flew up to 10 hours a day for months on end, without the benefit of navigational aids on the ground, and their great strength was that they knew the terrain of Laos like the backs of their hands. They were also more familiar with the tactical situation on the ground than either the US Embassy or the Royal Lao general staff. When you were shot at as often as they were, you had to be.

After Bill Dawson had skilfully landed the Courier on Kong Le's rough, muddy mountain-top airstrip, I had a co-ordination meeting with the enthusiastic leader of the Neutralist Army. As an army attaché, my

Operation Triangle July 1964

In the summer of 1964, a North Vietnamese-backed offensive in northern Laos threatened to overwhelm the troops of the American-supported Royal Laotian government. The Pathet Lao held large areas of northern Laos, including the road between the key towns of Luang Prabang (the royal residence) and Vientiane (the administrative capital).

On 22 July, Royal Lao and neutralist forces backed by the airlift capability of Air America, began their attacks against Pathet Lao forces along Routes 7 and 13 – Operation Triangle.

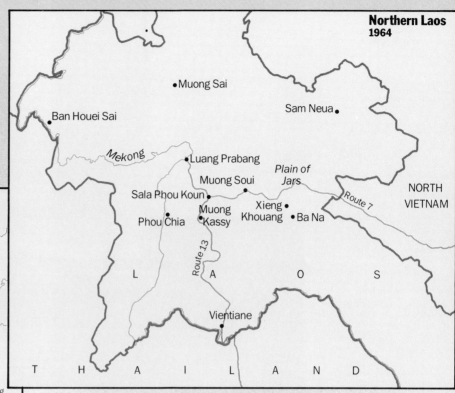

Northern Laos 1964

- Muong Sai
- Ban Houei Sai
- Sam Neua
- *Mekong*
- Luang Prabang
- *Plain of Jars*
- Muong Soui
- NORTH VIETNAM
- Sala Phou Koun
- *Route 7*
- Phou Chia
- Muong Kassy
- Xieng Khouang
- Ba Na
- *Route 13*
- L A O S
- Vientiane
- T H A I L A N D

Southeast Asia

- NORTH VIETNAM
- Hanoi
- Haiphong
- Luang Prabang
- L A O S
- Vientiane
- Hue
- Da Nang
- Quang Ngai
- Qui Nhon
- T H A I L A N D
- Bangkok
- C A M B O D I A
- Nha Trang
- Phnom Penh
- SOUTH VIETNAM
- Saigon
- SOUTH CHINA SEA

Far left above: Claire Lee Chennault, whose Civil Air Transport line (far left below) was the parent firm of the CIA 'proprietary' Air America.

Below left: An Air America Pilatus Porter races down the dirt airstrip at Sam Thong. Below: Two Laotian C-47 transports with an Air America C-123 in the background.

CIA INVOLVEMENT IN LAOS

In July 1962, a neutralist coalition government was established in Laos. The country remained split, however, between anti-communist forces in the south, neutralists, and the communist Pathet Lao in the north.

The general policy of the United States in Southeast Asia during the early 1960s was to secure the neutrality of Laos and Cambodia, while actively defending South Vietnam and Thailand. Aiming to reinforce the neutrality of Laos, in 1962 President John F. Kennedy concluded an agreement with the North Vietnamese that involved the withdrawal of US and North Vietnamese military forces from the country. Although the US withdrew, the North Vietnamese did not and the Ho Chi Minh Trail, running through Laos, was increasingly used to fuel the communist effort in South Vietnam.

In 1963, the US government was faced with a communist offensive that rapidly gained control of much of eastern and northeastern Laos along the border with North Vietnam. Deciding against the committal of regular US troops, it stepped up undercover activity in Laos. US Special Forces personnel were infiltrated into the south, while the CIA set about arming the Laotian hill tribes for war with the Pathet Lao and North Vietnamese. Eventually, some 30,000 tribal irregulars were trained and armed with light weapons and artillery. Meanwhile, bombing of the Ho Chi Minh Trail was conducted on an increasingly large scale. The CIA-organised units of Meo tribesmen ceased to be of military significance when their main base at Long Cheng was overrun in December 1971.

Right: US and Laotian personnel pack the cargo hold of an Air America C-47. Far right: The view from the flight deck of a C-47 as the pilot prepares to take off. Far right centre: An Air America C-123 makes a steep descent into Sam Thong airfield. Below: US advisors move to board an Air America chopper. Far right bottom: Air America planes, including a C-46, a C-47 and a Porter, lined up on an airfield in Laos.

job was not to advise on tactics or strategy. It was to co-ordinate the logistics so that the operation would be properly supported, and to report on events and conditions in the field – a considerable change from what I had become accustomed to in Vietnam. I quickly determined that Kong Le had an excess of ammunition and supplies at Ba Na, and more were expected. I finally convinced him that his force had to be moved in one day, and with 25 miles to cover by helicopter he would have to abandon much of his stockpile of rice. The Air America H-34 helicopter fleet was going to have enough difficulty with the altitude and temperature conditions of Ba Na as it was. He would just have to take it on faith that we would support him at his new base at Moung Soui.

The plan to eliminate the Pathet Lao from Route 13 involved three co-ordinated attacks. Two Royal Lao regiments would attack north against the Pathet Lao regiment at Muong Kassy, north of Vientiane. One Royal Lao battalion would attack south on Route 13 from Luang Prabang. That attack was actually a feint and it was hoped that the Pathet Lao regiment at Sala Phou Koun, the intersection of Routes 7 and 13, would be drawn off to the north to oppose the feint. At the same time, Groupe Mobile 11 (GM 11), a 500-man force, was to attack Sala Phou Koun, approaching out

of the jungle from the west. Since Kong Le's move to Muong Soui was to occur on the same day as the three attacks, GM11 would not be able to use the Air America fleet of Helicopters. D-day was to be 22 July 1964.

My assignment for Operation Triangle was to supervise the logistical support for GM 11, set up a radio station at a Meo village, and accompany GM 11 on its attack. Several days before the jump-off, Air America deposited myself, a Collins KWM2A radio, a generator and other paraphernalia at the Meo village of Phou Chia, high in the mountains. The Pilatus Porter barely managed the landing on a tiny open field. GM 11 arrived two days later, after an exhausting jungle trek south from Luang Prabang. The plan was for me to resupply the unit while it rested for a day, after which we would head for Sala Phou Koun, 35 miles to the east through very difficult terrain. GM 11 needed rice, and I arranged an air drop for that afternoon.

Two hours before daylight the next morning, 21 July, we were off. Plunging through thick foliage, GM 11 headed east towards Sala Phou Koun. Moving in single file, we rarely had a trail to follow, and we continued until two hours after sunset. When the word to stop was passed down, no-one took the time

to eat. We simply lay down to sleep in our tracks, and two hours before dawn the next day, we were on our way again. By noon on the 22nd (D-day), we were within five kilometres of Sala Phou Koun and the intersection of Routes 13 and 7.

After an hour of rest, I saw our Air America C-47 reconnaissance plane coming at a high altitude from the direction of Vientiane, and I grabbed a VHF portable radio to make contact: 'Mustang, this is Bobcat.' The pilot replied, 'This is Mustang, over.' I asked, 'How is the fishing?', and his reply came over, 'Good, pull in your line, you'll get about 15.' I turned to the colonel of GM 11 who was standing beside me and told him that the pilot had seen 15 trucks departing from Sala Phou Koun. The Pathet Lao had taken the bait. They were depleting the garrison at the vital road intersection in order to reinforce their units under attack to the north and south. So far undetected by the Pathet Lao, there was no reason that we should not achieve complete surprise, and we moved east at a rapid clip.

Operation Triangle was a success. We had little trouble pushing what remained of the Pathet Lao garrison out of Sala Phou Koun, and when the last helicopter load of Kong Le's troops arrived at Moung Soui we had complete command of Route 7. The Pathet Lao units on Route 13 found that they were cut off, caught between our forces positioned to the north and south of them along the road. Within a few days they abandoned their vehicles, gave up the

Air America Bell 204B (UH-1B) choppers (above and below) were involved in the evacuation of US nationals when Saigon fell in 1975. Bottom: An H-34 helicopter hovers over a village in Laos.

fight, and started a long retreat eastwards through the jungle towards the Plain of Jars.

In the summer of 1964, the fortunes of the Royal Lao government, the Meo tribesmen and the Americans in Laos looked bright. The victory that had been won over the Pathet Lao during Operation Triangle seemed to provide just the event that was needed to ensure the ultimate neutrality of Laos. But we were all making a fundamental mistake. We were measuring our progress against that of the Pathet Lao. The real bench-mark was the strength and determination of the North Vietnamese. Hanoi never desired the neutrality of Laos, and 22 years later North Vietnam would conquer the territory. Although the American cause failed, for many reasons, none of them had anything to do with Air America. That airline had been one of the few things in Laos that had worked. Air America had lived up to its motto: 'Anything, Anytime, Anywhere – Professionally'.

THE AUTHOR Colonel Rod Paschall served six years in Laos, Vietnam and Cambodia during the Second Indochina War. Afterwards, he was the Delta Force commander.

The light helicopters of 3 Commando Brigade Air Squadron were seldom out of the line of fire as they operated at the front during the Falklands campaign of 1982

Below: Aircrew of a 3 Commando Brigade Air Squadron Aérospatiale Gazelle check their machine and (bottom) make a pre-flight instrument check.

ON FRIDAY, 2 May 1982, the men of 3 Commando Brigade Air Squadron were about to go on leave. Their Commanding Officer, Major Peter Cameron, was already skiing in France. Then suddenly all leave was cancelled, and at 0315 hours the brigade was put on 72 hours' notice to move – 'the people down south are about to be invaded'.

A weekend of confusion followed, and there were constant changes of plan as men and equipment were frantically gathered together. Warehouses were ransacked for aircraft spares by the Army Air Corps at Middle Wallop, and shopping lists of vital items were written out by Major Cameron and Captain Andrew Eames, the Senior Pilot and second in command. Included were transponders to enable the ships to recognise friendly helicopters, infra-red suppressors for their exhausts, and night vision goggles (NVG); these and every other article were acquired in record time.

On Monday, 5 May, the squadron embarked its helicopters, nine of its 12 Aérospatiale SA341 Gazelles and all six of its Westland Scouts, onto the LSLs (Landing Ship, Logistics) which were to take them south. The British aircraft industry, realising where

CHOPPERS AT WAR

The British Army has had an air component ever since the Royal Engineers fielded a balloon section in 1873. Many of the functions of the army's original air units were finally given over to the Royal Air Force on its establishment in 1918, but in 1942 the need for a combined air and infantry force led to the formation of The Parachute Regiment and The Glider Pilot Regiment, both under the administrative control of the Army Air Corps (see badge below). After being temporarily disbanded in 1950, when The Parachute Regiment transferred to the infantry of the line, the Army Air Corps was re-formed in 1957 by amalgamating The Glider Pilot Regiment with the Royal Air Force Air Observation Post squadrons.

Today, the Army Air Corps shares its headquarters at Middle Wallop in Hampshire with such supporting arms as the Aircraft Engineering Wing REME, 70 (Aircraft) Workshop REME and 1 Aircraft Support Unit RAOC, and Middle Wallop is the main training base for personnel entering every branch of the corps. All potential pilots must complete groundcrew and aircrew training and service before they may apply to become pilots.

The Army Air Corps Centre is also responsible for the training of Royal Marine aircrew, including those of 3 Commando Brigade Air Squadron (see badge on far right). The squadron's pilots and aircrew are volunteers from the Royal Marines, the Army Air Corps and the Royal Artillery . Based at RNAS Yeovilton in Somerset, the squadron receives full logistical and training support from the Army Air Corps.

they were going – and why – were incredibly helpful in every way, and by the next day the squadron had embarked and sailed for Ascension Island. During the passage south, the four flights of the squadron, all on separate ships settled into practising day and night landings and flightdeck procedures. The aircrewmen trained to do emergency deck landings in daylight in case their pilots were wounded.

A huge pile of stores was waiting for them at Ascension Island. Groundcrews scavenged for spares and technicians fitted furiously. The Gazelles test-fired their newly acquired SNEB rockets and the Scouts their SS11s. Flying tactics were discussed and decided in the shade of the verandah at the Exiles Club. Then, as the ships resumed their journey, training continued, including the usual preparations for commando operations. Three Scouts of No.656 Squadron, Army Air Corps, joined the ships, coming under Peter Cameron's command.

'Then suddenly there was death. We realised what going to war in a helicopter was all about'

On 21 May, the day of the first landings at San Carlos on East Falkland, there was an abrupt transition from preparation to the reality of combat. Captain Nick Pounds, Officer Commanding M Flight, recalled the moment:

'The light helicopters had never been in a war before. It was a lovely morning; there was a gradual feeling of relaxation on the radio net; everything was going really well. Then suddenly there was death. We realised what going to war in a helicopter was all about.'

Flying started well before dawn on that fateful day, when the light helicopters took off to make deck space for Sea King helicopters arriving to take the first wave of troops ashore. The second wave, which was to go ashore in landing craft, was delayed for about an hour by problems loading the craft and by mist at the northern entrance of Falkland Sound. The air and sea landings were slipping out of sequence.

Once the first wave got ashore, the highest priority was to off-load the Task Force's Rapier anti-aircraft missiles by Sea King before first light, when the Argentinian air force was certain to appear on the scene. The two Gazelles of C Flight were tasked to recce and clear some Rapier sites and then act as escort for the Sea Kings as they brought in the launchers. Since the landing craft had not yet landed the second wave, the helicopters would now have to fly over ground which had not been secured.

The Gazelles flew ahead of the Sea Kings. They were told to stick together, a strict rule because lone aircraft are very vulnerable. But a hard fact of life had to be accepted, that 'Gazelles were more expendable than Sea Kings', and the crews knew that if they drew no ground fire while flying over the intended Rapier sites it would be safe for the Sea Kings to deliver their valuable underslung loads. Taking off from RFA *Sir Galahad*, the Gazelles flew ashore. After a time it was clear that something had gone badly wrong.

A Gazelle had been shot down by smallarms fire while flying over the high ground east of Port San Carlos. The pilot, Sergeant Andy Evans, was mortally wounded yet somehow managed to bring the helicopter down safely into the sea. His crewman, Sergeant Eddie Candlish, inflated Evans' life-jacket and managed to swim 650yds in icy water towards the shore, pulling Evans behind him while a group

Right: A Gazelle prepares for take-off from HMS *Fearless*. The helicopter's armament control switches have been lashed onto the main control panel and were not part of the original machine. Above right: A Gazelle returns to an LSL (Landing Ship, Logistics) in San Carlos Water.

THE GAZELLE

The Gazelle is one of three helicopters produced jointly by Aérospatiale in France and Westland at Yeovil in Somerset, the other models being the Puma and the Lynx. Its French prototype first flew on 7 April 1967, and now several versions are assembled at Yeovil. They include the British Army SA341B (designated Gazelle AH Mk 1), the Royal Navy's SA341C (designated HT Mk 2), the RAF's SA341D trainer (HT Mk 3) and SA341E (HHC Mk 4) communications version. Replacing the Bell Model 47 Sioux as the light general purpose helicopter of the Army Air Corps, the AH Mk 1 is powered by a 590shp Turboméca/Rolls Royce Astazou 111N engine and has a cruising speed of 164mph. Its range is 416 miles and it accommodates a crew of one or two, and three passengers. More can be carried if the rear seats are removed.

The armament of the Gazelle can include two pods of 68mm rockets, two forward-firing Miniguns, or two 7.62mm machine guns, the latter either mounted behind the pilot to fire out to the side or fitted in pods over the landing skids. The missiles that may be carried include four AS.11s, four or six HOTs or TOWs, or two AS.12s, all of them with their appropriate sight system. The British Army's AH Mk 1 is fitted with a radio to allow it to communicate on ground troop nets and there is an additional blade aerial under the tail boom.

of Argentinians machine-gunned them from the bank. Miraculously, Candlish escaped unscathed and brought Evans ashore. Despite desperate efforts by Candlish and Falkland Islanders Thora Alazia and Suzanne McComish, Sergeant Evans died.

On the brigade headquarters ship HMS *Fearless*, Brigadier Julian Thompson was expecting a counter-attack. It was now essential for him to know whether this incident indicated an enemy force capable of jeopardising the operation at this most critical stage. He was not helped by the fact that the grid reference of the enemy position supplied by the Sea King pilot was wrong by 2000yds.

Lieutenant Robin Makeig-Jones was sent to join the second Gazelle (piloted by Lieutenant Ken Francis) in order to investigate. Before he reached the helicopter, however, Francis and his crewman, Corporal 'Giff' Giffin had moved off, probably searching for the missing Gazelle. From the shore, Candlish watched in horror as the Gazelle flew over the same enemy position east of Port San Carlos. A burst of fire disintegrated the helicopter's perspex bubble and knocked the machine like a stone into the hillside. Both men were killed instantly. Francis and Giffin probably never saw the enemy patrol, for it was a bright, clear day and flying into the sun made observation very difficult.

Makeig-Jones avoided further damage and, his craft vibrating like hell, he struggled back

Unable to make contact with the two Gazelles, Robin Makeig-Jones flew cautiously into the area. Probing very carefully, using stomach-wrenching porpoise loops to get a quick look ahead before plunging down into the cover of the hills, he rounded The Knob, a hill just east of Port San Carlos. Immediately he was fired upon, losing a blade from the tail rotor and collecting 12 shots along the tail boom. One bullet shot through the cockpit, narrowly missing his crewman, Corporal Roy Fleming. With great flying skill Makeig-Jones avoided further damage and, his craft vibrating like hell, he struggled back to *Sir Galahad*, sending the first accurate report of the enemy's position to the brigadier. He had seen 40 Argentinians retreating from Port San Carlos, and at

last his Brigade Commander knew that no counter-attack was imminent.

With these tragedies behind them, 3 Commando Brigade Air Squadron entered the battle for Darwin and Goose Green as hardened and cautious veterans. Before the battle, aircrew of the squadron climbed up into the Sussex Mountains to study the lie of the land with members of the 2nd Battalion, The Parachute Regiment (2 Para), for whom they were to be flying. Captain Eames went to the battalion's tactical headquarters as liaison officer to co-ordinate the work of the helicopters.

Two Gazelles of M Flight and two Scouts of B Flight were allocated to the paras. Their first task would be to resupply the battalion at Camilla Creek House, 11 miles south of San Carlos. On the night of 26/27 May the paras, carrying what they could, marched south to the house to lie up, and all the following day the squadron's helicopters crept up the gullies to bring in Blowpipe missiles and ammunition, taking every precaution to avoid alerting the Argentinians.

The battalion attacked the Darwin isthmus the next night, and at first light on the 28th the helicopters flew south to help. With an early morning fog over the Sussex Mountains it was difficult to monitor the progress of the battle. They brought ammunition forward to Camilla Creek, and from there the battalion moved it south using a commandeered tractor and two Bv202 tracked over-snow vehicles. The ammunition, particularly mortar bombs, was being used too quickly for this process, however, and the helicopters were soon delivering to the mortar

Above: A pipe deflector can be fitted to the jet exhaust of the Gazelle to direct hot gases away from the aircraft, thus minimising the danger from heat-seeking missiles.

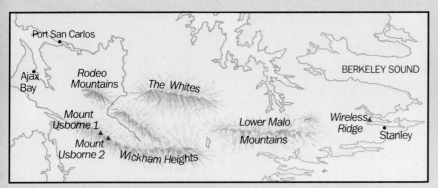

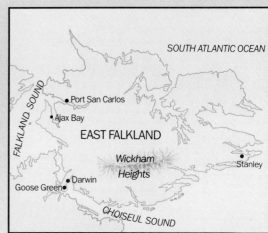

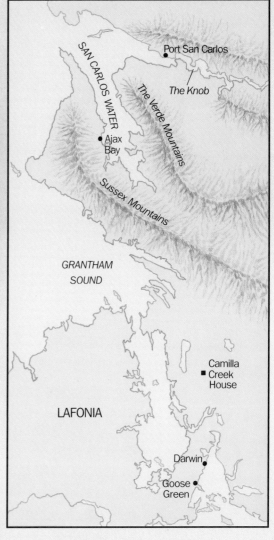

Above far left: Major Peter Cameron, Commanding Officer of 3 Commando Brigade Air Squadron, well equipped – including World War II tin helmet!

Top far left: Stretcher bearers lift a casualty from a Scout following the disastrous bombing of RFA *Sir Galahad* at Bluff Cove on 8 June. Top left: A Gazelle of 3 Commando Brigade Air Squadron fires its Matra 68mm SNEB rocket pods over Ascension Island. Above right: A Rapier surface-to-air missile system is delivered by Sea King to a site near Port San Carlos. Left: A Gazelle lies shattered after sustaining smallarms fire.

teams. Only two mortars were firing, the crews of the remainder acting as ammunition porters, but even so they were always on the verge of running out.

At around 1000 hours the battalion began to sustain casualties. The helicopters went forward to pick them up, bringing ammunition to the forward company positions and then delivering the wounded to Camilla Creek House. From there they were collected by the larger Sea King and Wessex support helicopters and flown back to the Main Dressing Station (MDS) at Ajax Bay. Serious cases were flown there directly from the battlefield.

At midday the British force received its first raid by Argentinian Pucará light attack aircraft from Goose Green. Heading for the company positions of 2 Para, they saw two Scouts, piloted by Lieutenants Jeff Niblett and Dick Nunn, which were on their way forward from Camilla Creek to pick up casualties.

Since the Falklands campaign 3 Commando Brigade Air Squadron has had two COs, Major David Mynords and Major A.D. Wray (left). In his turn Major Wray will relinquish command in August 1987. Right: Captain Andy Wellesley, RA, flying low-level in a Gazelle. Inset from top: Lynx pilots Lieutenant Tony Menzies, RN, (left) and Sergeant Kevin Gleeson, RM, during training; a pilot wears infra-red night vision goggles (NVG); Gazelles and a Lynx participate in a 3 Commando Brigade Air Squadron exercise.

The two Pucarás immediately changed their attack profile. Coming in from between 100ft and 200ft at around 200 knots, the unarmed Scouts could not avoid them. The standard fighter evasion manoeuvres employed by the helicopter pilots simply did not work with the much slower Pucarás.

In a desperate attempt to escape back to the Blowpipe air defence screen at Camilla Creek House, the two Scouts split left and right to dodge and weave northward. The Pucará pilots were very good indeed, slowing to stalling speed with flaps and wheels down in order to trap and shadow the Scouts. Jeff Niblett evaded three Pucará attacks but Dick Nunn was caught by rocket and machine-gun fire during the Argentinians' second try and was hit just as he reached cover. Everyone was firing up at the Pucarás, and it was amazing that they were not hit.

The two helicopters vanished out of sight to those on the ground, and then there was a plume of smoke. Captain Pounds flew to investigate and found the first Scout on the ground with Sergeant Bill Belcher beside it. He appeared to be kneeling over Nunn's body. Pounds dropped his crewman, Sergeant Priest, to help and went back to find Jeff Niblett and collect a stretcher. Niblett had landed and was in a state of shock, but he immediately got back into his Scout and flew to help.

It turned out that Dick Nunn was dead inside the burnt-out helicopter. Belcher had appeared to be kneeling over Nunn because his severely shot-up legs were broken and lying bent at unnatural angles. The men used debris from the wreck to splint Bill

Belcher's legs, and within 15 minutes he was back at Ajax Bay. One leg was saved – and his life.

The encounter had taken less than two minutes, with the Pucarás each taking one helicopter. Against the unarmed Scouts, it had been a cat-and-mouse game with the Pucarás enjoying all the advantages. Jeff Niblett had been greatly aided by his crewman, Sergeant John Glaze, who had darted about in the back shouting instructions as to which way to fly, such as, 'He's coming in now. Stand by to break right. Break now!' Sergeant Belcher had been doing the same, but once he was hit in the legs there was little hope for Dick Nunn to evade further attacks. Nunn was killed instantly by machine-gun fire while airborne, and then Belcher was again wounded in the legs. As the pilotless Scout slammed into the ground it swung round 180 degrees, throwing Belcher clear, and caught fire. Bill Belcher, thrown onto the ground with both legs badly injured and one nearly severed, calmly injected morphine into his better leg, deciding that the other was probably a write-off.

While all this was taking place, casualties were building up on the Goose Green battlefield. Every return flight was laden with wounded, now mostly Argentinian, and 2 Para was established on Darwin Ridge. Further Pucará attacks had been sustained without loss, and one Pucará had been shot down. The battle for Goose Green lasted for 33 hours and by the end the groundcrews were exhausted, having worked flat out refuelling, repairing and loading the aircraft. Repairs had been designed to get the helicopters back into the air as fast as possible and the rule book was often disregarded. On 30 May a Scout hit a telegraph wire in no-man's land. The perspex bubble on the pilot's side was smashed, and the vertical stabiliser and the top of the tail were sliced off. The damage was repaired in less than two hours by the 'Downbird' team of 'Q' Hopkinson and Sergeant Charlie Walker of the Royal Electrical and Mechanical Engineers. The aircraft flew for the rest of the war with its ingenious lash-up repair of polythene, wire, and black masking tape intact.

The NVG picture, a green video image, was often hazy and demanded great concentration

The final battles of the Falklands War, as the British closed in around Stanley, saw the light helicopters ferrying ammunition to the front line and casualties back to the Main Dressing Station. Continuing after dark, either flying totally beyond the normal and accepted rules or using NVG, the pilots evacuated 85 casualties over a 24-hour period.

Initially, the pilots most practised in the use of NVG were Sergeant Bill O'Brien and Captain Nick Pounds, who were flying Gazelles. Robin Makeig-Jones and Sergeant Jim Chapelle later joined them in NVG casevac missions. NVG was very tiring to use. The goggles covered only a narrow span of vision and the pilots felt blinkered, constantly having to move their heads up and down and from side to side in order to see. The picture, a green video image, was often hazy and demanded great concentration. The equipment was heavy and caused headache, a sore neck and a cut nose where it continuously dug in. Although the endurance of the pilots increased the more they used NVG, three hours were usually enough to wear down their stamina. Nevertheless, Pounds and O'Brien were to fly on NVG for over seven hours at one stretch during the battle for Port Stanley.

Bottom: Royal Marine aircrew prepare for a training flight after returning from the war. The large cabin doors to the front and the smaller interlocking doors to the rear open back to admit awkward loads such as stretcher cases. The flotation bags here visible on the skids were removed in the Falklands to lighten the aircraft, thus allowing more to be carried aboard. Those who have flown in the Gazelle have described it as the 'E-type' of helicopters, extremely fast and capable of astonishing aerobatics. For passengers in the back, though, sitting in front of the powerplant, it is easy to become very airsick from vibration and the swooping movements of the aircraft.

The most hazardous NVG flying took place when the helicopters emerged from the battle zone into airspace where non-NVG aircraft were operating. It was especially 'hairy' near the busy LZs where the NVG Gazelles were invisible to other aircraft. One pair of Scouts, led by WO2 'Robbie' Robinson, and a Gazelle flown by Captain Andy Newcombe, were even flying NVG jobs without NVG. The aircrews knew that wounded men needed them on the battlefield, and they ran a coolly calculated very high level of risk in order to get them out.

Today, 3 Commando Brigade Air Squadron has a different role – tank hunting with twin-engined Westland Lynx helicopters armed with TOW wire-guided missiles. The squadron acts as the brigade commander's mobile anti-tank weapon and reserve. Its tasks are to stop unexpected assaults by enemy tanks, to cover approaches that the brigadier chooses not to defend with ground troops, and to concentrate fire during decisive points in battle. In terrain which offers limited movement to tanks, such as the steep-sided fjords of Norway, these swift ambushes would be devastatingly effective.

While the squadron's Scouts have now been re-placed by the Lynx, the Gazelles remain. Their present role is to find enemy tanks and prepare airborne 'HELARM' ambushes, where the speed and high mobility of helicopters are utilised to the maximum. HELARM operations require close co-operation between all the elements involved – helicopters, ground troops, fighter ground-attack aircraft and artillery – all of whom have key parts to play.

A HELARM operation begins as enemy tanks approach a designated armoured killing zone (AKZ). The Gazelles move forward, flying low over the tops of hills and ridges, to determine how the armoured attack will be carried out. Pinpointed by the recce Gazelles, the tanks may then be subjected to artillery fire to force them to close down and to damage their optics and radio aerials. The commander calls the Lynx fire teams forward to a final rendezvous (FRV),

from where they are led into their fire positions by the Gazelles. The commander then orders them to 'unmask' and they rise up from their low defensive altitude to get a clear shot with their TOW missiles. At this point they are at their most vulnerable to enemy anti-aircraft and ground fire. Following an attack, the Lynxes will move to new fire positions, continually withdrawing to allow the enemy into fresh AKZs.

Within the Army Air Corps and its affiliated units there is constant revision of the function of military aviation. Light aircraft, flown by soldiers who understand what is happening on the ground and who have themselves fought there, can perform virtually any task that may suddenly be required of them in the course of a conflict. This ability to adapt quickly was exemplified by 3 Commando Brigade Air Squadron on the first tragic morning at San Carlos. In the future, the role of light helicopters is likely to change every time they enter operations, provided that the aircraft themselves do not become too specialised to be able to adapt.

If there was ever any doubt as to the value of the light helicopters in the Falklands, it was never shared by one doctor of The Parachute Regiment: 'Just when you thought, "God, I really need a helicopter now", there it would be, coming over some fold in the ground like the Seventh Cavalry. They were the bravest of anyone.' The pilots themselves did not see it quite like that. One was to say, 'Oddly enough, it's easy to be calm. The point is that the helicopter engine makes such a noise that you can't hear the gunfire outside. It's quite peaceful, in a way.'

THE AUTHOR Major Hugh McManners, as a captain, was one of the Naval Gunfire Forward Observers of 148 Commando Forward Observation Battery during the Falklands campaign of 1982. The author and editor would like to thank Lieutenant-Colonel Peter Cameron, MC, RM, Major A.D. Wray, RM, Captain Nick Pounds, RM, and Captain Andy Wellesley, (RA), for their help in the preparation of this article.

Air gunner, Army Air Corps, Falklands 1982

This corporal is wearing a British Army DPM combat smock with a gunner's brevet on the breast. He has 'lightweight' OG trousers, black flying boots, olive gloves as issued to aircrew, and a MK IV flying helmet with boom microphone.

Any military hardware making an incursion into Soviet air space can expect an extremely hot reception from a vast array of radar-guided air defence weapons

SKYWATCH

SOVIET AIR DEFENCE FORCES: WEAPONS AND DEPLOYMENT

THE SOVIET UNION has the most formidable air defence system in the world. Within its organisation are no less than half a million troops, 13,600 strategic and tactical surface-to-air missile (SAM) launchers, 2600 interceptor aircraft and an estimated 10,000 radar units. The National Air Defence Command, PVO (Protivo-Vozdushnaya Oborona) Strany, even has a little-known space defence division that in wartime would be tasked with destroying US strategic nuclear and conventional missiles in space.

PVO-Strany ranks third in the Soviet order of precedence after the Strategic Rocket Forces, with which it is at some levels interlocked, and the Ground Forces. (The Ground Forces, incidentally, have their own air defence units, armed with some 25,000 shoulder-fired SAM launchers, but these units are quite separate from PVO-Strany.) Fourth and fifth in the Soviet order of precedence are the Air Force and the Naval Forces. PVO-Strany covers the entire Soviet Union, stretching from the frozen wastelands of the Arctic Circle to the Black Sea. The air defence system is integrated with the Warsaw Pact forces on the Soviets' western flank, adding another 100,000 troops and their missiles and fighters to its strength and providing a vital outer line to its vast network.

The overall system is controlled by a centralised command centre in Moscow under Marshal of Aviation A.I. Koldunov. It covers 16 air defence districts, six of them in the Warsaw Pact zone. Until the time of the Soviet invasion of Afghanistan in December 1979, PVO-Strany was probably the most combat-experienced wing of the Soviet armed forces since World War II. The force's systems and weaponry specialists were deployed in North Vietnam against the US Air Force, in Syria, Lebanon and Egypt against the Israelis, and in the Korean War, when the Soviet air defence system was in its infancy.

The Soviets have been obsessed with artillery and the concept of massed firepower since the 14th century. For hundreds of years, the artillery was the elite of the Russian Army. Peter the Great was fascinated by rockets as an arm of artillery, and Soviet interest in rocketry has continued to the present day, with the military commanders increasingly focusing on developing surface-to-air and air-to-air missiles for the strategic defence of the homeland. The Air Defence Command now has much of the responsibility for meeting the threat of US intercontinental ballistic missiles (ICBMs), as

Previous page, top: The Rockwell B-1B succeeded the B-52 as America's principal long-range, multi-role strategic bomber and is well equipped for high-subsonic low level penetration. However, the proliferation of such mobile Soviet air defence weapons as the SA-4 Ganef surface-to-air missile (previous page, bottom) and the SA-3 Goa SAM (below) has helped to shift NATO emphasis from long-range bombers to stand-off and cruise weapons. Right: Marshal of Aviation A.I. Koldunov, commander-in-chief of the National Air Defence Command in Moscow.

well as the low-level dangers posed by NATO's air forces and by the growing airpower in China.

PVO-Strany has four main component arms: anti-aircraft missile troops (Zenitno-Raketmye Voiska, or ZRV), anti-aircraft artillery troops (Zenitnaya Artilleriya, or ZA), radar and technical troops (Radiotekhnicheskie Voiska, or RTV), and fighter aviation (Istrebitel'naya Aviatsiya, or IA-PVO).

Soviet tactics of deep defence are aimed at locat-

ing and engaging enemy aircraft at maximum range with interceptors, harassing them with both fighters and SAMs as they thrust deeper into the defensive system, and finally hammering them with missiles from their point defences in the target areas. As the menace has diminished from NATO long-range strategic bombers, such as the B-1 and the high-flying B-52, PVO-Strany's old adversary in Vietnam, so the threat has grown from low-level cruise missiles and stand-off weapons dropped by aircraft. Soviet concepts of air defence have adapted to meet the new threats and PVO-Strany possesses weapons to combat high-, medium- and low-level attacks. They include the fearsome ZSU-23-4 Shillka self-propelled anti-aircraft mount, the four-barrelled 23mm anti-aircraft gun and the 20m Galosh anti-ballistic missile, which some believe can loiter in flight while incoming warheads are separated from decoys and then home in for the kill.

Moscow remains the most heavily defended capital against air attack in the world

Unlike the United States, which over the last 20 years has made little serious effort to counter tactical air attack, the Soviets use every available weapon in air defence. The Soviet organisation includes half a million personnel, while US air defence employs only 10,000 men, excluding the continental fighter squadrons. The Soviets learnt the value of air defence during the trauma of the Nazi invasion in World War II, and those lessons form the basis of much of their military wisdom today.

Before that conflict, all Soviet anti-aircraft, artillery, searchlight and sound-detection units were split between various military commands. When war broke out, a more cohesive system was developed by necessity and air defence began to become a separate structure, so that by 1945 a million men were involved in air defence. The technology they used was primitive, however. It was not until the 1950s, for example, that the Soviets perceived the shortcomings of their radar systems as the nuclear bomber concept was developed in the West.

Some of the lessons of World War II had an immediate effect on subsequent Soviet air defence strategy. When the Luftwaffe unleashed hundreds of bombers on Moscow in the summer of 1941, the Soviets rushed their crack artillery units to defend the capital. In the process, they assembled one of the greatest concentrations of anti-aircraft firepower ever to be gathered in one target area, and the Heinkel and Junkers bombers were driven off by the

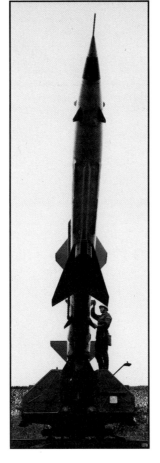

Left: A soldier of the Polish Army checks an SA-2 Guideline missile on a fixed launcher. The Guideline is the most widely used of Soviet anti-aircraft SAMs, and one destroyed a high-flying American U-2 spyplane over the Soviet Union on 1 May 1960. Below: PVO-Strany personnel with a MiG-23 Flogger interceptor. Its large radome houses the powerful High Lark radar and the aircraft is armed with specially developed medium-range and dogfighting missiles.

storm of fire. This success provided the embryo of PVO-Strany's air defence doctrine of today, and Moscow remains the most heavily defended capital against air attack in the world. Around the city are stationed a potent array of SAMs, including the most advanced types in the Soviet armoury, and no less than 400 MiG-23, MiG-25 and Su-15 fighters are based around Moscow in four air defence zones.

The Soviets combined air defence under one command in 1948. Six years later, PVO-Strany was made an independent arm of service, responsible for defending military and industrial targets against all forms of air attack. According to Pentagon studies, since the 1950s the Soviets have invested enormous resources in air defence. They are now concentrating on countering the threat of low-flying cruise missiles and aircraft by intensifying the integration of strategic and tactical air defence systems and upgrading their computerised command and control system, which for long has been one of the weakest points of their network. They have recently added to the system the Tupolev Tu-126 surveillance aircraft, codenamed Moss by NATO, which is the Soviet

Although the Soviet Air Defence Command uses every weapon available, the core of its network is an integrated missile and interceptor package. The Soviets are currently believed to be intensifying the integration of their strategic and tactical air defences with ever more sophisticated data control systems.

Between these two arms of their elaborate and potent defence system the Soviets can deploy 9000 strategic SAM launchers, 4600 tactical SAM launchers and more than 1200 interceptors, backed by an additional 2800 fighters deployed by the Soviet Air Force's Frontal Aviation. This last is a separate entity from PVO-Strany and is the Soviet equivalent of NATO's tactical air forces. Because PVO-Strany has a different role to those of the Strategic Rocket Forces and the Air Force, the Soviets have for decades designed combat fighters specifically for air defence. The planes have a rapid rate of climb and heavy firepower to tackle bombers and missiles, rather than the sturdier strike, ground-attack and reconnaissance aircraft flown by Frontal Aviation. Three PVO-Strany interceptors that have emerged are the big, long-range Tu-28 Fiddler, deployed mainly in the northern sector of the Soviet Union and armed with four AA-5 Ash air-to-air missiles, and the Su-15 Flagon and MiG-25 Foxbat all-weather fighters for low-level combat.

The supersonic fighters are closely integrated with SAM defences which include the long-range SA-5 Gammon, designed to neutralise stand-off missiles launched from high-flying bombers, the SA-2 Guideline high-altitude command guidance missile, and the low-altitude SA-3 Goa and SA-10 Grumble, both designed to kill cruise weapons.

The Soviets are now deploying mobile batteries of SA-10s and are believed to be flight-testing a new mobile SAM-system, the SA-X-12, that can intercept aircraft, as well as cruise missiles and short-range ballistic missiles.

Right: First deployed by PVO-Strany in 1978, the swing-wing MiG-23 Flogger may be regarded as an advanced, scaled-down version of the McDonnell-Douglas F-4 Phantom in terms of the range of roles it was designed to fulfil. The Su-24 Fencer (below) is flown primarily by Frontal Aviation as an all-weather support aircraft for the MiG-23's successor, the MiG-27, which is also codenamed Flogger. Bottom: MiG-23 aircrew discuss battle tactics before a training exercise.

ability to confuse and blind defensive radar systems. Although Soviet air defence hardware, manned by Syrians, fared badly against Israeli strike planes in the Beqaa Valley in 1982, the Soviets are understood to have made a great effort to upgrade the systems.

Manning the Soviet missile systems are the anti-aircraft missile troops of the ZRV. These are split into brigades, each with 10-12 launch battalions. Each regiment has between three and five launch battalions, which in turn have up to eight launchers, depending on their function and the type of missile with which they are armed. Each battalion has between 80 and 120 men and deploys several 23mm and 57mm anti-aircraft guns to protect its batteries from low-level air strikes. Although until now the batteries have been mostly fixed installations around key target zones, the Soviets appear to be boosting their complement of mobile batteries with four-launcher units carried aboard converted BMP personnel carriers.

The organisation of the larger PVO-Strany units, such as divisions and corps, depends on the target areas they are assigned to defend. A division, for example, could be assigned to protect a major power station or industrial complex. For this mission it would probably comprise one SAM brigade in fixed positions, plus two or three regiments for point defence, as well as mobile, independent battalions to fill operational gaps or reinforce hard-pressed units. On top of these, the divisional commander

version of NATO's Airborne Warning and Command Systems (AWACS) aircraft. The Soviets are also improving their air surveillance system with over-the-horizon radar in the Far East to give early warning of US submarine-launched ballistic missiles in the Pacific Ocean.

Despite the introduction of a new range of advanced fighters with improved radar capabilities, the main Soviet defence from air attack comes in the form of a wide range of strategic and tactical SAMs, and 40,000 of them are produced a year. The Soviets regard the command of air space as vital to both offensive and defensive strategies, and the SAMs would pose a formidable threat to NATO strike forces, even given the major advances in NATO's

Right: Soviet citizens look on as the huge bulk of an ABM-1B Galosh anti-ballistic missile is hauled through the streets in its ribbed cylindrical container. The missile is thought to break through the end-cap of the launcher when fired. Right centre: Mounted in a mobile range-station, this manually operated target-tracking equipment may now be replaced by computerised technology. Right top: Around Moscow the Soviets have the world's only operational anti-ballistic missile system. Originally including 64 reloadable ABM-1B launchers, the total is being upped to the 100 launchers permitted by the 1972 ABM Treaty. The missiles are fully linked to early-warning radar systems.

would have at his disposal at least one air regiment of between 30 and 36 interceptors from IA-PVO to provide air cover, along with radar battalions to give early warning and control.

A PVO-Strany corps comprises three or four SAM brigades, a radar regiment and two regiments of fighters, one for long-range defence and the other for high-altitude operations.

The mainstay of the Soviet SAM arsenal is the SA-2, codenamed Guideline by NATO. It is probably the most widely deployed system of its kind in the world and has been used extensively in the Middle East and Asia. Commanded by radar-guided controls, it is effective from altitudes as low as 2000ft to as high as 80,000ft; it has a range of 31 miles and packs a 286lb high-explosive warhead.

The SA-5 Gammon missile is used for high-altitude, long-range interception and is widely deployed around Moscow and Leningrad, two cities which happen to be centres of SAM production. The SA-5 is effective up to 95,000ft and has a range of about 100 miles at speeds reaching Mach 5. Medium and low-range threats can be countered with the tracked SA-6 Gainful, a weapon which was tested in combat in the 1973 Yom Kippur War.

To meet the threat of low-level air attack, now the favoured NATO approach, the Soviets have the SA-10 Grumble, a Mach 5 missile believed to be designed to kill incoming terrain-hugging cruise weapons. These missiles, which can hit targets as low as 300ft, are now being widely deployed among the PVO-Strany units.

Soviet air defence tactics emphasise far stricter control of missiles and interceptors than is current in the West, where pilots are permitted greater individual freedom of action and initiative. In many ways, this inflexibility is seen as a major failing of the rigid Soviet system, one which pervades through all arms of all services.

PVO-Strany officers are well educated and well motivated after years of going through the Soviet military academies, but Western analysts consider them over-constrained by the highly centralised Soviet military organisation. The Soviet officer corps, one million men strong, forms the backbone of the organisation and, as in other branches, PVO-Strany officers undergo extensive academic, technical and military training at such military institutions as the Higher Anti-Aircraft Missile Engineering School in Kiev and the Higher Anti-Aircraft Missile Command

Schools in Leningrad and Orenburg. The radar and communications specialists in PVO-Strany are usually graduates of the Signal Academy in Moscow, while electronics schools in Leningrad, Riga, Novosibirsk, Kiev and Moscow turn out specialists for the Air Defence Command.

Most air defence troops are conscripts who must serve two years. The NCOs, most of whom are drawn from conscript ranks, are usually men who have received pre-induction training or who have been educated to an advanced level. They therefore tend to lack military experience, and Western analysts see this as a serious weakness in the Soviet military structure, for experienced NCOs are the backbone of Western armies. However, the military authorities have in recent years tried to establish a corps of highly qualified NCOs, or ensigns, roughly the equivalent of warrant officers, to give the air defence

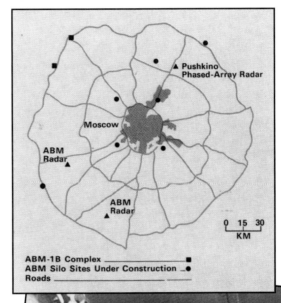

ABM-1B Complex _____ ■
ABM Silo Sites Under Construction _ ●
Roads _____

MOSCOW AIR DEFENCE DISTRICT

Defending Moscow against NATO's missiles and strike planes is PVO-Strany's highest priority. The Moscow Air Defence District, one of six PVO-Strany zones in the USSR, includes the Kremlin, government offices, military command centres (including that of PVO-Strany itself), plus key factories and industrial areas. The district is split into four operational zones, each with its own fighter, missile, anti-aircraft artillery and radar components. The Moscow Air Defence District is manned by a complete PVO-Strany army, comprising a corps of five or six SAM regiments with up to 300 launchers, a radar regiment, and a specially expanded fighter strength of 11 air regiments (instead of the usual two or three). It is estimated that 400 of the most advanced Soviet interceptors are stationed at Moscow, including MiG-29 Fulcrums, MiG-25 Foxbats and Su-25 Flagons. They co-operate closely with Tu-126 Moss early-warning planes, as well as the vastly improved Tall King and Hen House ground radar systems, which can detect incoming missiles and aircraft from ranges of up to 3000 miles. Moscow also has its own anti-ballistic missile defences, including over 60 ABM-1B Galosh anti-ballistic missiles, believed to be the only weapon of its type operational in the world. The Galoshes are linked with both the gigantic Hen House long-range early warning radars, and Dog House radars, which can discriminate between warheads and decoys from a range of 1500 miles. According to the latest Western intelligence reports, the Soviets are continuing to upgrade their defences around Moscow. It is a measure of the paramount importance of Moscow Air Defence District that new fighters, missiles and radar systems always see their earliest deployment in that zone.

forces a command level that bridges the big gap between officers and men.

Air defence troops lead tough, regimented lives. PVO-Strany barracks offer the most rudimentary amenities, and the authorities have only recently tried to improve conditions by installing indoor toilets and central heating for their troops. Some soldiers are allowed no leave at all during their two years of service, and at best leave is rare. Pay for a private soldier seldom exceeds five roubles a month (about six pounds sterling). Discipline is harsh, as befits an elite unit, and the Soviets are at pains to provide training that reflects the rigours of war.

The operational PVO-Strany units also undertake the training of new recruits. Inductions take place every six months, when as many as 25 per cent of the experienced soldiers are replaced by raw recruits.

Above: The formidable ZSU-23-4 self-propelled anti-aircraft mount presents a very potent threat to NATO's tactical aircraft. Equipped with a Gun Dish radar, its four AZP-23 23mm cannon reach out to an altitude of 5.1km, each barrel firing 200rpm. Below: The six-wheeled SA-8 amphibious launch vehicle carries four SA-8 Gecko SAMs and the multi-purpose Land Roll radar, making it an entirely independent, integral anti-aircraft system.

These immediately begin several weeks of basic training skills before advancing to specialised training. Each man must learn other skills apart from his assigned speciality to reduce unit vulnerability to losses in combat. Units are frequently pitted against one another in simulated combat to test their efficiency and improve their readiness. Marshal V.F. Tolubko, commander of the Strategic Rocket Forces, believes that a powerful means of increasing mastery of combat skills is found in competition… 'under the banner of striving for the utmost in combat readiness and rigorous adherence to required military procedures'.

The fighter units in PVO-Strany get the pick of the Soviet pilots, taking precedence over the tactical air regiments of the Soviet Air Force. In keeping with their status, the PVO-Strany airmen receive the best food in the Soviet armed services – Ration No.5, which includes one pound of meat daily, three ounces of butter and other fats, as well as rye and white bread. Non-flying personnel also eat better than most of their comrades in the military. They receive Ration No.6, which is similar to the pilots' fare but with smaller portions of meat and butter. The technical personnel within PVO-Strany receive Ration No.2, which is coarser than the others and contains more bread and cereals. The meat content is only four ounces per day.

Regardless of the specific duties they perform for the Soviet Air Defence Command, the pilots, missile troops, technicians and other personnel within the PVO-Strany organisation are well aware that they have a unique responsibility. The command structures of the various elements of the Soviet armed forces are highly centralised, and in the event of conflict the major cities of the Soviet Union would be

Top: A BRDM armoured reconnaissance vehicle, armed with a pair of SA-9 Gaskin SAMs. A quadruple mounting is more common, and usually a regimental anti-aircraft battery comprises four quadruple SA-9 launchers and four ZSU-23-4 anti-aircraft guns. Above: The SA-6 Gainful SAM launcher. Left: The Ilyushin 76 Mainstay AWACS aircraft.

prime targets for military as well as political and industrial reasons.

Beyond the limited objective of protecting the nerve centres of the Soviet Union, PVO-Strany is charged with the air defence of the homeland itself. Deeply embedded in the consciousness of the Soviet people is the traumatic memory of Hitler's savage attempt to destroy their nation, and it is certain that PVO-Strany will use every weapon in its gigantic arsenal to prevent such an event occurring again.

THE AUTHOR Ed Blanche is a journalist of The Associated Press who specialises in military subjects. He has written extensively on many aspects of the Soviet armed forces and on current Soviet military strategy worldwide.

KAMPF-
GESCHWADER 200

During World War I the German Air Service gave the hazardous task of landing agents in enemy-held territory to hand-picked, experienced aircrews from frontline squadrons. In early World War II the Luftwaffe saw no reason to depart from this practice and it was not until early 1944 that it became necessary to form a unit expressly for that purpose.

The change was precipitated by the 1944 depletion of the bomber and transport forces in favour of additional fighter units as the Luftwaffe, responding to increasing long-range B-17 bomber raids over Germany and the threat posed by the capitulation of Italy, reorganised itself for the defence of the Reich.

On 20 February, Kampfgeschwader 200 (KG 200) was formed under the command of Oberst (Colonel) Higer. Although it was originally intended to comprise two Gruppen (wings), with I Gruppe responsible for operations and II Gruppe providing technical support and training, KG 200 expanded to four Gruppen by the end of 1944. Agent-dropping operations were given to I Gruppe, with its 1st Staffel undertaking long-range missions, its 2nd Staffel organising flights nearer the front, and the 3rd Staffel providing replacement crew training. II Gruppe was given responsibility for developing the new Mistel composite aircraft, while III Gruppe operated as a torpedo-bomber unit with modified Focke Wulf Fw 190 fighters. Training and technical support thus devolved to IV Gruppe, which also became involved in the Reichenberg IV project, in which piloted V1 flying bombs were flown on suicide missions.

Above: The Luftwaffe's bomber qualification clasp.

In early 1944, a special Luftwaffe unit – Kampfgeschwader 200 – was formed to carry out hazardous clandestine operations behind enemy lines

KAMPFGESCHWADER (fighter group) 200 (KG 200), the Luftwaffe unit responsible for clandestine air operations behind enemy lines, inevitably attracted many myths. It was reputed to be a suicide group, its ranks bound by a special oath of allegiance and required to take their own lives by cyanide capsule rather than submit to capture. None of this was true. However, in the words of one of its officers:

'The fact is that KG 200 was the most secret unit of the Luftwaffe in its own lifetime, but whatever was

involved. Known to the Germans as V-Leute (Vertrauensleute, or trusted people), agents were often renegade Allied nationals and as such were frequently regarded with suspicion by the KG 200 crews, who wondered if their carefully planned operations were simply providing unreliable agents with an easy means of returning to their homelands. However, Hauptmann (Captain) P.W. Stahl, Commander of Detachment 'Olga' at Rhein-Main near Frankfurt, thought of the V-Leute that, 'they were not adventurers, as one perhaps would have expected, but quite the opposite [and] looked and behaved just like the proverbial man in the street.'

The agents' flights into enemy territory were very much trips into the unknown. For security reasons they were not told the airfield from which they were to fly, and, apart from a short briefing by KG 200

SECRET SERVICE

revealed to the public in detail after the war soon built into a legend that contains more misleading inventions than truth. Yet the truth is adventurous enough.'

Kampfgeschwader 200 had its headquarters at Gatow airfield near Berlin. Although its main airbase was established at Finow, also near Berlin, its operational airfields were scattered throughout Germany and the occupied territories. The insertion of agents was undertaken by semi-independent detachments, or Kommandos, with cover names such as 'Carmen', 'Clara', 'Olga' and 'Tosca', under the overall control of KG 200's I Gruppe (wing). They flew a tremendously varied mixture of aircraft, enabling them to undertake a wide range of different missions. The complement included Ju 188 and Heinkel He 111 bombers; transport aircraft such as the long-range Ju 290 and Arado Ar 232B Tatzelwurm; various cargo gliders; and maritime aircraft including the Ar 196 floatplane and the Blohm and Voss Bv 222 long-range flying boat. In addition to these German-built aircraft, the Geschwader operated various captured types of foreign manufacture, such as French Amiot 143s, Italian Savoia-Marchetti SM 79 and SM 82 trimotors and American B-17 Flying Fortresses and B-24 Liberators. The latter types, although frequently flown on clandestine missions over Allied territory, carried German rather than American markings. Indeed, they were pressed into service primarily to relieve the Luftwaffe's chronic shortage of long-range transport aircraft in 1944, rather than as a deception measure.

The agents carried by KG 200 were generally recruited by the RSHA (SS State Security Office) or the Abwehr (military intelligence), although sometimes Germany army special-forces troops were

Left: Leutnant Josef Thurnhuber of KG 200's Detachment 'Carmen' receives the Knight's Cross for his part in covert operations. Below: Kommodore Werner Baumbach in the cockpit and (bottom left) briefing his crew before a mission. Bottom: Among the numerous types of aircraft used by KG 200 to drop agents was the Focke Wulf Fw 200 Condor.

WERNER BAUMBACH

One of the Luftwaffe's most outstanding bomber pilots of World War II, Werner Baumbach was born at Cloppenburg in Oldenburg on 27 December 1916. Like many German airmen of the time, he began flying training on gliders, and in April 1936 he entered the Luftwaffe's academy at Gatow as a cadet. His early wartime service was with Kampfgeschwader 30, the first frontline unit to be equipped with the Junkers Ju 88. Baumbach was awarded the Knight's Cross for attacks on British naval forces in 1939 and for service in the Norwegian campaign of 1940. It was in anti-shipping bombing that Baumbach was to excel, and he participated in the Luftwaffe's raids on the Arctic Convoys in 1942. Later serving in the Mediterranean and the Black Sea, he was awarded the Swords and Oakleaves clasps to the Knight's Cross. Late in 1942 Baumbach was posted to Berlin where, as an officer on the staff of the General of Bombers, he had special responsibility for the development of such new weapons as the Henschel Hs 293 glider bomb. This work brought him into contact with Albert Speer, the Minister for War Production, and the two men became close friends. He ended the war as Kommodore of KG 200 and, after interrogation by the Western Allies, emigrated to Argentina in 1948.

personnel immediately before take-off, they had no prior instruction in parachuting techniques. For this reason, special equipment had to be developed for them. Their parachutes were opened automatically by means of a static line attached to the aircraft, and up to three agents were sometimes dropped together in a special container (the Personen-Abwuft-Gerat (PAG), or personnel drop device), which was carried under the aircraft's wing and parachuted in the same way as a supply container. Once they were strapped into this claustrophobic wooden canister, the agents' only outside contact was via an intercom link with the aircraft's crew.

KG 200's special-duty operations took their crews virtually everywhere in Europe, behind the Eastern and Western Fronts, and over much of North Africa and the Middle East as well. A typical night's activity began, as darkness approached, with crew briefings. Hauptmann Stahl recalled that:

'From around the airfield one could hear the sound of engines starting up as the mechanics carried out the final checks on the parked aircraft. A fuel bowser struggled along the bumpy road alongside the runway – the usual activities on an airfield before operations, only this time in the gathering dusk and not at first light.'

Good weather was essential for these missions and precise navigation was needed to find poorly marked dropping zones. Populated areas had to be avoided to prevent arousing suspicion. For the same reason, the aircrafts' engines were throttled back prior to the drops and the release points approached in a glide. Detachment 'Olga', equipped with six Ju 188s and a pair of B-17s, had an area of operations covering the United Kingdom, France and the Low Countries.

On the night of 23/24 November 1944, Stahl was flying one of three Ju 188s assigned to operations. His mission was to deliver supplies to a group of agents south of Rotterdam, then to carry on into Belgium and parachute an agent in, and finally to drop three Frenchmen in a PAG in the vicinity of Paris. Over Amiens airfield the Ju 188 was mistaken by the Allies for a friendly aircraft and given a green flare to signify that it was cleared to land. Ignoring the invitation, Stahl continued with his mission:

Below: The deadly Mistel combination of a Focke Wulf Fw 190 carrier and an explosive-packed Ju 88 airframe. Centre: The Heinkel He 177A-5 Greif (griffin) bomber, with a range of 5500km, was often used for KG 200's long-range agent drops. Bottom: Flying in the Fieseler Fi 103R piloted V-1 would have been a terrifying experience had it ever been used operationally, and although it was theoretically possible for the pilots to bale out, their missions would almost certainly have ended in death.

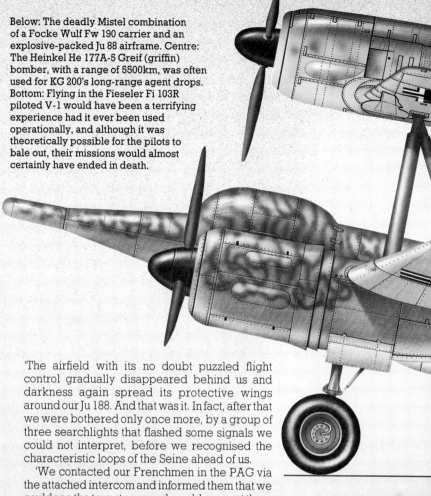

'The airfield with its no doubt puzzled flight control gradually disappeared behind us and darkness again spread its protective wings around our Ju 188. And that was it. In fact, after that we were bothered only once more, by a group of three searchlights that flashed some signals we could not interpret, before we recognised the characteristic loops of the Seine ahead of us.

'We contacted our Frenchmen in the PAG via the attached intercom and informed them that we could see the target area and would soon set them down in the agreed spot, a strip of meadow within a U-shaped bend of the Seine…

'Releasing the PAG was much less dramatic than dropping our Belgian with his parachute straight from the cabin. With throttled back engines, I let the 188 fly on at a slow speed in a flat glide towards the clearly discernible target and passed over the river bend in a westerly direction at 250m altitude. The moonlight was quite suf-

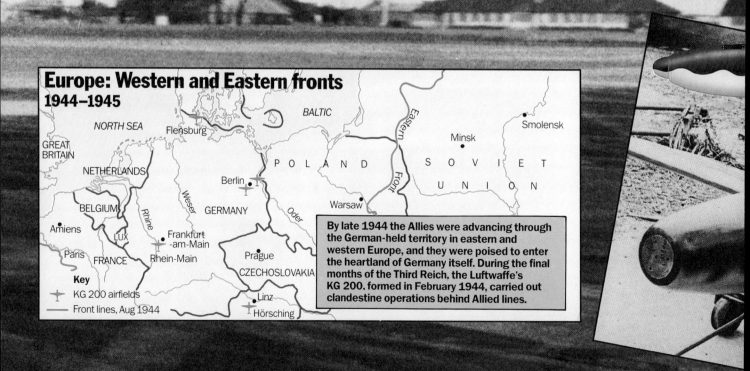

Europe: Western and Eastern fronts
1944–1945

BALTIC

NORTH SEA
Flensburg

GREAT BRITAIN

Minsk

Smolensk

NETHERLANDS

P O L A N D

S O V I E T

Berlin

Weser

GERMANY

Oder

Warsaw

U N I O N

BELGIUM

Rhine

Amiens

LUX

Frankfurt -am-Main

Prague

Paris

FRANCE

Rhein-Main

CZECHOSLOVAKIA

Key

✈ KG 200 airfields

— Front lines, Aug 1944

Linz

Hörsching

By late 1944 the Allies were advancing through the German-held territory in eastern and western Europe, and they were poised to enter the heartland of Germany itself. During the final months of the Third Reich, the Luftwaffe's KG 200, formed in February 1944, carried out clandestine operations behind Allied lines.

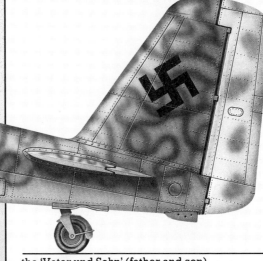

THE MISTEL PICK-A-BACK BOMB

Since the Germans had no equivalent to the British Lancaster heavy bomber and the powerful 12,000lb 'Tallboy' deep-penetration bomb, it was proposed in 1943 that, as a substitute, obsolescent Ju 88 airframes should be packed with explosives and converted into pilotless missiles of great destructive power. Each would be carried to its target by a fighter plane, usually a Messerschmitt Bf 109 or a Focke Wulf Fw 190; it would then be released to fly on under the control of its automatic pilot. Known as the Mistel (mistletoe) composite, or the 'Vater und Sohn' (father and son) combination, the weapon went into limited production in' 1944.

Clearly, such a potent missile would be used only against targets of the greatest importance. The first targets selected were major ships of the British Home Fleet, but by late 1944 priorities had changed. New plans were being drawn up to eliminate the great power stations near Moscow and Gorky, in order to paralyse the whole electricity-generating network of western Russia. With the rapid advance of the Soviet Army on Germany in early 1945, however, Hitler became more concerned with targets of immediate tactical importance.

In March 1945, KG 200 was ordered to carry out repeated attacks on bridges over the River Oder. Although several of the structures were successfully knocked out, the Soviet army engineers were able to replace them almost immediately with pontoon bridges. One raid, that on Steinau bridge on 31 March, was masterminded in almost every detail by Hitler himself. Six Mistels were despatched, and although three failed to reach the target, the rest struck home and wiped out the bridge. This last-ditch operation was completed with the loss of only two Bf 109s of the bombers' escort, and yet within days the bridge was again fully serviceable.

Despite the missile's great drawback, that it could not be controlled once it had been released by the 'Sohn', the Mistel was an imaginative weapon that could have presented a serious threat to Allied installations in the closing months of the war.

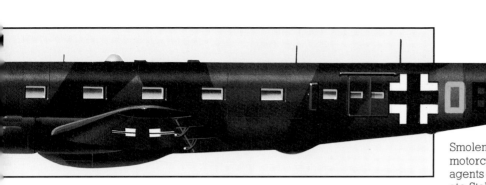

ficient to help me avoid overflying any houses and once I had reached the right spot it was only a matter of pressing on the bomb release button. Then the aircraft jumped in the air, now almost 800kg lighter, and then a second jolt as the strong steel rip-cord jerked off the cap and pulled out the parachutes.

'Without opening the throttles, I continued flying in the same direction to avoid drawing the attention of any casual observer to the PAG dropping area. Only when the ground had come dangerously close did I carefully open the throttles and slowly began to gain height again to make a wide curve in a southerly direction before setting the course for home.'

Many of KG 200's most hazardous missions required the aircraft to land in enemy territory. Operation Zeppelin, carried out in September 1944, called for an Ar 232B to fly a team into a landing field near

Above: A Junkers Ju 290A, seen here in night camouflage, tailored for clandestine nocturnal missions. Left: Men climb aboard a Blohm und Voss Bv 138 three-engined flying boat. Its nickname, the 'Fliegende Holzschue' (flying clog) was inspired by its characteristic shoe-shaped hull. Below: This Allied B-17F served with KG 200 in Luftwaffe markings. Bottom left: Kommodore Baumbach introduces Hitler to young KG 200 members. Bottom right: Another long-haul plane, the Ju 352A trimotor.

Smolensk. After touchdown, they were to unload a motorcycle combination which would carry the agents on to Moscow. Their mission was to assassinate Stalin. This audacious plan was thwarted when the aircraft crashed while attempting to get down within too short a landing run and the agents were quickly captured. Another of KG 200's operations on the Eastern Front required the supply of a group of German troops reported to be cut off well behind enemy lines in the swamps and forests east of Minsk. Many supply drops were made, at considerable risk to the crews, before it was realised that the German High Command had been taken in by a Soviet 'radio game' and that the isolated troops had never existed. A much more creditable mission, which was perhaps the greatest feat of airmanship performed by KG 200, was the flight of a Ju 290 to Mosul in Iraq in late November 1944. Its crew, captained by Hauptmann Braun, successfully completed a 13-hour flight and, after parachuting five agents over the dropping zone, returned to the German-occupied island of Rhodes.

The Geschwader Kommodore, Oberstleutnant Baumbach, recalled being told by one young fanatic, 'We stand under a higher law!'

Perhaps the most bizarre of all KG 200's varied operational tasks was that of readying the 'self-sacrifice' crews for their one-way missions aboard manned V1s. These pilots were not regular Luftwaffe aircrew, but volunteers from the Hitler Jugend with gliding experience. They were regarded with suspicion, not untinged with derision, by the KG 200 regulars. The Geschwader Kommodore, Oberstleutnant Baumbach, recalled being told by one young fanatic, 'We stand under a higher law!', when paraded before his commander on a charge of overstaying his leave. Fortunately for these young men, the war ended before the determination of the self-sacrificers could be put to the test.

By late April 1945 the regular work of KG 200 had come to an end, but one final task remained. The Nazi leadership had to be ferried to safety. At Flensburg a group of Bv 222 flying boats was prepared for a long-range mission to a secret hideout on the coast of Greenland, while at Hörsching near Linz, Hauptmann Braun stood by with his Ju 290 to fly a similar evacuation mission to Madrid. In the event, none of these fanciful missions was flown. The advancing Allies overran the surviving aircraft of KG 200 on their airfields and the personnel of the top-secret Geschwader disappeared into the anonymous ranks of the defeated Luftwaffe.

THE AUTHOR Anthony Robinson was formerly on the staff of the RAF Museum, Hendon, and is now a freelance military aviation writer. He has edited the books *Aerial Warfare* and the *Dictionary of Aviation*. The publishers would like to acknowledge gratefully permission to reproduce from *KG 200: the true story* by P. W. Stahl, published by Janes.

HARRIER STRIKE

The Harriers of No. 1 Squadron RAF, streaking in on low-level ground attacks, played a vital role in the fighting to wrest the Falklands back from Argentinian forces

Below left: An RAF Harrier GR3 is checked at Ascension Island before continuing to the Falklands. Bottom left: No.1 Squadron's first team, the pilots who went south with the initial wave. They are (from left to right) Squadron Leader Peter Harris, Flight Lieutenants Jeff Glover, Mark Hare and John Rochford, Squadron Leader Jerry Pook, Wing Commander Peter Squire (the commander) and Squadron Leader Bob Iveson. Seated is Flight Lieutenant Tony Harper. Below: No.1 Squadron's GR3s first operated over the Falklands in the interceptor role, and they were consequently armed with Sidewinder missiles. Bottom: Closely ranged on the flight-deck of HMS *Hermes*, GR3s await deployment with Royal Navy Sea Harriers, two of which have been camouflaged in grey-white during the voyage.

THE HISTORY OF No. 1 Squadron, the premier Royal Air Force flying squadron, dates back to 1912 when it formed with non-rigid airships. Since then, the unit has been involved in almost every conflict in which the Royal Flying Corps and the Royal Air Force have participated. The Falklands war of 1982 was to prove no exception.

Throughout the planning of Operation Corporate to retake the Falkland Islands, the most serious single limitation on the British side was seen to be the shortage of Sea Harrier short take-off and vertical landing naval fighters: only 28 of these aircraft were available, and any loss would deplete the already meagre fighter cover available to the Task Force. The only other jet aircraft that could possibly take part in the operation were the Harriers of the RAF, but these were ground attack aircraft, not interceptors, and they were not equipped for carrier operations. Nor were their pilots trained for them.

Following the Argentinian landings on the Falklands at the beginning of April 1982, and the decision to send RAF Harriers to the South Atlantic, No. 1 Squadron's base at Wittering near Peterborough became a hive of activity as pilots and aircraft were readied for the task. The pilots flew their Harriers to the Royal Naval Air Station at Yeovilton in Somerset for a short course in the technique of 'ski-jump' take-offs from aircraft carriers. They also received briefings on air-to-air combat and took part in exercises against Phantom and Lightning fighters. Meanwhile, those Harrier aircraft earmarked to go south were prepared for the interceptor role; each was fitted with the fixed equipment to enable it to fire Sidewinder infra-red homing missiles. The Harriers were also modified for deck operations with the fitting of lashing rings, radar transponder units, and changes to the aircraft's inertial navigation equipment to allow it to be aligned on the deck of a ship.

By the beginning of May the unit was ready to move south. Staging through St Mawgan in Cornwall, the first six Harriers flew to Ascension Island, taking fuel en route from the Victor tanker aircraft accompanying them. After arrival on Ascension the ferry tanks were removed and the Harriers flew over to the container ship *Atlantic Conveyor*, anchored off the coast, and landed on her foredeck. Once on board, No. 1 Squadron's Harriers and the Sea Harriers and helicopters also in transit to the Task Force were lashed down on the open deck. On the evening of 6 May the container ship set sail for the South Atlantic. On the 18th, *Atlantic Conveyor* joined up with the British naval task force and the RAF Harriers transferred to the aircraft carrier *Hermes*, which was to be their operational base.

On arrival on *Hermes* the Harriers were still

NO. 1 SQUADRON

Officially formed as a balloon unit on 13 April 1912, No. 1 Squadron did not receive aircraft until May 1914. During World War I it flew with the British Expeditionary Force in Nieuport 17 cls and SE5as, claiming over 200 enemy aircraft in a series of furious air battles.

Disbanded after a postwar period of service in India and then Iraq, the squadron was re-formed at Tangmere in 1927. It flew Siskin IIIas, Hawker Fury Is and Gladiators, and one year before the onset of World War II it received its first Hurricanes. These flew in the Advanced Striking Force in France, and later in the Battle of Britain. In 1941, many Czechs and Poles joined the squadron and it came to specialise in night-flying. Between 1942 and 1943 Typhoons were flown in the ground-attack role, and then Spitfire IXs were used on anti-V1 patrols; 39 flying-bombs were downed.

After the war, No. 1 was again in the front line with Meteor F.4s, F.8s, and Hunter F.5s. Though No. 1 was disbanded in June 1958, No. 263 Squadron was redesignated No. 1 a month later and equipped with Hunter F.6s and FGA.9s. These were flown until April 1969, when the squadron received its first British Aerospace Harriers, later to be deployed with such success in the Falklands. Above: The badge of No. 1 Squadron, with its motto 'Foremost in everything'.

fitted out as interceptors, and during the initial flights to familiarise pilots with deck operations the aircraft carried Sidewinder missiles. With the landings on the Falklands due to begin on the night of 20 May, however, and the Sea Harrier losses somewhat lower than had been feared, it was decided to use the Harriers in their accustomed ground attack role. Their first attack was in the late afternoon of the 20th, when Wing Commander Peter Squire led his two flight commanders, Squadron Leaders Jerry Pook and Bob Iveson, in a three-aircraft attack on an Argentinian fuel dump at Fox Bay, West Falkland. Each Harrier carried two BL755 cluster-bomb containers each holding 147 bomblets. Later Iveson recalled:

'We swept in low over the hills, then suddenly in front of us was our target: rows of jerricans and 40-gallon drums laid out carefully on the ground, so that supposedly a single bomb would not set off the lot. But in fact they had laid them out in almost a perfect shape for a cluster-bomb pattern! I saw the boss go in first, his cluster bombs hit and the fuel dump started to go up with a lot of secondary explosions. Then I went in, attacking from 30 degrees to the right of the boss's line. Finally Jerry Pook came in on a similar line to the boss and put down his bombs. So far as I could see, not a shot was fired at us. We ran out past East Head, turned north-east up Falkland Sound and then started our climb back to high altitude to return to the carrier.'

On the following day, the 21st, the squadron was in action in support of British troops going ashore at San Carlos Water. At first light Jerry Pook and Flight Lieutenant Mark Hare took off to attack Argentinian helicopters which an SAS patrol had reported on the ground beside Mount Kent. The helicopters had been sent into the hinterland to safeguard them from attack, but the move was unsuccessful. Pook and Hare arrived to find a Chinook, two Pumas and a Bell UH-1 sitting on the ground well apart. The two pilots made repeated strafing attacks with 30mm cannon and afterwards Hare recalled:

'I did a level strafing pass on the Chinook. I saw my exploding rounds walking along the ground towards the helicopter; when I saw them exploding on it I held my sight there, then it blew up with a spurt of flame and I pulled away.'

During a subsequent strafing run Hare destroyed a Puma and the two pilots shared the destruction of a second. On the final firing pass Hare's aircraft was struck by a burst of smallarms fire and he was forced to break off his attack. On return to the carrier it was found that the Harrier had taken three hits, but the damage could be easily repaired and the aircraft was flying the next day.

Questioned after the conflict on why he had made no immediate attempt to drive the British troops into the sea, once he knew they were ashore at Port San Carlos, Argentinian commander, General Menen-

Harrier GR3 pilot, No.1 Squadron RAF

The anti-gravity suit worn under this pilot's Mk 10 immersion coverall is supplied via the hose at his hip. In front of his M22 life-preserver he has a V8 oxygen mask and regulator, and the pouch on his left breast contains a personal locator beacon (PLB). The blue garters at the knee are attached to the Harrier's seat to prevent leg injury should the pilot be forced to eject.

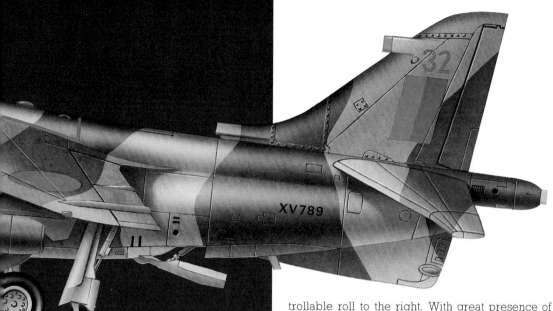

XV789

It is no exaggeration to state that the outstanding all-round performance of the RAF and Royal Navy Harriers in the Falklands heralded a new era in military aviation. Not only were the aircraft able to deploy from landing strips that would be quite unserviceable for any other modern fighter, but they allowed radically new air combat tactics to be brought into play.

The Harrier's V/STOL (vertical/short take-off and landing) performance derives from the application of its Rolls-Royce Pegasus 103 vectored-thrust turbofan powerplant. Its 21,500lb of thrust is channelled through four swivelling nozzles, and for a vertical take-off these are rotated to point straight downwards. Once airborne, they are eased back to point aft, and conventional flight begins. For a short take-off, which allows a greater load of weaponry and fuel than a vertical one, the nozzles are set at an intermediate angle.

In effect, the Harrier's V/STOL capability enables it to dispense with the fixed airbase, and in wartime Harrier forces can operate from separate and concealed locations, making their destruction on the ground a near impossible task.

Following its introduction into service, it was demonstrated that the Harrier's vectored thrust could be manipulated to gain advantage in combat. Known as vectoring in forward flight ('viffing'), a pilot can suddenly reduce his forward speed by applying a rear air-brake, simultaneously making a sharp gain in altitude. This tactic is effective in throwing off a heat-seeking missile, and invariably causes an enemy fighter to overshoot, thus leaving him exposed to the Harrier's armament.

z stated that he lacked sufficient helicopters to fly ops and weapons to mount an effective counter-ack. Before news of the landings reached the gentinian general, Pook and Hare had deprived n of a significant part of his helicopter lifting pacity.

Also that morning No.1 Squadron lost its first rrier in action. Flight Lieutenant Jeff Glover was king a low-altitude photographic run over Port ward when his plane was hit by ground fire. The ot saw nothing of the enemy: the first he knew of eir presence was when his aircraft shuddered der the impact of cannon shells. Almost imme-tely the Harrier flicked into a violent and uncon-

trollable roll to the right. With great presence of mind Glover waited until the aircraft had rotated through 320 degrees, then pulled the handle to fire the ejector seat. When the seat fired, the aircraft was the right way up but even so Glover was blasted out into a 600mph airflow which wrenched back his left arm. His arm, shoulder and collar bone were immediately broken and he passed out. He regained consciousness to find himself underwater and struggling to reach the surface. Deep in shock, the injured pilot forgot to inflate his life-jacket but fortunately there was sufficient air trapped in his rubberised immersion suit to keep him afloat. He later told this author:

'I had a good look around and saw the shore about 200yds away. I started trying to swim towards it on my back but I got nowhere fast – I had not released my parachute harness. So I gave that up and started to think things out. I was in the process of releasing the pack connectors, before inflating my dinghy, when I heard voices and shouts. I looked around and saw about ten Argentinian soldiers standing on the shore. Then a rowing boat put out with half a dozen soldiers on board.'

Jeff Glover was taken prisoner and flown to the Argentinian mainland, where he remained until his release early in July.

Peter Harris led a three-aircraft raid on Argentinian positions at Goose Green in support of 2 Para

During the days that followed, the squadron was in action whenever the weather permitted, striking at targets on East and West Falkland. One noteworthy attack was late on the afternoon of the 28th, when Squadron Leader Peter Harris led a three-aircraft raid on Argentinian positions at Goose Green in support of men of the 2nd Battalion The Parachute Regiment (2 Para) advancing on the settlement. The attack knocked out the artillery weapons on which the defence hinged, and the following morning the Argentinian force surrendered.

The squadron lost two further Harriers to ground fire during attack missions on 27 and 30 May, though on each occasion the pilots, Bob Iveson and Jerry Pook, were able to eject safely. This reduced the number of RAF Harriers in the South Atlantic area to three and necessitated a reinforcement from Ascension. On 1 June, Flight Lieutenants Murdo Macleod and Mike Beech flew a pair of Harriers 3800 miles from the island direct to *Hermes* in eight hours and 25

Below: While several of No.1 Squadron's aircraft received battle damage in the Falklands, only one required a complete change of engine. The work was carried out in the hangar of *Hermes* when other priorities permitted, and a combined team of RAF and RN personnel had her flying again in three days.

HARRIER AVIONICS

The RAF GR3 Harrier, an aircraft already exceptionally well endowed with the advantages of unsurpassable manoeuvrability and a formidable system of armaments, further benefits from an array of advanced electronic 'eyes' and 'ears'. The Harrier is equipped with the Ferranti laser ranging and marked target seeker (LRMTS), fitted into the aircraft's extended nose. This can pick out targets fixed by a ground-controller's laser designator and then supply precise target ranges. Approaching aircraft are scanned by the Harrier's identification friend or foe (IFF), and at night the pilot is alerted to their presence by his Marconi ARI 18223 radar warning receiver (RWR), located in the tail-fin, which operates by detecting incoming radar waves. The Harrier's navigation equipment includes the Ferranti FE541 inertial navigation and attack system, which supplies positional data that is projected onto the pilot's head-up display (HUD) in the cockpit. It also drives a moving map display in front of the pilot. Navigation through interpretation of radar signals received from fixed source beacons, normally achieved with the Tacan system, was set up in the Falklands using I-band transponders compatible with Royal Navy ships. In order to maintain contact with fellow aircraft and with ground-control, the Harrier is equipped with both UHF and VHF radios.

minutes, taking fuel along the route from Victor tankers. Had anything gone wrong with either aircraft it would almost certainly have been lost, for after leaving Ascension there were no land airfields within reach. Quite apart from the length of the flight there was the problem of the deck landing at the other end: before the operation neither pilot had landed a Harrier on the deck of a ship. But nothing did go wrong and the two Harriers landed safely on *Hermes*. It was a remarkable test of both the Harrier and the pilots' flying skills, and neither was found wanting. On 8 June two more Harriers flew from Ascension to *Hermes*, piloted by Flight Lieutenants Ross Boyens and Nick Gilchrist.

Once the beach-head at Port San Carlos was secure, men of the Royal Engineers began laying aluminium matting for a Harrier operating strip immediately to the west of the settlement. The first pair of Harriers, piloted by Bob Iveson and Tony Harper, landed there on 5 June. Harriers were to use the strip as a forward refuelling point for the remainder of the conflict, though they had to return to *Hermes* for re-arming and servicing.

Throughout the fighting the Harriers had frequently taken hits from smallarms fire, but on 12 June only superb flying saved one of the aircraft. During a strafing attack in support of British troops advancing on Sapper Hill, Murdo Macleod's aircraft was hit in the rear fuselage. The bullet passed clean through the duct carrying air to the rear reaction-control jet, which provides control for the aircraft when it is hovering. During his flight back to the carrier the pilot had no indication that anything was amiss, but as he entered the hover alongside *Hermes* before

landing, all sorts of unpleasant things began to happen. As he lowered the jet nozzles, the reaction-control jet pipes were fed with super-heated air at high pressure and this leaked into the rear fuselage. The electrical wiring and systems there immediately began to 'cook', presenting Macleod with some very odd indications in the cockpit. Peter Harris, who had landed in front of Macleod, watched the drama unfold from the deck of *Hermes*:

'Flyco [the flight deck control officer] called, "No.2, are you dumping fuel?" I looked over my shoulder to see what was happening, and it patently was not fuel. I called on the radio, "Its not fuel, its smoke!" Murdo continued to decelerate. Then the Flyco called "You'd better land quickly, there are bits falling off your aircraft!" In fact the "bits" were large flakes of paint blistering off the heated rear fuselage and blowing away; but I didn't know that and Murdo certainly didn't. He brought the Harrier into an immediate hover alongside the ship, eased it to the right and landed. It wasn't a "controlled crash" on the deck, it was an immaculate vertical landing.'

Once on the deck Macleod shut down the engine and the fire crew converged on the aircraft to blanket the rear with foam. For saving his aircraf

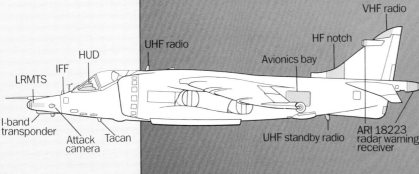

LRMTS
IFF
HUD
UHF radio
Avionics bay
HF notch
VHF radio
I-band transponder
Attack camera
Tacan
UHF standby radio
ARI 18223 radar warning receiver

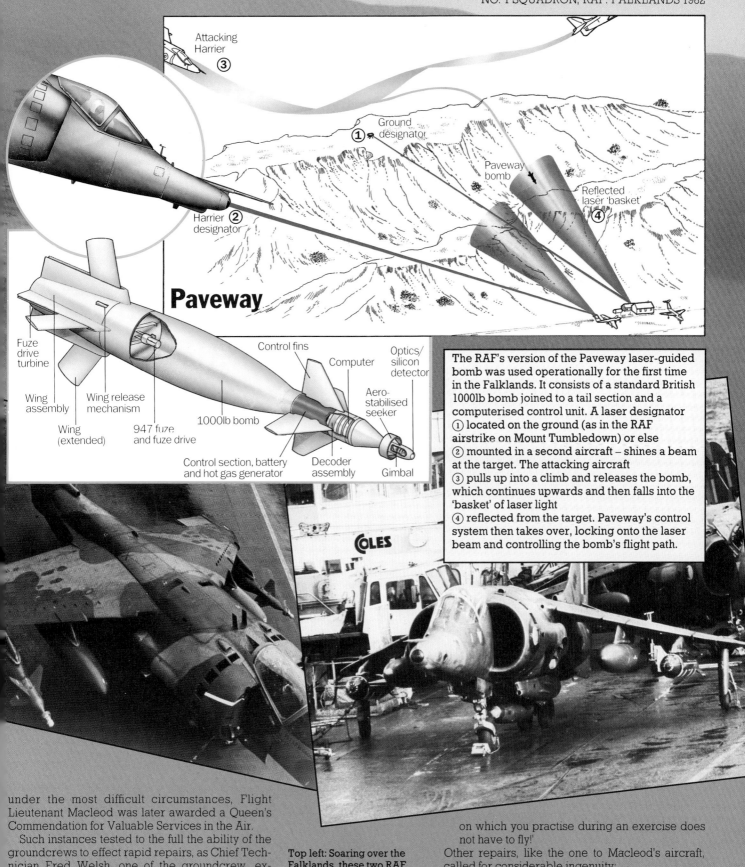

Paveway

Attacking Harrier ③

Ground designator ①

Harrier designator ②

Paveway bomb

Reflected laser 'basket' ④

Fuze drive turbine

Wing assembly

Wing release mechanism

Wing (extended)

947 fuze and fuze drive

Control section, battery and hot gas generator

1000lb bomb

Control fins

Computer

Decoder assembly

Optics/ silicon detector

Aero-stabilised seeker

Gimbal

The RAF's version of the Paveway laser-guided bomb was used operationally for the first time in the Falklands. It consists of a standard British 1000lb bomb joined to a tail section and a computerised control unit. A laser designator ① located on the ground (as in the RAF airstrike on Mount Tumbledown) or else ② mounted in a second aircraft – shines a beam at the target. The attacking aircraft ③ pulls up into a climb and releases the bomb, which continues upwards and then falls into the 'basket' of laser light ④ reflected from the target. Paveway's control system then takes over, locking onto the laser beam and controlling the bomb's flight path.

under the most difficult circumstances, Flight Lieutenant Macleod was later awarded a Queen's Commendation for Valuable Services in the Air.

Such instances tested to the full the ability of the groundcrews to effect rapid repairs, as Chief Technician Fred Welsh, one of the groundcrew, explained:

'Some of the battle damage could be repaired on deck between sorties. If it was a simple hole and nothing inside had been hit, we could cut away the rough edge and cover the hole with Speedtape – thick aluminium foil with a self-adhesive backing, rolled on by means of a special tool. We had done it all before on exercises – but the hulk

Top left: Soaring over the Falklands, these two RAF Harriers are armed with 68mm rockets. Each underwing multi-tube launcher carries 18 rockets. Above left: The laser-guided Paveway bomb in position. Above right: A GR3 with two BL755 cluster-bomb containers.

on which you practise during an exercise does not have to fly!'

Other repairs, like the one to Macleod's aircraft, called for considerable ingenuity:

'The batteries and cable looms in the rear compartment had all started to melt. We repaired the bullet holes and the ducting. On the electrical side, two of the cables had to be spliced. Two of the radio sergeants used cables out of one of their test sets to improvise a repair.'

Surprisingly, in view of the damage it had suffered, Macleod's Harrier would be flying again within three days.

Mark Hare believed that the success of the No. 1 Squadron pilots in avoiding further losses stemmed from the quality of their previous training, especially that in high-speed low-altitude operations.

'The important thing is to conceal your approach to the target; if you have to fly behind a 50ft contour to achieve surprise, then you must do that. If you can arrive out of nowhere and hit your target, then you've won. If they get 15 seconds warning to line up their guns and missiles then you've blown it, you might as well crash immediately after take off! Unless you train to fly really low in peacetime, in war you will stand a good chance of killing yourself by flying into the ground. You must learn to concentrate your entire attention in front of you. During an approach to the target at 50ft and 500 knots, the ground on either side and in front to about 600yds is just a blur.'

During the final 10 days of the conflict, up to the Argentinian surrender on 14 June, No.1 Squadron was in action every day flying attack missions in support of British troops advancing on Port Stanley. During this period the unit flew more sorties making contact with the enemy than all the other flying units engaged in the conflict, on both sides, put together. This phase ended with a couple of highly successful attacks on enemy troop positions with Paveway laser-guided bombs, immediately before the Argentinian surrender.

Because it is smaller than comparable attack aircraft, some had commented before the Falklands campaign that the Harrier was rather like a 'Dinky Toy' – pretty to look at, even able to do clever tricks, but not of much practical use. The success of the aircraft in war has demolished that view completely. In fact, the small size of the Harrier has proved a

Above: Squadron Leader Bob Iveson, whose GR3 was shot down by flak as he strafed Argentinian positions in support of 2 Para's attack at Goose Green. Below: The famous 'ski-jump' on *Hermes*, which thrust the aircraft into the air at the end of their short take-off. Right: Port Stanley airfield was pitted by the bombs of No.1 Squadron.

positive advantage in combat as, other things being equal, a small attack aircraft will take less hits from enemy gunfire than a large one. Such was the Harrier's fine combat record and great versatility that the aircraft is now established as a symbol of the modern British armed forces.

Tony Harper, who flew during the conflict as a Flight Lieutenant, feels that the Harrier has come out of its first taste of action showing itself to be a very effective ground attack aircraft:

'It is a very good aeroplane; it seems to be able to survive battle damage well. Its small size and absence of smoke make it difficult for the enemy to see it coming, and the camouflage is effective. It is fast enough at low altitude – if you went much faster you wouldn't have time to pick out the target. It is able to operate from stupidly small strips.'

During the conflict the squadron flew a total of 126 tasked sorties and lost three Harriers to enemy action, in each case to ground fire. A further Harrier was damaged beyond repair when it suffered an engine failure as it was coming in to land at Port San Carlos. No Harriers were lost to battle damage which a comparable conventional aircraft would have survived; and all Harriers which returned with battle damage were repaired within three days using only the resources on *Hermes*. But the most significant aspect of No.1 Squadron's operations over the Falklands is the fact that they happened at all. With only a minimum of training on land, a normal RAF line squadron was able to deploy to an aircraft carrier more than 8000 miles from its base; and when it reached the carrier the unit went straight into action without the lengthy work-up training usually considered necessary for deck operations. By any standards it was a remarkable feat, and had the unit been

East Falkland

Key

✈ Airfields
✈ Temporary airstrip (British)
✺ Major air strikes by No. 1 Squadron RAF

Douglas

Port
San Carlos

Teal Inlet

San Carlos

EAST FALKLAND

24 May
30 May
21 May *Mt Kent* **31 May**
28 May △ **9 June**
29 May *Sapper Hill* △ Stanley
Bluff Cove **9 June**
Fitzroy **12 June**
14 June

Darwin
Goose Green
27 May
28 May

equipped with any aircraft other than the Harrier it would have been quite impossible. The term 'flexibility of operation' is used so often when describing the Harrier that it has become a cliché, but nobody minds living with a cliché if it refers to that sort of capability.

Tony Harper summed up his feelings on combat flying over the Falklands in words that will be all too familiar to pilots who flew over Europe during air operations in World War II:

'The worst bit of any mission was sitting in the aircraft on deck at five minutes cockpit readiness waiting to go, when there was time to worry about what might happen. Once the order came to go it was not so bad, you were too busy to worry. By the end of the conflict all of the squadron pilots were starting to get a bit twitched – it was only a matter of time before somebody got hurt. In the event nobody was: we were bloody lucky nobody on the squadron was killed or seriously injured.

'I expected war to be far more dangerous than it apparently was. And I expected it to be far more spectacular than it was. Beforehand people had said war is three per cent sheer panic and 97 per cent boredom, and that is absolutely true.'

THE AUTHOR Alfred Price served as an aircrew officer in the RAF for 15 years, specialising in electronic warfare, aircraft weapons and air-fighting tactics. He has written extensively on aerial warfare.

SPECIAL DUTIES

The Special Operations Executive (SOE) was set up in July 1940 after the fall of France with the aim of nurturing and sustaining the newly-emergent resistance movements in Nazi-occupied Europe.

One of the SOE's most urgent requirements was for a means of supplying the resistance groups with agents, arms and other essential supplies. The Secret Intelligence Service (SIS, better known under its cover designation MI6) also needed a clandestine transport service to deliver and pick up agents from deep inside enemy territory. During World War I, aeroplanes had often been used to carry agents behind enemy lines, and in August 1940 the practice was revived when No. 419 Flight was formed for Special Duties, as these clandestine missions were termed, and it was equipped with Westland Lysanders and Armstrong Whitworth Whitleys. No. 419 Flight's first pick-up mission was carried out on the night of 19/20 October 1940.

The RAF's Special Duty operations were slow to gain momentum, however, as suitable aircraft were in short supply and little ordnance could be spared for the resistance groups. Nevertheless, No. 419 Flight was expanded to become No. 138 Squadron in August 1941, and in February 1942 it was joined by No. 161 Squadron (whose badge is shown above), led by Wing Commander E.H. 'Mouse' Fielden. The squadron's 'A' Flight was equipped with Lysanders for pick-up missions, while 'B' Flight operated Whitleys (and later Halifaxes and Stirlings) for parachute drops.

Flying by moonlight, No. 161 Squadron, RAF, slipped into occupied France to deliver precious cargoes of secret agents.

AS THE FIST of Germany tightened on the European nations subjugated by the Blitzkrieg operations of 1939 and 1940, hitherto isolated groups of resistance were consolidating and organising links with the free world. Knowing that their assistance would be invaluable in the struggle against Germany, Britain was anxious to encourage them with agents and supplies of equipment. With the expansion of the French partisan movement, known as the maquis, and similar movements elsewhere in occupied Europe, including Czechoslovakia, Poland and Yugoslavia, Britain was soon in need of air squadrons specialising in serving the resistance groups.

No. 161 Squadron, brought into the fray in February 1942, was formed at Newmarket in Suffolk around a nucleus supplied by elements of the disbanded King's Flight and of No. 138 Squadron. Wing Commander E.H. 'Mouse' Fielden, who previously was captain of the King's Flight, became No. 161 Squadron's first commanding officer, and the new squadron's aircraft, an assortment of Lysanders and bombers, included one Lockheed Hudson from the disbanded unit.

On the night of 27/28 February 1942, Flight Lieutenant A.M. 'Sticky' Murphy, piloting a Lysander, carried out the squadron's first pick-up operation. Everything went according to plan, unlike an earlier sortie flown by Murphy when he was serving with No. 138 Squadron. On that occasion he had landed in a field in Belgium and come under fire from German troops lying in ambush. Although wounded in the neck and losing a lot of blood, he, nonetheless, succeeded in flying his Lysander back to Tangmere. In March 1942, Murphy was promoted to squadron leader and took command of 'A' Flight. His next mission to France was rather unusual, as it was the only occasion on which an Avro Anson – borrowed from a training unit – was used for a pick-up operation. It was needed because four passengers were to be collected from a field near Issoudun, and the

SPECIAL DUTIES

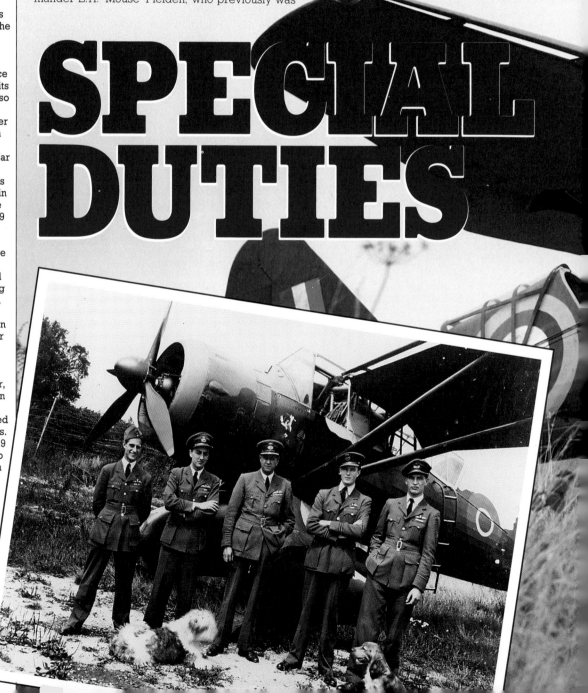

Below: The redoubtable Lysander, with its near-revolutionary short take-off and landing (STOL) capabilities, was the king-pin of British pick-up operations. Bottom left: Standing before Squadron Leader Hugh Verity's Lysander, with its distinctive 'Jiminy Cricket' insignia, are Flight Lieutenant Jimmy McCairns, Verity, Group Captain P.C. Pickard, DSO, and Flight Lieutenants Peter Vaughan-Fowler and Frank Rymills. Bottom centre: Frank Rymills in the cockpit. Right: Wing Commander Pickard, commanding officer of No. 161 Squadron before his promotion to group captain, and his successor, Wing Commander Lewis Hodges (bottom right).

Lysander's normal passenger load was only two. Although visibility was poor, which made visual navigation difficult, Murphy eventually reached the landing zone. 'Landing completed without trouble and the four passengers embarked very rapidly,' he later reported. One of these passengers was Squadron Leader J. 'Whippy' Nesbitt-Dufort, a Lysander Special Duty pilot of No. 138 Squadron who had been forced by heavy ice to crash-land in France during a pick-up operation on 28 January. After a month in hiding with the resistance, he was relieved to be rescued and breezily reported of his homeward flight: 'The skill of the pilot and the navigator proved in this case to be exceptional, as we were only lost the majority of the way home.'

In March 1942, No. 161 Squadron moved from Newmarket (where it had operated from the famous race course) to Graveley in Huntingdonshire, before settling at Tempsford, Bedfordshire, in April. This airfield, which it shared with No. 138 Squadron, then became the centre of RAF Special Duty operations. 'It was not much of a station,' thought Squadron Leader Hugh Verity. 'It was a rush job quickly built in wartime, like hundreds of others. Officers' mess, station headquarters, squadron offices and all the rest were temporary huts.' A farmhouse on the site, Gibraltar Farm, was used by the SOE to prepare agents for parachute drops and to store supply containers, while the Lysander missions were generally flown from the forward base at RAF Tangmere in Sussex, where No. 161 Squadron used a cottage opposite the main gates as their crew room.

The Lysanders used for pick-up operations were

THE 'LIZZIE'

The Westland Lysander, known by the RAF as the 'Lizzie' and the 'Flying Carrot', was designed for operations to support the British Army and it entered

stripped of all armament and carried a 150-gallon auxiliary fuel tank beneath the fuselage in order to increase endurance to eight hours. A ladder was fitted to provide easy access to the rear cockpit, which usually accommodated two persons but could take three or even four adults cramped together. Since the pilot had to navigate himself over enemy territory, usually relying solely on map-reading, it was essential that operations took place within the full-moon periods. Wing Commander Lewis Hodges, commanding officer of No. 161 Squadron during 1943/44, who was destined to retire from the

RAF as Air Chief Marshal Sir Lewis Hodges, recalled:

'Our lives were governed by the phases of the moon. We needed moonlight to map-read by; we needed moonlight to find our way to the dropping zones for parachuting and to the small fields that served as landing grounds; and we needed moonlight to be able to see the ground clearly enough to make a safe landing.'

The resistance 'reception committees' were warned by a cryptic radio message over the BBC's French service that a pick-up or parachute drop was scheduled for them that night. The pre-selected landing fields had to have an approach unobstructed by tall

RAF service in 1938. With the outbreak of World War II it was soon in action supporting the British Expeditionary Force in France, dropping supplies to the beleaguered troops around Dunkirk and carrying out reconnaissance and ground-attack missions. When the SOE began to look for a reliable light aircraft which could land and rapidly take off from short, rough-and-ready strips in the open countryside, the Lysander was an obvious choice. Not only did it have one of the best STOL performances of the war, but surplus stocks were immediately available. Its wings were fitted with slats and flaps which allowed slow flying speeds and very high take-off angles, and the high-wing design afforded the pilot an excellent view of the ground. Another feature of the Lysander which made it particularly suitable for clandestine landings was its immensely strong fixed undercarriage.

The first Lysanders used for pick-up operations were painted black overall. However, this camouflage presented a hard silhouette against low cloud to German nightfighters flying above, and the Lysanders' upper surfaces were subsequently repainted in dark green and pale grey.

Below: The pilots and groundcrew of 'A' Flight, No. 161 Squadron, at Tangmere in 1943. When Squadron Leader Hugh Verity (seated at centre below the propeller blade) joined the flight in December 1942 it was operating six Lysanders, with one in reserve, each fitted with a long-range fuel tank and a ladder to speed access to the rear cockpit.

trees or other obstacles, and were expected to provide a firm and level surface of at least 600yds in length. However, in practice many fields fell far short of these requirements, sometimes with serious consequences. The reception committee was responsible for laying out a rudimentary flare path, consisting of three lamps, to mark a landing run into the direction of the wind. Once the Lysander pilot had found the field, an identifying code letter was flashed to him in morse to signal that all was well. The Lysander would come in to land and turn into the wind to be ready for take-off, before disembarking its agents, (invariably known as 'Joes' or 'Janes', according to sex) and picking up those to be carried out. The time on the ground was naturally kept to a minimum, and a smooth pick-up could be accomplished within three minutes.

Parachute dropping operations, which were far more frequent than landings, employed broadly similar procedures. The dropping zone was marked by a pattern of lights, and the reception committee again identified itself to the Special Duty pilot by a code letter. The supply containers, sometimes accompanied by agents, were then dropped from an altitude which was sufficiently high to ensure that the parachutes deployed properly, but not so high that the containers were scattered over a wide area. This kind of operation called for precise flying skills if the loads were to be delivered within the designated dropping zone. By 1944 the job of supply dropping had been made easier by the introduction of the Eureka/Rebecca navigation beacon system, which enabled the aircraft to home onto the dropping zone.

The pilot and reception committee were also able to communicate using the 'S-phone'. In theory, all the Special Duty pilots were proficient in French and at least one member of each reception committee was to have received training in basic flying control techniques, but since, in practice, these requirements were often relaxed, the S-phone was not

always particularly useful.

Despite the operational dangers it faced; 161 Squadron's casualties were not especially heavy, a fact attributable largely to the high standards of navigation and airmanship achieved by its crew. Enemy action was an ever-present threat, with the Special Duty aircraft being vulnerable to German flak and nightfighters when in the air, and to ambush when landing in France. In the event, two Lysanders were lost to German anti-aircraft fire, but the only ambush attempted by the enemy failed to prevent Flight Lieutenant 'Sticky' Murphy from returning to base. Bad weather, especially when it involved poor visibility and ice, was another hazard. On one disastrous night, 16/17 December 1943, two Lysanders were lost and their pilots killed when they crashed in fog while trying to land at the end of a mission. Again, aircraft were frequently damaged or bogged down after landing on unsuitable fields. For example, on 16/17 April 1943, Flight Lieutenant John Bridger's Lysander hit a high-tension cable when attempting to land on a field south of Clermont-Ferrand. The blinding flash temporarily destroyed his night vision, but he kept control of the aircraft and landed to disembark his passengers. One of the mainwheel tyres had burst and Bridger decided to puncture the other with a shot from his revolver in order to make his take-off easier. Fortunately the wheel rims did not dig into the ground and he was able to return safely to base.

The landing strips were sometimes found to be too boggy to take the weight of an aircraft, and on several occasions pilots were forced to abandon their trapped aircraft in France. One of the less serious of these incidents took place on the night of 24/25 February 1943 and involved a twin-engined Lockheed Hudson. Its pilot was Wing Commander P.C. Pickard, who had relieved Fielden as commanding officer of No. 161 Squadron on 1 October 1942, when the latter was promoted to group captain and given command

FORCED-LANDING IN OCCUPIED FRANCE

On 28 January 1942, Squadron Leader J. Nesbitt-Dufort collected two agents in northern France. After seven hours in the air, during which heavy icing had rendered his Lysander unmanageable, he was forced to crash-land near Chateauroux:

'I force-landed in the most likely looking field which unfortunately had a ditch running across the far end, which could not be seen in the dark. This resulted in the aircraft breaking the undercarriage, and turning up on its nose. No-one was hurt, my passengers jumped out, and I tried to extract the axes, which had, however, got firmly wedged in the cockpit. A jack-knife was used to tackle the bottom of the auxiliary petrol tank, which being self-sealing gave some difficulty. Eventually I managed to get petrol flowing, and having exploded the IFF, I fired the two 'sisters' (recognition flares) and one Verey cartridge to set the aircraft on fire. Owing to shortage of petrol I had some difficulty getting the aircraft to burn. After two more cartridges, however, it seemed well alight, and we all ran for it, as we were only about 75yds from a house. I am afraid that when we were about 2km away the fire must have gone out as we could see no glow coming from the direction of where we had left the aircraft.'

Squadron Leader Nesbitt-Dufort was concealed from the Germans for 30 days by the French Resistance; he and three agents were then rescued in an Avro Anson flown by Flight Lieutenant A.M. 'Sticky' Murphy. It was later discovered that the Lysander was totally destroyed by a locomotive at a level crossing while being towed away.

Above and top: Photographs of Squadron Leader Nesbitt-Dufort's Lysander, resting disconsolately on its nose after the crash, were passed to the British. The aircraft's long-range fuel tank is clearly visible below the fuselage.

of RAF Tempsford. Pickard was probably the best-known bomber pilot in the RAF at that time, thanks to his role as the captain of the Wellington 'F-for-Freddie' in the documentary film 'Target for Tonight' – he was subsequently to be killed in action in February 1944 when leading the famous Mosquito raid on Amiens prison. Pickard had carried out the first pick-up sortie flown by a Hudson on the night of 13/14 February and this had gone according to plan. However, on the more eventful mission 11 nights

F/O BRIDGER   SIR ARCHIBALD SINCLAIR   W/cdr PICARD   G/Capt SIR L.G.

Top left: Philip Schneidau was one of the first Allied agents to parachute into occupied France. He was later picked up by a Lysander which was forced to crash-land on the Scottish coast by a fierce southwesterly gale. Top right: On a visit to RAF Tempsford, Sir Archibald Sinclair, Secretary of State for Air (before aircraft on right), speaks with Flight Lieutenant John Bridger.

later, his aircraft had become stuck in a patch of muddy ground and, as one squadron member recalled, 'his crew were armed to the teeth with revolvers, Sten guns and so on, but not so much as a teaspoon to dig themselves out.' Eventually they succeeded in freeing the aircraft – hindered rather than helped by an excited crowd of French villagers – only to see the aircraft become bogged down again. By the time that the Hudson had been freed a second time dawn was approaching, and the aircraft was fortunate to reach England unmolested by German fighters.

The experience of Flight Lieutenant Robin Hooper on 16/17 November 1943 was even more nerve-racking. His outward flight was uneventful and he recalled:

'After two unsuccessful attempts I got down off a very tight low circuit (even for a Lizzie!), dropping in rather fast and rather late through the mist. I soon realised that the ground was very soft indeed ... At first, when I braked the wheels just locked and slid; but very soon it was a question of using quite a lot of throttle to keep moving at all – and it seemed best to keep moving at all costs. Turning was all but impossible since the wheels dug into deep grooves. Finally we managed to turn 90° to port and there stuck. The aircraft was immoveable even with +6 boost, so I told the passengers to get out and got down myself to inspect. We were bogged to spat level; the ground appeared to be wet, soggy water-meadow. The reception committee came running up: I organised them to push and we attempted some more +6 boost without the slightest effect, except perhaps to settle the wheels a little more firmly in their ruts ...

'At this point someone suggested getting some bullocks from the nearest farm; after a certain amount of fuss this was agreed to and a small, well-armed party set off to collect bullocks, spades and some planks or brushwood ... The rest of us continued to dig trenches in front of the wheels with the idea of making a kind of inclined

plane up which they could be pulled. About 20 minutes later an odd procession loomed out of the mist; two very large bullocks trailing clanking chains, the farmer, his wife, his two daughters and the three chaps from the reception committee. The farmer shook me warmly by the hand and asked me when the British were going to land in France, and got to work.'

Despite the efforts of this team, later augmented by a further two bullocks, the Lysander remained firmly stuck. Flight Lieutenant Hooper decided to burn the aircraft and go into hiding with the resistance. He was picked up by Wing Commander Hodges a month later.

The liberation of France greatly reduced the calls on the Special Duty squadrons' services, although drops of supplies and agents continued over other areas under enemy control. No. 161 Squadron's last pick-up operation was flown on 5/6 September 1944, by which time over 200 such missions had been successfully accomplished. The squadron's contribution to the Allied war effort was greater than that figure suggests. In all some 6700 agents had been flown into Occupied Europe, of which not many more than 400 had been carried during pick-up operations. Yet the latter flights had extracted more than 600 persons out of enemy territory – and it was this service which was so uniquely valuable to the Allied resistance and intelligence networks. Moreover, No. 161 Squadron had made a significant contribution to the dropping of supplies to resistance forces, which in all received some 42,800 tons of materials supplied by air.

For the crest of its official badge, No. 161 Squadron adopted the motif of an open fetterlock. Its motto is 'Liberate'. Neither is an overstatement of the vital role played by the squadron in releasing Europe from the yoke of Nazi occupation.

THE AUTHOR Anthony Robinson was formerly on the staff of the RAF Museum, Hendon, and is now a freelance military aviation writer. He has edited the books Aerial Warfare and the Dictionary of Aviation.

NO.11 SQUADRON PAF

At Partition in 1947 the Royal Indian Air Force was divided between India and Pakistan according to religious allegiance, with some 20 per cent of its personnel opting to serve the new Muslim state of Pakistan. This gave the Royal Pakistan Air Force (the Royal prefix was dropped in 1956) a frontline strength of only two fighter squadrons, flying Hawker Tempest Mk IIs, and a transport squadron flying Douglas Dakotas. A third fighter unit was formed in 1949, and in 1951 the PAF received its first jet fighters, Supermarine Attackers. No.11 Squadron had the distinction of being formed to operate the jets, and it remained the only jet unit in the PAF until the United States began to supply Pakistan with F-86F Sabres in 1955.

No.11 Squadron replaced its Attackers with F-86Fs in 1956, and by the beginning of the 1965 war it formed part of the elite No.33 Wing based at Sargodha in West Pakistan. The wing had a strength of 30 Sabres, 22 of which were fitted with the Sidewinder air-to-air missile. These were to prove a major factor in No.11 Squadron's formidable performance against the superior numbers and more modern aircraft of the Indian Air Force.
Above: Pakistan Air Force insignia.

THE SABRES STRIKE

Flying outmoded aircraft, the elite pilots of No. 11 Squadron, Pakistan Air Force, proved their flying skill against Indian Hawker Hunters

Left: Squadron leader Alam (on left) with his wingman. Right: Unlike its principal opponent, the Hawker Hunter, the Sabre could carry GAR-8 Sidewinder missiles. Bottom: An IAF Hunter falls victim to the Browning machine guns of a Sabre flown by No.11 Squadron PAF.

SQUADRON LEADER Mohammed Mahmood Alam of No.11 Squadron, Pakistan Air Force (PAF), first opened his account with the Indian Air Force (IAF) on 6 September 1965, in a dusk attack on the IAF base at Adampur. Flying in a section of three F-86F Sabres, Alam suddenly spotted four IAF Hawker Hunters slightly higher, at 500 feet, and crossing directly in front of him. Alam ordered the PAF pilots to jettison their drop tanks and the Hunter formation released theirs at the same moment. The two formations then turned towards each other. Alam put his sights on the rearmost Hunter and opened fire. After a brief burst of fire his opponent flew into the ground in a great ball of flame. The remaining fighters then engaged in a swirling dogfight at just above treetop level. 'I never fought at such low altitudes again or at such low speeds,' Alam recalled. He succeeded in outmanoeuvring a second Hunter and shot it down,

while another Sabre damaged a third. However, the PAF fighters were by then running short of fuel and Alam ordered his formation to break off combat and return to base. While making his escape at low level, Alam came upon another enemy formation of two IAF Hunters and opened fire on the wingman. He thought that his shots had found their mark, but the Hunter continued flying and Alam was too low on fuel to continue the fight.

This was an impressive start for the PAF in the Indo-Pakistan War of 1965, particularly as their combat strength of about 140 aircraft was dwarfed by the 500-plus jet machines of the IAF. Moreover, the PAF's most numerous fighter type, the North American F-86F Sabre, was an older design than its IAF counterpart, the Hawker Hunter, which was not only much more powerful but also carried a heavier gun armament. It had seemed that the tiny PAF would be hard-pressed even to defend its own airspace and so would have little opportunity to carry out offensive

air operations against India. Yet in the vitally important attributes of pilot training and tactical leadership the PAF had a clear advantage. The IAF was in the process of rapidly expanding its strength at that time and, as a consequence, training standards and operational efficiency had suffered. Therefore, the PAF was able to operate in a far more aggressive and effective manner than its shortage of numbers indicated. The ascendancy established by Pakistan's fighter pilots over those of the IAF was typified by the operational career of No.11 Squadron PAF, and its commanding officer, Squadron Leader Mohammed Mahmood Alam, who emerged as the leading air ace of the conflict with nine victories gained during the course of only three engagements.

The Pakistan Army had begun its offensive across the ceasefire line in the Chhamb sector of Kashmir on 1 September. Early the next morning Squadron Leader Alam led four Sabres, armed with 2.75in rockets, in a ground-attack mission against Indian troops. Alam, then aged 32, was a slightly-built man

THE 1965 INDO-PAKISTAN WAR

The Partition of 1947 signalled the end of the British Empire in India, and the establishment of two independent states, India and Pakistan. They took opposite sides over Kashmir's struggle for independence in 1947-49, and although open war was averted, India lost 6000 men in the conflict. India annexed Kashmir in January 1957 and there followed a long period of tension with Pakistan. Armed clashes in the Rann of Kutch in western India during January 1965 and Pakistan's recruitment of a 'Free Kashmir' guerrilla army finally erupted into open warfare in August 1965.

The ground forces of the two countries appeared to be evenly matched, and their respective offensives (although involving approximately 6000 casualties on each side) were indecisive. The Pakistan Air Force, however, emerged with great credit from its conflict with the Indian Air Force, destroying 22 IAF aircraft in air-to-air combat for the loss of only eight of its own – a remarkable achievement considering that the PAF faced odds of nearly four to one.

During the conflict India and Pakistan came under strong international pressure to end the war, and arms supplies to both sides were cut off by Britain and the US. A ceasefire imposed by the UN Security Council then reduced the conflict to a series of sporadic minor clashes, and the national leaders were persuaded to attend a peace conference at Tashkent in January 1966. Their decision to renounce the use of force finally ended the war.

THE F-86F SABRE

The F-86F Sabre was powered by a General Electric J47 turbojet giving 6000lb of thrust against a clean aircraft weight of 15,000lb. This compared unfavourably with the more modern Hawker Hunters of the Indian Air Force, which weighed 18,000lb (without external stores) but had 10,000lb of thrust from their Rolls-Royce Avon 203 engines. The Sabre was not only a slower aircraft than the Hunter, but it was also outgunned: its six 0.5in machine guns did not have the hitting power of the Hunter's four 30mm cannon. One advantage the F-86F had over its opponent, however, was that it could be fitted with air-to-air missiles, and 22 of the Pakistan Air Force's Sabres were armed with infra-red-guided Sidewinders. Since IAF Hunter pilots could never be certain whether their opponents were carrying AAMs or not, they were often reluctant to use their aircraft's better acceleration to pull away from trouble, since this would present an easy target to a Sidewinder. Squadron Leader Alam, who had flown Hunters himself on training missions with the RAF in Britain, was aware of another advantage which the Sabre enjoyed. In a turn, especially at low speed, the Hunter slowed down more quickly than the Sabre – a fact Alam used to his advantage when he shot down four Hunters in a single manoeuvre on 7 September 1965.

who had no trouble fitting into the cramped cockpit of an F-86F. He was a highly experienced Sabre pilot with over 1400 flying hours on the type, and had achieved the best air-to-air gunnery scores of the PAF during weapons training. Alam's experience was tested to the limits on 4 September, during an armed reconnaissance sortie in the vicinity of the Indian airfield at Jammu. Flying at low level and at a speed of more than 400 knots, his Sabre was hit by groundfire and its cockpit canopy shattered. Despite being temporarily blinded by debris, Alam maintained control and continued with his mission. Spotting Indian artillery positions in the battle area, he carried out two firing passes before his guns jammed through overheating and he was forced to return to base.

The IAF had been slow to react to the PAF's incursions, but on 7 September a counterstroke against the main Pakistani bases was anticipated. Accordingly, at first light Sargodha was covered by an airborne combat air patrol and further fighters, including a section of Sabres led by Squadron Leader Alam, were at readiness at the end of the runway, with the pilots strapped in to the cockpits ready to take off at a moment's notice. The first warning they had of an enemy raid was the sight of six IAF Mystère IVA fighter-bombers pulling up prior to a strafing and rocket attack on the crowded airfield. Fortu-

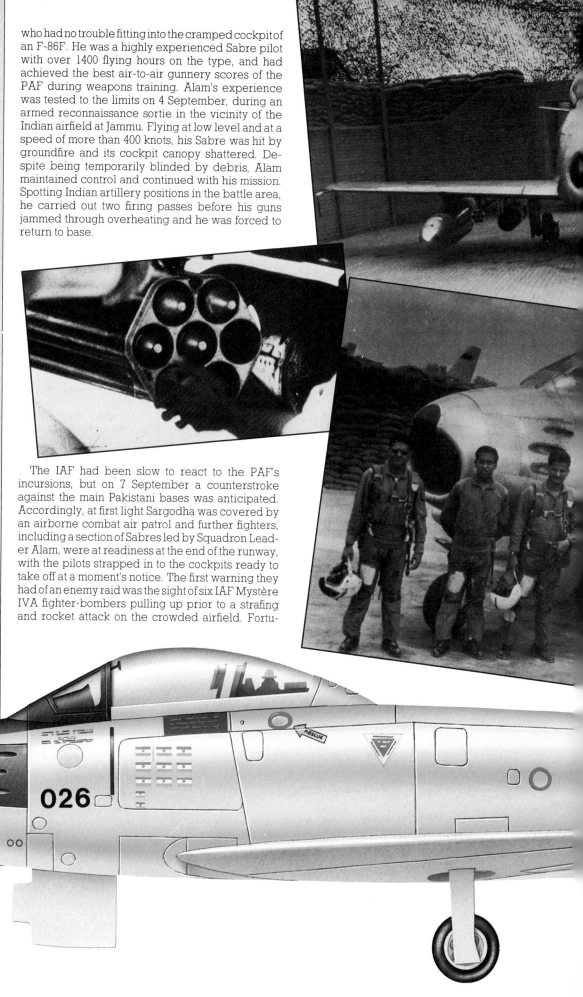

026

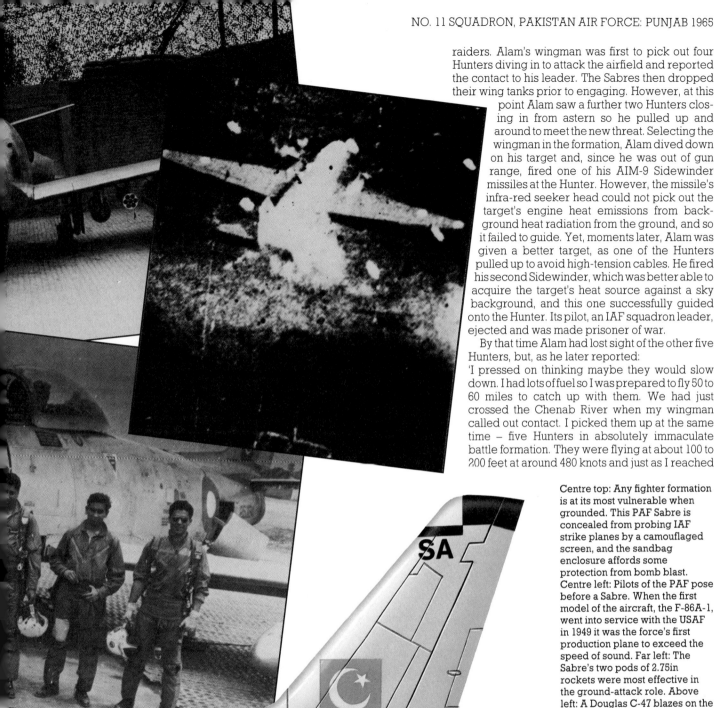

raiders. Alam's wingman was first to pick out four Hunters diving in to attack the airfield and reported the contact to his leader. The Sabres then dropped their wing tanks prior to engaging. However, at this point Alam saw a further two Hunters closing in from astern so he pulled up and around to meet the new threat. Selecting the wingman in the formation, Alam dived down on his target and, since he was out of gun range, fired one of his AIM-9 Sidewinder missiles at the Hunter. However, the missile's infra-red seeker head could not pick out the target's engine heat emissions from background heat radiation from the ground, and so it failed to guide. Yet, moments later, Alam was given a better target, as one of the Hunters pulled up to avoid high-tension cables. He fired his second Sidewinder, which was better able to acquire the target's heat source against a sky background, and this one successfully guided onto the Hunter. Its pilot, an IAF squadron leader, ejected and was made prisoner of war.

By that time Alam had lost sight of the other five Hunters, but, as he later reported:

'I pressed on thinking maybe they would slow down. I had lots of fuel so I was prepared to fly 50 to 60 miles to catch up with them. We had just crossed the Chenab River when my wingman called out contact. I picked them up at the same time – five Hunters in absolutely immaculate battle formation. They were flying at about 100 to 200 feet at around 480 knots and just as I reached

Centre top: Any fighter formation is at its most vulnerable when grounded. This PAF Sabre is concealed from probing IAF strike planes by a camouflaged screen, and the sandbag enclosure affords some protection from bomb blast. Centre left: Pilots of the PAF pose before a Sabre. When the first model of the aircraft, the F-86A-1, went into service with the USAF in 1949 it was the force's first production plane to exceed the speed of sound. Far left: The Sabre's two pods of 2.75in rockets were most effective in the ground-attack role. Above left: A Douglas C-47 blazes on the ground after a successful raid by the PAF on Srinager airfield in Kashmir.

gunfire range they saw me. They all broke in one direction, climbing and turning steeply to the left, which put them in close line astern.

'This, of course, was their big mistake. If you are bounced, which means a close range approach by an enemy fighter within less than about 3000 feet, the drill is to call a break. This is a panic manoeuvre to the limits of the aircraft's performance, splitting the formation, getting you out of the way of an attack and freeing you to position yourself behind your opponent. However, in the absence of one of the IAF sections initiating a break in the other direction to sandwich our attack, they all simply stayed in front of us.

'It all happened very fast. We were all turning very tightly – pulling in excess of 5G, or just about on the limits of the Sabre's very accurate A-4 radar

nately, the Indian pilots' marksmanship was not as good as their navigation and the damage inflicted on Sargodha was slight. Alam and his wingman, Flying Officer Masood Akhtar, were scrambled, together with another pair of Sabres and an F-104A Starfighter of No.9 Squadron, to reinforce the airfield's defences.

Shortly after 0610 hours a second IAF force approached Sargodha and the covering fighters were directed by ground control to intercept the ranging gunsight. I think that before we had completed more than about 270 degrees of the turn, at around 12 degrees per second...four Hunters had been shot down! In each case I got the pipper of my sight around the canopy of the Hunter for virtually a full deflection shot. Almost all our shooting throughout the war was at very high angles off – seldom less than about 30 degrees. Unlike some Korean combat films I had seen, nobody in our war was shot down flying straight and level.'

Alam's remarkable achievement in shooting down five enemy fighters in a single sortie was all the more noteworthy because he was flying the less modern fighter aircraft. Alam was awarded credit for five confirmed victories, although the crashes of only three of them could be found in Pakistani territory.

Alam's last clash with the IAF occurred on 16

Below: Squadron Leader Mohammed Alam, whose expertise claimed nine IAF planes in only three clashes with the rival air power.

Indo-Pakistan war
Sept 1965

From 1949 until 1965 Jammu and Kashmir, although claimed by both India and Pakistan, was divided along the 1949 cease fire line. With the outbreak of hostilities in September 1965, the area was the scene of a hard-fought air war in which the pilots of the Pakistan Air Force, flying F-86F Sabres, gained an unquestionable superiority over the Indian Air Force's Hunters.

Gilgit
Indus
JAMMU AND KASHMIR
1949 cease fire line
Indus
Peshawar
Srinagar
Rawalpindi
JAMMU AND KASHMIR
Jhelum
Chamb
Jammu
Jhelum
Chenab
Sargodha
Bavi
PAKISTAN
Lahore
Amritsar
Adampur
PUNJAB
PUNJAB
Sutlej
Fazilka
Halwara
Bhatinda
I N D I A

AFGHANISTAN
JAMMU AND KASHMIR
CHINA
Indus
Lahore
PAKISTAN
Bahawalpur
Dehli
NEPAL
Karachi
INDIA
RANN OF KUTCH

Key
Disputed areas
Limits of Pakistani claims
Limits of Indian claims
✈ Airfields
○ Radar sites

Bottom: Flying the outclassed Sabre, the PAF pilots succeeded by dint of their superior training.

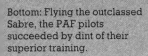

September, when he and his wingman Flying Officer Shaukat penetrated Indian territory to within 10 miles of the airfields at Halwara and Adampur. Two Indian Hunters were scrambled to intercept them and dived into the attack at a speed of about Mach 0.95. The Pakistani pilots turned to meet them head-on, forcing the Hunters to zoom above them. Alam then reversed his turn, putting the Hunters in front of his section. The two Indian fighters broke in different directions, one climbing up to about 20,000 feet and the other diving. Alam followed the first aircraft into his climb and fired three short bursts with his machine guns which turned the Hunter into a ball of flame. Shaukat had followed the other Hunter down, but being inexperienced, had been outmanoeuvred and hit by his opponent and was forced to abandon his damaged Sabre. He parachuted into enemy territory and was made prisoner of war. Alam gave chase to the second Hunter and when nearing its airfield at Halwara, launched two Sidewinders against it. The first failed to guide properly, but the second hit the Hunter in the wing root. Alam was then forced to break off the combat because he was short of fuel, and so did not see the Hunter crash, but he was credited with two victories in this combat.

The PAF claimed a total of 35 IAF aircraft shot down in air combat (plus a further 75 destroyed on the ground or by anti-aircraft fire), for the loss of seven F-86F Sabres and one F-104A Starfighter to the Indian fighters. The enemy's actual casualties have

been impossible to reconcile satisfactorily with these claims, as the IAF only admitted to losing 35 aircraft from all causes including accidents. It is likely that the PAF exaggerated its success in the 1965 War, and a figure of 22 aircraft shot down in air-to-air combat is a reasonable estimate. What cannot be disputed is the degree of mastery that it exerted over its opponents. Squadron Leader Alam flew 36 patrol missions and several ground-attack sorties during the war and only met IAF fighters on the three occasions described. That he could shoot down nine aircraft in only three sorties is a tribute to his courage and professional skills. Alam was promoted to the rank of wing commander after the war and was responsible for overseeing the Mirage III interceptor's introduction into service. His old squadron exchanged its venerable Sabres for Shenyang F-6s (Chinese-built MiG-19s) in 1966, and in 1983 became the first PAF unit to operate the US-supplied F-16 Fighting Falcon.

THE AUTHOR Anthony Robinson was formerly on the staff of the RAF Museum, Hendon and is now a freelance military aviation writer.

ISRAELI AIR FORCE

The Israeli Air Force (IAF) has its roots in various civilian flying clubs that came under the control of the Sherut Avir (Aviation Service) of the Hagana in 1947.

After the Sherut Avir was disbanded and replaced by the IAF during 1948, agents were sent to Britain, Czechoslovakia and North America to purchase a variety of war surplus aircraft.

Although the infant IAF performed adequately in the 1948 War of Independence, senior Israeli officers soon recognised that the air force would have to be forged into a highly trained professional body if it was to outfight the superior forces of its Arab neighbours.

In 1953 Dan Tolkovski took charge of the IAF and immediately set in motion a series of changes that were to form the basis for the modern air force. Realising that only qualitative superiority would offset the Arab numerical superiority, he set about intensive training, to ensure that pilots were capable of flying the most advanced machines then available.

Tolkovski also devised a strategy that would enable the IAF to inflict heavy losses on enemy air forces in the early stages of a war. He believed that the IAF had two basic roles to perform: the destruction of enemy machines on the ground and, after this aim had been achieved, to provide air support for ground forces.

In the wars fought since Tolkovski took charge, the IAF has grown into one of the most sophisticated air forces in the world. In terms of the skill of its pilots and the quality of its machines it is more than a match for its enemies.
(Above: The badge of the Israeli Air Force.)

In the skies over Lebanon, the Israeli Air Force launched a devastating attack against Syrian missile sites in the Beqaa valley

AS THE TANKS and armoured personnel carriers of the Israeli Defence Forces (IDF) rumbled northwards in the first days of Operation Peace for Galilee, the drive to clear the Palestine Liberation Organisation out of Lebanon, senior officers of the Israeli High Command steeled themselves for the inevitable clash with the Syrian forces stationed ahead of them. The Syrians had entered Lebanon in June 1976 in an interventionary peacekeeping role during the Lebanese civil war, and, by June 1982, their presence comprised a number of armoured and mechanised brigades positioned in the strategic Beqaa Valley under a protective umbrella of at least 19 Soviet-supplied surface-to-air missile (SAM) batteries. The choice facing the Israelis was clear – if they were to gain air superiority, the SAMs would have to be destroyed.

Many of the Israeli Air Force (IAF) pilots viewed the prospect of delivering a knock-out blow against the Syrian's air defences with a great deal of trepidation. Indeed, the IAF's experience of Arab anti-aircraft missiles had not been happy. After the loss of 105 aircraft during the Yom Kippur War of 1973 – most of them to ground defences – the service considered SAMs to be much more of a threat than enemy interceptors.

At the time of the invasion the missile threat was twin pronged: the man-portable, heat-seeking SA-7

EAGLES IN THE SKY

Main picture: Two F-4 Phantoms of the Israeli Air Force dive to attack Syrian SAM sites in the Beqaa Valley on 9 June 1982. The lead aircraft carries bombs used to take out enemy radar installations. Below: An F-15 Eagle taxis along a runway before flying a high-cover sortie to protect the main Israeli strike force.

Grail system, deployed by most Syrian units, and the radar-guided SA-2 Guideline, SA-3 Goa and SA-6 Gainful batteries concentrated in the Beqaa. Of the two types of system, the latter group of missiles were the most dangerous to the Israeli airmen. The SA-7s were not considered overly troublesome as IAF pilots were well versed in dropping high-intensity flares to decoy the missiles from their intended target.

By the summer of 1982, the Syrian defences in the Beqaa consisted of two SA-2, two SA-3 and at least 15 SA-6 batteries, along with their associated radars and control centres. The system as a whole had been in existence for a year prior to the Israeli invasion, a factor which had allowed the Israelis ample time to plot their locations.

Since the Yom Kippur War, the IAF had acquired some of the most advanced electronic surveillance

equipment available, and had made great use of this hardware to identify the enemy's SAM installations in advance of Operation Peace for Galilee. Two methods were used: ground stations scanned the atmosphere for the tell-tale electronic 'finger prints' generated by Syrian radars, and RF-4E Phantoms or remotely-piloted vehicles (RPVs) provided detailed photographic coverage.

Based on this and other intelligence, an all-out strike against the Beqaa missile batteries was finalised and then executed on 9 June, immediately before the IDF's first clash with Syrian ground forces. The plan for the anti-missile operation was complex in the extreme, involving every type of aircraft and weapon at the IAF's disposal. Electronic-warfare aircraft, including military versions of the Boeing-707 passenger jet, and ground stations were to open the attack by jamming the Syrian Air Force's (SAF) early-warning and Ground-Controlled Interception (GCI) radars, together with their air-to-ground communications network.

Once the electronic counter-measures were under way, a multi-wave strike force, armed with special Shrike 'anti-radiation' missiles (ARMs) capable of homing in on a transmitting radar set, TV-guided Maverick stand-off weapons and cluster bombs, would hit the SAM sites. In addition, the Israeli Army's Wolf short-range ground-to-ground missiles were to be used. The IAF also took measures to protect their attack aircraft: a fighter force

made up of the latest F-15 'Eagle' and F-16 'Fighting Falcon' interceptors was earmarked to deal with enemy fighters, and E-2C Hawkeye airborne early-warning (AEW) aircraft would be on hand to provide both radar coverage of the valley and control facilities for the operation as a whole.

The first strike wave of 24 F-4E Phantoms was scheduled to open the attack in the early afternoon, and by midday the groundcrews on the airfields at Mahanayim, Haifa, and Ramat were making the final pre-flight checks and adjustments to the aircraft. Preparations for the attack had been made that bit more difficult by the specialist nature of the munitions being used; both the AGM-45 Shrike ARM and the AGM-65 Maverick systems required special 'plumbing' before they could be carried by the F-4s.

Pre-combat tension showed on the faces of the

McDONNELL DOUGLAS F-15A EAGLE

The proposed development of a new US all-weather air superiority fighter was given added impetus when the Soviet Union unveiled their formidable MiG-23 and Mig-25 interceptors in July 1967. McDonnell Douglas won the contract in 1969 and the first F-15A Eagle off the St Louis production line flew on 27 July 1972.

The design of the F-15A had the great advantage of simplicity over its closest rival, the Grumman F-14 Tomcat. Single-seated with a fixed wing, the Eagle introduced a completely new power plant, two 10,800kg-thrust Pratt and Whitney F100-PW-100 afterburning turbofans, which enabled the plane to seize the world take-off and vertical ascent records from the MiG-25 Foxbat. With a maximum speed of mach 2.5 and maximum altitude of 30,000m the Eagle has decisive superiority over the MiG-23 Flogger. Primarily an air-to-air combat aircraft, the F-15A is also designed for surface strikes and is capable of delivering 7258kg of ordnance at supersonic speeds. Its air-to-air weaponry consists of four AIM-9L sidewinders and a 20mm M61A1 cannon. The Eagle is a true fighter-pilot's aircraft. It is highly manoeuvrable, the bubble canopy gives direct all-round vision, and the pilot is provided with a head up display. At the heart of the F-15A's electronics lies an advanced Hughes APG-63 pulsed Doppler radar, capable of tracking targets over a range of 160km.

One Israeli pilot has testified: 'You have to be super-fast when you fly an F-15...it can do anything. No matter how fast your reaction speed is, the F-15's is faster. The things you can do with it are amazing. Your only limitation is your own endurance. Not only is the F-15 a perfect aircraft – it really loves its pilot!'

aircrews attending their final briefings. Apart from the normal adrenalin flow stimulated by the prospect of seeing action, the pilots and their 'back seaters' had to suffer the discomfort of wearing cumbersome 'G-suits' in the heat of the midday sun. The crews were also concerned about firing the AGM-45, a weapon requiring considerable skill in its use which the IAF had not used in anger since 1973. Although the pilots had trained with the missile until its launch characteristics were second nature to them, there was a vast gulf between a training mission and the reality of a combat sortie. However, the crews did receive one piece of good news: the Syrians were using the highly mobile SA-6s in static positions, making them much easier to find and destroy.

As the strike crews made their final preparations, the support elements of the operation began to assemble. At least one of the IAF's four Hawkeyes lumbered into the air and then headed out over the sea to take up its station off the Lebanese coast. As the pilots settled down to flying their designated 'beat', the three-man systems crew crammed into the E-2C's centre fuselage checked and re-checked their sensitive electronic equipment. Each operator sat at a work station dominated by a circular display onto which would flash the information gathered by the

aircraft's powerful APS-125 radar and other receiver systems. The aftermost member of the team, who would act as the airborne controller in the coming battle, paid particular attention to his VHF and UHF radio links along which his warnings and instructions would flash to the waiting 'top cover' fighters.

With all the check lists completed, the operators settled back to wait on events: dim shapes, barely visible in the necessarily subdued cabin lighting. To add to everything else, one of the operators, new to Hawkeye, fought back the motion sickness brought on by the curiously flat turns made by the aircraft in order to keep the antenna in its enormous 'rotodome', turning above the fuselage, correctly aligned. The desire to vomit passes quickly enough after a few flights, but he had not reached this point yet.

From other airfields the electronic warfare Boeing-707s smoked their way skywards shortly after the Hawkeye. Perhaps the most secret machines in the IAF's inventory, the 707s' job was to blot out the Syrian air defence network by transmitting jamming signals at the appropriate moment. Specially converted for this type of task, the aircraft were festooned with antennae and carried large amounts of electronics. Gone were the rows of seats carried in their former civilian days. Now the fuselages were crammed with racks carrying the 'black boxes' necessary for their 'black art', neat operator consoles and literally miles of wiring.

A little after 1300 hours local time, the strike-force crews boarded their F-4s, which then shattered the peace of the Israeli airfields with the ear-splitting

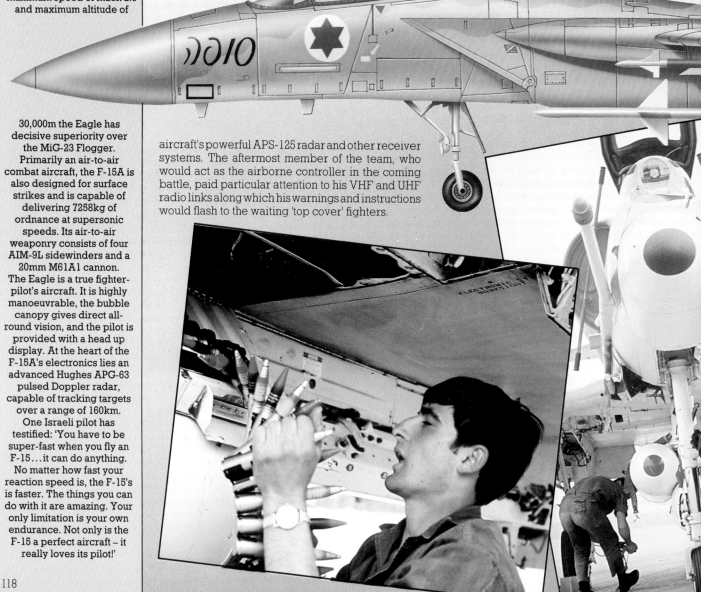

BLOODING THE EAGLE

On 27 June 1979 an F-15 pilot of the IAF claimed the aircraft's first kill worldwide, a MiG-21J of the Syrian Air Force. The pilot (whose name was not released for security reasons) described the action from the moment his strike force received warning of enemy aircraft approaching over Sidon: 'We headed for them at once – we all knew that whoever got in close fastest would down the first MiG. Within seconds, I was on the tail of one of them, in fire position. Locking the IR missile, I fired immediately. The MiG never even had a chance to break away – my missile got it at close range and it exploded in mid-air. I had apparently hit the fuel system. I broke away at once, toward the second MiG – but it wasn't there any more. While I'd been blasting "my" MiG out of the sky, my buddies had taken care of four more!'
Later the squadron opened and drained five bottles of champagne – one for each MiG downed.

Above left: Recorded by the nose camera of an Israeli jet, a Syrian MiG 21 explodes after being hit by an air-to-air missile. Most of the combats were fought at altitudes between 10,000 and 20,000ft and most were over within a few seconds. Left: A profile of an Israeli F-15 interceptor.

Far left: A member of an Israeli Air Force groundcrew arms a jet with cannon shells, while (left) other men give a final check to an A-4 Skyhawk. Flights of A-4s were used to mop up Syrian positions in the Beqaa after the main strike force had dealt with the SAM sites. Above: An F-4 Phantom, armed with either US sidewinder or Shafrir missiles, waits for the order to begin its take-off run.

roar from their 48 powerful jet engines. Shimmering in the heat haze, the shark-like Phantoms waddled from their shelters and lined up for the 'last chance' checks. Groundcrews, their ears protected by padded muffs, swiftly gave each aircraft a visual check, after which they gave the universal 'thumbs up' and then cleared the area. With the engine roar building to a climax as the afterburners were cut in, the F-4s climbed into the sky, leaving the characteristic smoke trails and stench of JP-4 fuel behind them as they headed for the Beqaa.

Once in the air, the Phantoms went 'down on the deck' and split into their attack formations. Maintaining radio silence, they raced northwards with the parched landscape below showing up as little more than a sandy blur to the crews. Flying at high speed at very low levels requires consummate skill and split-second reactions. With the pilots concentrating all their attention on not hitting the ground, the systems operators sitting behing them calmly checked their equipment. At this stage of the mission, their most important job was to monitor the flight and engine instruments. Each man was ready to tell his pilot the moment any indicator was not as it should be, and also had a wary eye on the vulnerable six o'clock position for any signs of hostile aircraft.

The Syrian radar operators and their Soviet advisers had already picked up the first signs of trouble

Ahead of the approaching Phantoms, the Syrian radar operators and their Soviet advisers had already picked up the first signs of trouble. What they did not realise, however, was that the phosphorescent blips registering on their screens were generated not by IAF aircraft, but by Israeli reconnaissance RPVs fitted with radar reflectors to give them the same 'signatures' as full-size machines. Once the Syrian SAMs had swung into action against this 'threat', the RPVs had achieved the desired effect: the air was full of signals for the receivers in the Phantoms' Shrike ARMs to home in on.

As the Syrian radars locked on to the 'spoof' targets, the radar warning sets on board the F-4s came alive with alarm signals. Despite the danger of attack the IAF crews pressed on. At 1400 hours, the Phantoms pulled up into a gut-wrenching climb to bring them to the optimum altitude for launching their weapons. As the aircraft raced upwards the crews' vision began to blur due to the effect of gravity, only to be arrested by the 'bite' of the G-suits as they inflated to control their blood supply. Those aircraft carrying the AGM-45s slammed over on their backs at the top of the climb, releasing their missiles before diving back towards the earth. In the Maverick-carrying aircraft, the systems operators settled down to steer their AGM-65s for the seconds it would take the missiles to cover the 22 miles to their targets.

Moments later, the first Shrike found its target, completely destroying a Syrian unit's big radar antenna, showering the battery's control cabin with debris and concussing the operators inside. Not far away, a Maverick ploughed into a second radar, pulverising both it and its crew in the ensuing explosion. Perhaps even more frightening for those on the ground were the much bigger explosions generated by the Wolf missiles, which now began to arc out of the sky adding to the general slaughter.

Away to the north, in Syria itself, horrified early-warning and GCI crews realised what was happening and set in motion a frantic scramble of SAF

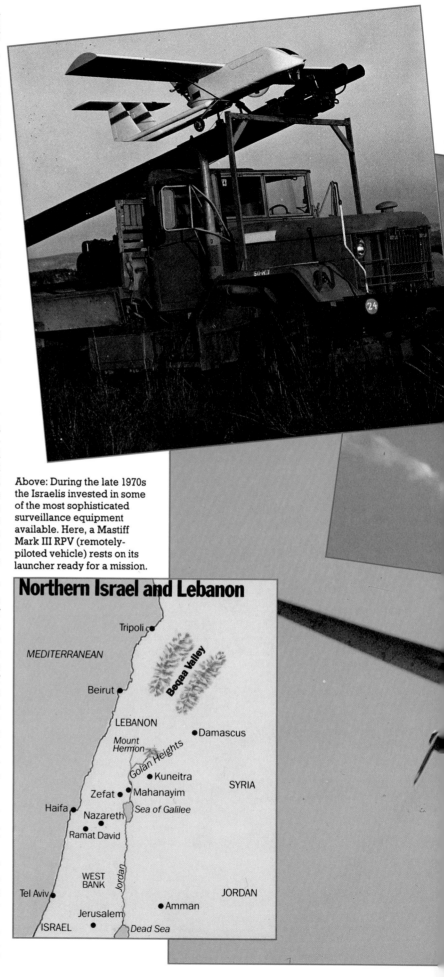

Above: During the late 1970s the Israelis invested in some of the most sophisticated surveillance equipment available. Here, a Mastiff Mark III RPV (remotely-piloted vehicle) rests on its launcher ready for a mission.

Northern Israel and Lebanon

Tripoli

MEDITERRANEAN

Beqaa Valley

Beirut

LEBANON

Damascus

Mount Hermon

Golan Heights

Kuneitra

Zefat

Mahanayim

SYRIA

Haifa

Sea of Galilee

Nazareth

Ramat David

WEST BANK

Jordan

Tel Aviv

JORDAN

Jerusalem

Amman

ISRAEL

Dead Sea

Below: Afterburner aglow, an Israeli F-16 Falcon streaks towards the Beqaa to meet and defeat the cream of the Syrian Air Force. During the combats of 9 June the Israelis destroyed 70 enemy aircraft for no loss. Bottom: An E-2C Hawkeye, packed with electronic surveillance gear, scans the sky for signs of approaching MiGs.

MiG-21s and MiG-23s. As the Soviet-supplied fighters headed into Lebanon, the IAF's Hawkeye controller calmly issued his first 'MiG warning' to the covering force and began vectoring the F-15s and F-16s available to him on an interception course. Aboard the patrolling 707s, flying high above Israel, jammers were turned on full blast. This, combined with ground-based jamming and Skyhawks carrying jamming and chaff dispensing pods under their wings, contrived to fill the SAF's radar screens with 'grass', through which nothing could be clearly seen. The jamming effectively cut the radio links between the enemy's ground controllers and their aircraft,

making it almost impossible for the Syrians to guide their interceptors on to the IAF's strike force.

In the Beqaa itself, the first Israeli attack was over in seconds, the strike force leaving behind columns of oily smoke rising into the afternoon sky as the surrounding mountains echoed to the roar of its departing jets. The Syrians' misery was not over yet; for, as the first Israeli strike wave headed for home, another 40 Phantoms, Kfirs and Skyhawks were heading for the valley. Using Mavericks and cluster bombs, the second wave struck at 1435 hours, creating yet more devastation.

High above the second strike wave, at 15,000ft, the IAF's Falcons and Eagles were fighting a sprawling battle against the cream of the SAF's pilots. Using their radars, the Israeli pilots had identified the enemy at a range of 10 miles. Immediately, the pilots swooped down on their prey. The MiG-21s and MiG-23s tried to break away, but most never had a chance; the Eagles and Falcons had already locked on to them and were preparing to fire their air-to-air missiles. As they dived, the Syrian planes would grow larger and larger in their gunsights until they abruptly disappeared, shrouded in a vivid ball of red and orange flame after being hit by a missile.

Remarkably, the Israelis had not lost a single aeroplane in the opening attacks; it was a situation which was to continue throughout the remainder of the action. The second strike force was followed by a third and then a fourth wave, the latter harassing the Syrians in the valley until darkness fell. Of the 100 or so MiGs despatched to meet the Israeli attacks, only 30 made it back to their home bases, so effective was the 'top cover' provided by the IAF's Eagles and Fighting Falcons.

After the last Israeli aircraft had landed in the gathering twilight, the inevitable debriefings began. It soon became clear to the jubilant crews that the whole operation had been a tremendous success. Not only had the primary target, the Beqaa SAMs, been destroyed, but the IAF had also proved itself immeasurably superior in air-to-air combat against even the latest Soviet-made equipment fielded by the Syrians.

In purely military terms, the air superiority won over the Beqaa Valley on that June day was never lost or even seriously contested. Indeed, it was only three years later, that the Syrians managed to re-build a credible air-defence system in the region, at a time when the Israelis were beginning to pull out of Lebanon. However, the most gratifying aspect of the mission was the simple fact that all the Israelis involved returned home to fight another day.

Sadly, Israel's security consciousness means that the detailed story of this operation or, for that matter, any of the operations the IAF has undertaken since 1948, remains to be told. What is clear however, is that it will be a remarkable one, ranging from the service's humble beginnings with a rag-tag collection of second-hand aircraft garnered from all corners of the globe in 1948, through the achievements of the Six-Day and Yom Kippur Wars, to the Eighties.

The IAF, flying some of the most modern and sophisticated machines available in the Middle East, contains more jet 'aces' than any other air arm in the world, and can call on a wealth of operational experience which is the envy of the world.

THE AUTHOR Martin Streetly is an aviation and electronic warfare historian who has contributed to various military and aviation journals. His publications include *World Electronic Warfare Aircraft.*

'Puff the Magic Dragon', 'Spooky', 'Shadow' and 'Spectre' were a family of gunships that struck terror in the hearts of the enemy in Vietnam

THE VIETNAM WAR prompted the development of a remarkable family of fixed-wing gunships. These planes, all of which evolved from cargo aircraft, performed a variety of missions, including night interdiction of enemy units, support of ground troops in contact with the enemy, the defence of isolated hamlets and outposts, and the destruction of enemy vehicles. The effectiveness of this elite force was based on the relatively simple principle of exploiting a 'pylon turn' in order to aim side-mounted guns at a fixed ground target. Initially, the United States Air Force (USAF) lacked an aircraft capable of performing these tasks. Attempts to use the Martin B-57 Canberra twin-engine bomber for this role failed, largely because of its light armament, and excessive speed and fuel consumption. Although the Douglas A-26 Invader, a veteran of World War II and Korea, flew missions against the Viet Cong along the infamous Ho Chi Minh Trail, structural problems made it inadequate for night interdiction.

Indeed, it was not until Captain Ron Terry, a former fighter pilot, became involved in a study known as Project Tailchaser that using a reliable gunship in Vietnam became a realistic possibility. After drafting a scenario using a side-firing weapon system in defence of a small fort or hamlet, Terry participated in a flight test for an armed C-131 'to determine the feasibility of firing guns with the lateral sighting system'.

At Eglin Air Force Base, Florida, Terry installed on the aircraft a 7.62mm General Electric SUU-11 A/A Gatling gun pod, capable of firing between 3000 and 6000 rounds per minute. Using the airborne pylon-turn manoeuvre, whereby the aircraft flew a left bank, circular pattern around a fixed reference point, the C-131 scored 100 hits on two rubber rafts with a one-second burst. Following additional tests, Captain Terry accompanied members of the newly established Project Gunship I team to Bien Hoa, South Vietnam. Arriving on 2 December 1964, this team was responsible for mounting three gun pods on a C-47 of the 1st Air Commando Squadron.

Terry's ingenuity proved invaluable in transforming this lumbering cargo plane, affectionately known as a 'Gooney Bird', into a formidable weapons system. He installed a gunsight from an A-1E Skyraider fighter-bomber in the plane's left cockpit window, and a trigger button, which fired the three guns individually or simultaneously, on the pilot's control wheel. Terry also modified the C-47's forward cargo hold to accommodate 24,000 rounds of 7.62mm ammunition and 45 200,000-candlepower flares. Other changes involved the installation of VHF and UHF radios, and an FM command radio for communication between the aircraft and ground units. The redesignated AC-47 carried a crew consisting of pilot, co-pilot, navigator, three gun mechanics and a South Vietnamese observer, responsible for estab-

Right centre: The awesome power of the multi-barrelled minigun is unleashed on enemy troops during an AC-47 'Puff the Magic Dragon' mission over South Vietnam.
Right top: A cascade of fire from two AC-47s pulverises Viet Cong positions on the outskirts of Saigon in 1972.
Right: 'Spectre', the gunship version of the C-130 Hercules.

FIREBIRDS

lishing and maintaining communications with South Vietnamese ground troops.

Only 13 days after Terry's arrival in South Vietnam, the AC-47 flew its first combat mission against a variety of targets, including sampans, trails, buildings, and enemy staging areas. On 23/24 December, the gunship undertook its first night mission, successfully attacking Viet Cong outposts at Thanh Yend and Trung Hung in the Mekong Delta area. After witnessing the aircraft's devastating performance in another night mission over the Mekong Delta, a *Stars and Stripes* magazine news correspondent reported that tracers fired from the plane resembled 'dragon's breath'. When this account appeared in the *Stars and Stripes*, the 1st Air Commando Squadron commander christened the gunship 'Puff', after the popular song 'Puff the Magic Dragon' by the folk trio Peter, Paul and Mary. Shortly after, rumours began to circulate that some Viet Cong refused to attack the AC-47 because they believed it was a mythical monster.

Word of Puff's capabilities quickly spread throughout the war zone, and soon almost every ground commander in South Vietnam wanted gunship air cover. To satisfy this growing demand, the USAF refitted four C-47s that had been flying as mail carriers from South Vietnam to the Philippines. The government also contracted a civilian firm, Air International, to begin work reconfiguring 20 C-47s into gunships. In addition, the 4th Air Commando Squadron started an AC-47 training programme, known as operation Big Shoot, at Forbes Air Force Base, Kansas. Finally, in late 1965, the 4th Air Commando Squadron arrived at Tan Son Nhut Air Base, outside Saigon, and began operations with Air Inter-

Below: The old 'Gooney Bird' C-47 transport aircraft found a new and deadly role during the Vietnam War. Mounting three 7.62mm miniguns, their barrels protruding through the door and the two rear windows on the port side of the aircraft, the AC-47 version was able to lay down a devastating carpet of fire. With all three guns blazing at once, the gunship could put a round into every square foot of an area the size of a football field in three seconds!

Gunship deployment

Target spotter

AC-47 gunships were often used in the target-spotting and flare-dropping roles.

An AC-47 gunship flies into position over a North Vietnamese Army position in the Central Highlands of South Vietnam. As a flight of two USAF B-52s begins its final run-in, the gunship prepares for a flare-drop over the North Vietnamese position to illuminate the bombers' target.

Interdiction

AC-47s used the 'lateral sighting' system which was first used in action by US gunships in South Vietnam. By lining up the sights in the pilot's left cockpit window with a fixed reference point on the ground and flying continuously in a steeply banked circle, the pilot could aim the aircraft's side-mounted miniguns and bring a withering cone of fire down on his target.

Here, an AC-47 demonstrates the principle of the lateral sighting system as it concentrates its fire on the rear of a North Vietnamese column carrying troops and supplies southwards.

AC-47

B-52s

North Vietnamese base

Ho C

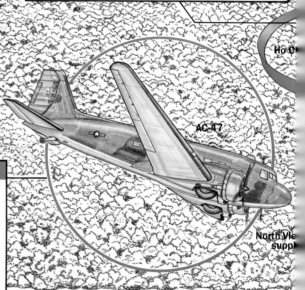

AC-47

North Vie
supp

Gunship attack

AC-47s were used against North Vietnamese troop concentrations and supply lines, pinning down enemy forces and giving fire support to friendly forces on the ground.

Here, an AC-47 gunship prepares to go into action as two McDonnell-Douglas A-1 Skyraiders bank steeply and pull away after dropping their payloads of napalm at the head of an enemy supply column. The AC-47 gunship banks sharply as it nears the trail, ready to line up its lateral sights on the leading trucks before opening fire.

Below: The AC-47 gunship version of the C-47 transport. This particular aircraft served in Vietnam with the 1st Special Operations Wing.

...mber 1964, a small ...under Captain Ron ...n South Vietnam and ...ting a veteran ...' transport aircraft ...p by the addition of ...ods, sights and ...mmunition and ...totype gunship, ...AC-47, flew its ...n mid-December.

AC-47

Douglas A-1 Skyraiders on napalm mission

national-built AC-47s. Eventually, the unit's personnel served at Udorn Royal Thai Air Base, Thailand and at installations throughout South Vietnam, including Nha Trang, Da Nang, Pleiku, Bien Hoa, and Binh Thuy. Within six weeks of commencing operations, the 4th Air Commando Squadron flew 277 combat missions and killed 105 enemy troops, while losing just two aircraft.

On the basis of this performance and numerous other combat successes, gunship operations slowly expanded and diversified. The AC-47 flew flare missions, worked as a target spotter for fighters or B-52 bombers, patrolled the canals and waterways of the Mekong Delta, and, with a loudspeaker mounted in its cargo door, supported various psychological warfare missions. For a short time in early 1966, the AC-47 even flew armed reconnaissance missions along the Ho Chi Minh Trail to stop the infiltration of North Vietnamese troops and supplies into South Vietnam. When an AC-47 went to the aid of a besieged Special Forces camp near Da Nang, a *Newsweek* correspondent on board witnessed the gunship's phenomenal firepower:

'Lieutentant James D. Goodman, the 26-year-old co-pilot, rolled his lumbering, old Gooney Bird over on its left side, peered into the sight of one of the Gatling miniguns mounted on steel pods and pulled the trigger. What resulted was an ear-shattering shriek as thousands of 0.3in calibre shells ripped from the six barrels of the gun and – seconds later – slammed into a group of Viet Cong

2000ft below us. Over the plane's radio came the jubilant message from the Special Forces camp: "Spooky One Two, this is Nathan Scalp. You were right on target . . . It didn't take us long to call you, and it won't again either!"'

Shortly before the Air Force's 53 AC-47s were phased out in early 1969, an incident occurred that earned a place in history for the gunship known as 'Spooky 71' along with one of its crew. On the night of 24 February 1969, the aircraft flew to the aid of besieged troops at Long Binh Army Base, northeast of Saigon. On board was 23-year-old Airman First Class John L. Levitow. During his previous 180 combat missions, Loadmaster Levitow had been responsible for setting the ejection and ignition controls of magnesium flares that provided illumination for ground troops and helped identify targets. After setting the controls, Levitow would pass the 27lb flare to a gunner, who activated the arming mechanism and then tossed it out of the AC-47's cargo door. Approximately 10 seconds later, the magnesium would ignite and generate a blindingly bright light source.

The airman threw himself on the flare, crawled to the open cargo door, and pushed it out

On this particular mission, Spooky 71 had been in the air for four and a half hours before arriving in the Long Binh vicinity. As the gunship manoeuvred into position for a flare drop, an 82mm mortar shell exploded on top of the aircraft's right wing, injuring all five crew members. In the confusion that followed, an armed flare, which had been knocked loose by the blast, started rolling around amidst several thousand rounds of minigun ammunition. Since the flare – which burned at 4000 degrees Fahrenheit – could easily eat through metal, the gunship could explode at any second. Levitow, despite sustaining 40 shrapnel wounds, dragged a wounded crew member away from the open cargo door. He then tried to pick up the smoking flare as it tumbled from one side of the plane to the other. This proved impossible, as Levitow was partially paralysed by his wounds and the gunship was still in a 30-degree bank. The airman

therefore threw himself on the flare, crawled to the open cargo door, and pushed it out just as it ignited. He then lapsed into unconsciousness. When Spooky 71 landed at its home base in Bien Hoa, ground personnel discovered that some 3500 shrapnel holes riddled the aircraft's wings and fuselage. Levitow was immediately flown to a military hospital in Japan. After recovering, he flew 20 more combat missions before returning to the United States. In recognition of his bravery, John Levitow was awarded the Medal of Honor by President Richard Nixon in a White House ceremony on Armed Forces Day, 14 May 1970.

Given the AC-47's unique capabilities and highly successful combat performance, the Air Force believed that a larger gunship with more firepower would make an even greater contribution to the war effort. After numerous tests in the United States, many of which involved the recently promoted Major Ron Terry, the Air Staff decided that the Lockheed C-130 Hercules transport plane could fulfil this role and instructed the Aeronautical Systems Division to begin a C-130 modification programme. Personnel installed four 7.62mm miniguns and four 20mm M-61 Vulcan cannon, the latter capable of firing 2500 rounds of high-explosive incendiary shells per minute. In addition, the modified C-130 gunship carried a night observation device, known as a Starlight scope, to detect troop movements and vehicle and riverboat traffic.

On 21 September 1967, a prototype C-130 gunship arrived at Nha Trang Air Base, South Vietnam, for a two to three month combat evaluation. During operations along the Ho Chi Minh Trail, this aircraft proved so effective that the Air Force immediately awarded a contract to a civilian firm to begin modifications on seven C-130s. Once in service, these planes, known as 'Spectre' gunships, quickly proved their worth in a variety of missions. In addition to normal sorties, the

redesignated AC-130As supported defenders of a fortified post in the southeast corner of Ban Thateng, Laos. Over a four-day period, the gunships fired 16,200 rounds of 20mm and 16,500 rounds of 7.62mm ammunition during their attempts to end the post's siege. During the 1972 North Vietnamese Easter Offensive, the planes destroyed scores of Soviet-built T-54 and T-55 tanks, and Lieutenant-General Tran Van Minh, chief of the South Vietnamese Air Force, also credited the AC-130A with helping to prevent an enemy takeover of the city of An Loc.

Despite these varied actions, the gunship's primary mission remained night interdiction, particularly along the Ho Chi Minh Trail. To enhance the aircraft's capabilities, a new proposal, called Surprise Package, recommended replacing the plane's standard armament with two 20mm Gatling guns and two 40mm Bofors anti-aircraft guns, and incorporating improved infra-red equipment. Other changes included a 105mm cannon as a replacement for one of the 40mm cannon. Thanks to the adoption of these and other modifications, the Spectre gunships compiled an impressive combat record. During the dry season from 10 October 1970 to 30 April 1971, 12 Spectre gunships assigned to the 16th Special Operations Squadron destroyed or damaged 12,741 trucks in night operations over Laos. In spite of these impressive statistics, however, the North Vietnamese still managed to get supplies through to their allies in South Vietnam. According to USAF analysts, the North Vietnamese ability to build or reconstruct roads at night and in bad weather all but neutralised the interdiction effort. Moreover, the interdiction mission lacked an overall strategy and sufficient information on road capacities, the number of available trucks, and travel time to transit points. To a greater or lesser degree, these problems plagued gunship operations for most of the war.

The old C-119 Flying Boxcar was another aircraft

Above: The view from the flight deck of a gunship as it goes in to provide fire support for embattled ground troops. Right centre: US Air Force personnel load a 7.62mm minigun on an AC-47 gunship before taking off on a mission against the Ho Chi Minh Trail. Right below: The minigun in action. Right top: As the role of the gunship in Vietnam expanded, so did the calibre of its armament and the weight of its firepower. This photograph shows the stern of an AC-130 gunship, mounting a 105mm howitzer, a weapon that was to prove deadly against enemy tanks during the North Vietnamese invasion of the South in 1972.

SUU-11B/A MINIGUN POD

The SUU-11B/A minigun pod is an extremely versatile weapon system, compatible for use on both high and low performance aircraft, including helicopters, provided they are equipped with a double-lug (14in) external stores rack.
The pod utilises the GAU-2B/A(M-134) minigun and a MAU-57 A/A linkless ammunition feed system. Both gun and feed system are extremely reliable and have shown an average stoppage rate of once every 35,000 rounds fired.
The pod carries 1500 rounds of 7.62mm ammunition and provides 15 seconds of sustained firepower at the high firing rate of 6000 rounds per minute. On the lower firing rate of 2000 rounds per minute, the pod can maintain a stream of fire for a full 45 seconds. The pod is reloaded without the aid of special ground-support equipment. Ammunition, belted in standard M13 links, is loaded into the pod with a MAU-69 A/A delinker loader which is stowed within the pod structure. The GAU-2 minigun is a rotary weapon with six barrels and is driven by an electric motor, powered by a battery pack located within the pod. Only a trickle of power for control and recharge of the battery is required from the aircraft. The whole system weighs only 325lb fully loaded with ammunition, and is 85in in length with a diameter of 12in.

POST-VIETNAM

Even before the US began withdrawing from Vietnam, the USAF was transferring gunships to the South Vietnamese and Laotian Air Forces. In December 1968 American personnel helped the latter to convert four of its C-47s into gunships by installing 0.5in machine guns. At the same time, the Air Staff despatched a mobile training team to Udorn Royal Thai Air Force Base to instruct Laotian pilots in gunship techniques.

On 2 July 1969, the Vietnamese Air Force's 817th Combat Squadron, popularly known as 'Fire Dragon', took delivery of five AC-47s, followed two years later by the first consignment of AC-119Gs. The USAF also made plans to continue using the Spectre AC-130 gunships in the aftermath of the Vietnam War. Thus, in 1979 an AC-130A flew a three-day mission monitoring fires and gas clouds after a massive train derailment in Florida. The following year, two gunships took part in the ill-fated Iranian rescue mission.

Today, AC-130s are assigned to the 16th Flying Squadron at Hurburt Field, Florida, as part of the 1st Special Operations Wing. They are also flown by the 711th Special Operations Squadron, a reserve unit based at Duke Field, Florida.

The United States Department of Defense intends to keep the AC-130s in service until the 1990s.

that saw duty as a gunship during the Vietnam War. On 17 February 1968, as part of Project Gunship III, the Air Force awarded a contract to Fairchild-Hiller Corporation to convert 26 C-119Gs into AC-119G gunships, and a further 26 into more advanced AC-119K gunships. The former, which became known as 'Shadows', supported ground troops and defended air bases, while the latter, called 'Stingers', were tasked to hunt and eliminate enemy vehicles. These aircraft – the successors to the AC-47 – initially carried four 7.62mm gun pods; however, a later modification changed the armament to custom-made General Electric MXU-470 minigun modules. Other equipment included ceramic armour, an AVQ-8 20KW Xenon light, a Night Observation Sight, a flare launcher, and a fire control system to ensure that the plane did not attack American or South Vietnamese forces.

After a combat evaluation report pointed out that the plane was slow, difficult to manoeuvre, and vulnerable to enemy anti-aircraft fire, the Air Force realised that the AC-119 was ill-suited to its assigned forward air control mission. Moreover, the lack of an all-weather capability hampered the aircraft's operation in fog and haze. The report therefore recommended that the AC-119 should not be used in high-threat environments. In spite of these shortcomings, the plane performed admirably. Between June and December 1969, for example, the 17th Special Operations Squadron flew more than 2000 sorties, fired in excess of 20 million rounds of ammunition, expended 12,000 flares, destroyed 150 sampans, and killed 800 enemy troops.

In addition to normal combat duty, the AC-119s also earned a reputation for versatility. In 1969, a

Below: 'The Super Sow' – an AC-119 Flying Boxcar gunship.

Right top: An AC-130 in action. Right: With many modifications and the addition of a great deal of electronic equipment, the AC-130 is still in service. This aircraft was photographed at Greenham Common in July 1981.

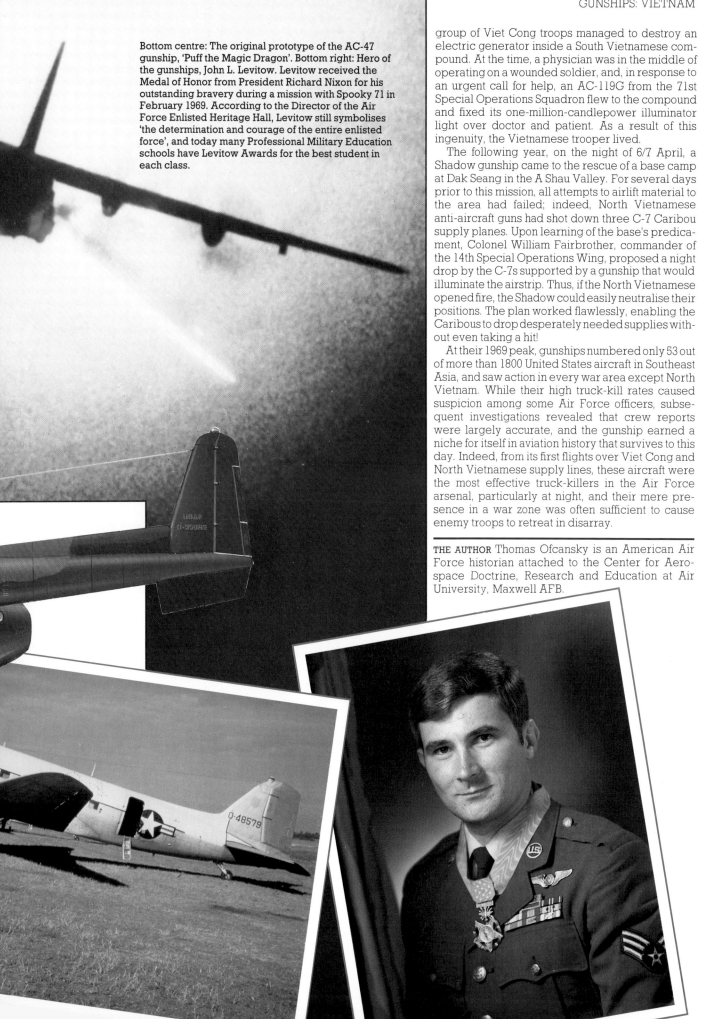

Bottom centre: The original prototype of the AC-47 gunship, 'Puff the Magic Dragon'. Bottom right: Hero of the gunships, John L. Levitow. Levitow received the Medal of Honor from President Richard Nixon for his outstanding bravery during a mission with Spooky 71 in February 1969. According to the Director of the Air Force Enlisted Heritage Hall, Levitow still symbolises 'the determination and courage of the entire enlisted force', and today many Professional Military Education schools have Levitow Awards for the best student in each class.

group of Viet Cong troops managed to destroy an electric generator inside a South Vietnamese compound. At the time, a physician was in the middle of operating on a wounded soldier, and, in response to an urgent call for help, an AC-119G from the 71st Special Operations Squadron flew to the compound and fixed its one-million-candlepower illuminator light over doctor and patient. As a result of this ingenuity, the Vietnamese trooper lived.

The following year, on the night of 6/7 April, a Shadow gunship came to the rescue of a base camp at Dak Seang in the A Shau Valley. For several days prior to this mission, all attempts to airlift material to the area had failed; indeed, North Vietnamese anti-aircraft guns had shot down three C-7 Caribou supply planes. Upon learning of the base's predicament, Colonel William Fairbrother, commander of the 14th Special Operations Wing, proposed a night drop by the C-7s supported by a gunship that would illuminate the airstrip. Thus, if the North Vietnamese opened fire, the Shadow could easily neutralise their positions. The plan worked flawlessly, enabling the Caribous to drop desperately needed supplies without even taking a hit!

At their 1969 peak, gunships numbered only 53 out of more than 1800 United States aircraft in Southeast Asia, and saw action in every war area except North Vietnam. While their high truck-kill rates caused suspicion among some Air Force officers, subsequent investigations revealed that crew reports were largely accurate, and the gunship earned a niche for itself in aviation history that survives to this day. Indeed, from its first flights over Viet Cong and North Vietnamese supply lines, these aircraft were the most effective truck-killers in the Air Force arsenal, particularly at night, and their mere presence in a war zone was often sufficient to cause enemy troops to retreat in disarray.

THE AUTHOR Thomas Ofcansky is an American Air Force historian attached to the Center for Aerospace Doctrine, Research and Education at Air University, Maxwell AFB.

The supply missions flown over the Balkans by No.148 (Special Duties) Squadron provided a vital lifeline to the Yugoslavian partisans

THE ROLE OF the Royal Air Force 'Special Duties' squadrons in World War II was to supply the Allied resistance movements with the guns, ammunition, food and intelligence agents they needed to wage their undercover war against the Axis. The work was very hazardous: drops were made from low level and the light aircraft were very vulnerable to anti-aircraft and machine-gun fire. Of these squadrons, perhaps the best known are Nos. 138 and 161, famous for their dropping of agents by Lysander aircraft into Occupied France. But special units operated in other theatres of the war, and on 4 January 1944 No.148 Squadron, RAF, had the honour of being made a Special Duties squadron. Late in January they moved to Brindisi in Italy and prepared for supply operations to Poland, northern Italy, the Balkans and Greece.

The move to Brindisi placed No.148 Squadron under the control of No.334 Wing. However, the bulk of the Balkan operations were undertaken by the US No. 62 Group operating Dakotas, which were more suitable than the Halifaxes of No.148 Squadron for short trips. To give the squadron a better short-flight capability, a Lysander flight was formed. Named C Flight, it was commanded by Flight Lieutenant Vaughan-Fowler, DFC, a veteran of the Lysander operations mounted by No.161 Squadron from Tempsford in England.

The partisan forces were in need of vehicles, and in April 1944 the squadron attempted to develop a technique for dropping a jeep from a Halifax. The bomb doors were opened and the jeep was suspended in the bomb bay. However, the possibility of damage to the aircraft should a vehicle snag during the drop led to the project being cancelled.

On 7 April, the officer commanding No.334 Wing, Group Captain Rankin, DSO, took part in his first operation as captain of an aircraft. His target was Durazzo in Albania, and in May many more operations were mounted against targets in Yugoslavia and Greece. The range of the Halifax allowed over 10,500lb of stores to be carried, as only a minimum of fuel was required for each trip. However, disaster later struck the squadron when Rankin crashed his Halifax on take-off. The aircraft burnt out, but all the crew escaped safely except the flight engineer, Sergeant Martin, who was badly hurt with a broken leg.

During the night supply drops, the crew member who was arguably most at risk was the despatcher. Operating in total darkness in order to ensure that no light showed from the aircraft when the bomb bay was open, he was obliged to attach himself to the plane via a static line and a rope tied to his parachute harness. A green light would go on and the parachuted loads would be forced out as rapidly as possible. A good despatcher, assisted by the wireless operator, could drop half a ton of supplies in three seconds.

The run-up to the dropping point was controlled by the bomb-aimer. The Halifax would begin the run over the target with the bomb doors open, the flaps partly down and the engine throttled back. With the bomb-aimer calling out instructions, the pilot would finally call on the despatcher to release the containers in the bomb bay. Dropping height was set at between 500 and 800ft, for below 500ft the parachutes would have insufficient time to open, and above 800ft dropping accuracy would deteriorate.

Arms for Yugoslavian partisans are packed into containers (right), later to be loaded into a Halifax's bomb bay (below). After a low-level run over smoke marking the drop zone (centre right), the pilot prepares to open the bomb doors (bottom right).

SUPPLYING THE PARTISANS

The rear gunner would act as observer, reporting whether the containers had overshot or undershot the landing zone. In the development of dropping techniques the squadron owed much to Flying Officer Guest, whose experience had been gained on 82 missions, a total of 615 hours on operations.

At the end of May 1944 the area of top priority became Yugoslavia. The squadron was informed that the Germans had mounted a major offensive aimed at eliminating Marshal Tito's headquarters near the coast, and there was bitter fighting in its defence. A maximum effort was required of the Special Duties squadron to keep the partisans supplied with arms, ammunition and especially food, since the Germans had been destroying crops and livestock to starve them out. On 28 May, Tito called for urgent drops to assist the partisans' blocking of the German advance. Of the 13 aircraft sent, 11

NO. 148 SQUADRON

Formed at Andover in Hampshire on 10 February 1918 and equipped with the F.E.2b bomber, No. 148 Squadron, RAF, moved to France in April for night operations against German airfields and railheads. After a short but successful combat period, during which four DFCs and one DFM were won by the squadron, No. 148 returned to England on 17 February 1919. The squadron was disbanded on 30 June.

It was not until 7 June 1937 that No. 148 Squadron was re-formed, this time as a long-range medium bomber unit equipped with the Wellesley, an aircraft newly designed by Barnes Wallis. These were eventually replaced by Heyfords, Wellingtons and Ansons. Following another disbandment in April 1940, the squadron was reactivated at Malta in December, where Sergeant Raymond Lewin was awarded the George Cross for rescuing a man from a crashed and burning aircraft. Moving to North Africa, it played an important role in support of the Eighth Army, and from December 1940 until December 1942, when it was again temporarily disbanded, it lost 106 aircraft missing or destroyed and 206 men killed or missing. Among the 79 decorations won during the squadron's 2862 sorties were 29 DFCs and 38 DFMs.

In March 1943 the squadron was re-formed and equipped with Liberators and Halifaxes for supply drops in the Balkans; at the same time being renamed. No. 148 (Special Duties) Squadron. From January 1944, the unit operated from Italy on bombing and partisan supply missions in Poland, Greece and the Balkans until the end of the war.

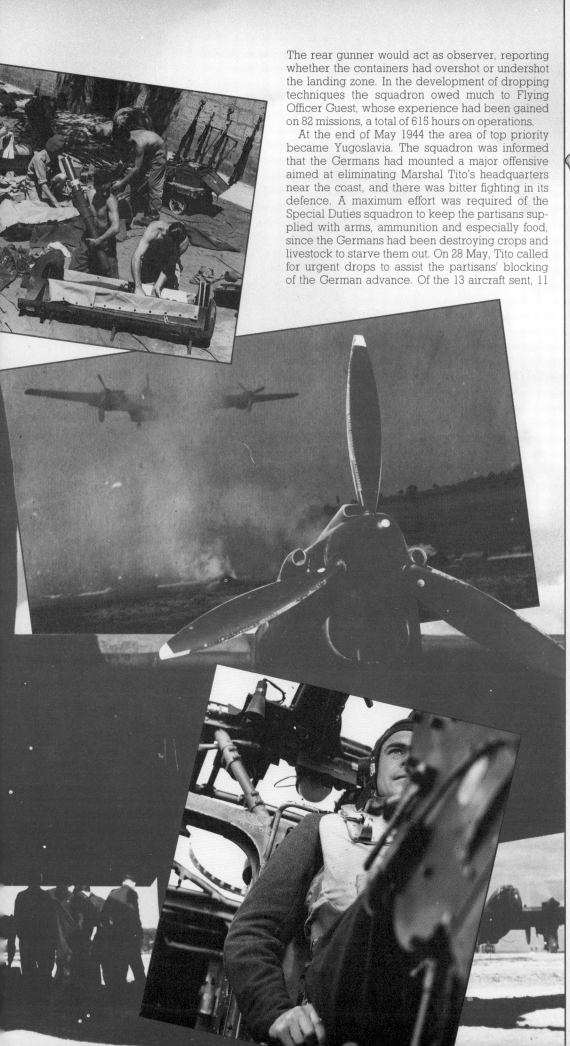

successfully dropped supplies, although the Germans later overran the target area.

Eleven more aircraft then delivered supplies to a point 15 miles away. The first six aircraft were successful, but as the seventh, flown by Pilot Officer

Leleu in Halifax JP 239, started to drop its load, Leleu saw several aircraft overhead with their navigation lights on. Below, parachutes were showering around the target accompanied by coloured parachute flares. Everything suggested that a paratroop landing was taking place, and so he called off the drop and shouted, 'Let's get the hell out of here.' The four aircraft following behind saw only scattered fires on the drop zone and, receiving no flashing signals from the ground, they brought their loads back to base.

Despite this partial failure, 11 aircraft were despatched two days later on 30 May, one of them

piloted by the undaunted Leleu. Nine completed their drops, and on 31 May members of the squadron were told at a briefing that they would be able to make squadron history that very night. Up to that point in the war, the squadron's record of sorties

Right: Flight Sergeants Stewart and Short push canvas bags of supplies through the fuselage hatch. Background and below right: The deploying parachutes were a welcome sight for anxiously waiting partisans. Daytime flying conditions in this area of the Balkans were often hazardous, with frequent thunderstorms and serious turbulence caused by the meeting of warm air currents rising off the sea and cold air from the mountains. The success of the daylight operations flown by No.148 Squadron was a tribute to the skill of its pilots.

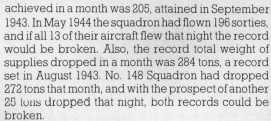

achieved in a month was 205, attained in September 1943. In May 1944 the squadron had flown 196 sorties, and if all 13 of their aircraft flew that night the record would be broken. Also, the record total weight of supplies dropped in a month was 284 tons, a record set in August 1943. No. 148 Squadron had dropped 272 tons that month, and with the prospect of another 25 tons dropped that night, both records could be broken.

This the squadron duly achieved, and a message was sent by Air Marshal Slessor, Deputy Acting Commander-in-Chief of the Mediterranean Allied Air Forces. Congratulating them on their excellent record for supply missions, it ended: 'Well done all, keep it up!' On 1 June the Balkan Air Force was formed, specifically for the task of supplying Tito's partisans. It was learnt on 12 June that the drops of 28/29 May had been crucial to the continued success of the partisans in the face of the relentless German siege. The partisans had been living solely on the supplies of food dropped, and their commander, Major-General Rodic, had sent a message saying simply: 'Thanks to all of you for your great effort.'

The squadron was, at this time, experiencing difficulty caused by aircraft tyres splitting on the rough runways at Brindisi. No.334 Wing heard that

The Handley Page Halifax Mk II Series 1A (above) had the aerodynamically-efficient moulded perspex nose and large rectangular fins for improved stability that subsequently became standard on all Halifaxes. It was powered by four Merlin XXII 1390hp engines that increased its cruising speed by 20mph to 217mph. The code letters FS show that the aircraft was flying Special Duties operations.

there was a supply of tyres to be found at Bari, and with great enterprise the men managed to purloin 14 tyres and have them fitted to their own aircraft. The owners of the tyres, No.204 Group, were very unhappy about the hijack and wanted them back. The only reply they received from No.334 Wing and No.148 Squadron was, 'the show must go on!'

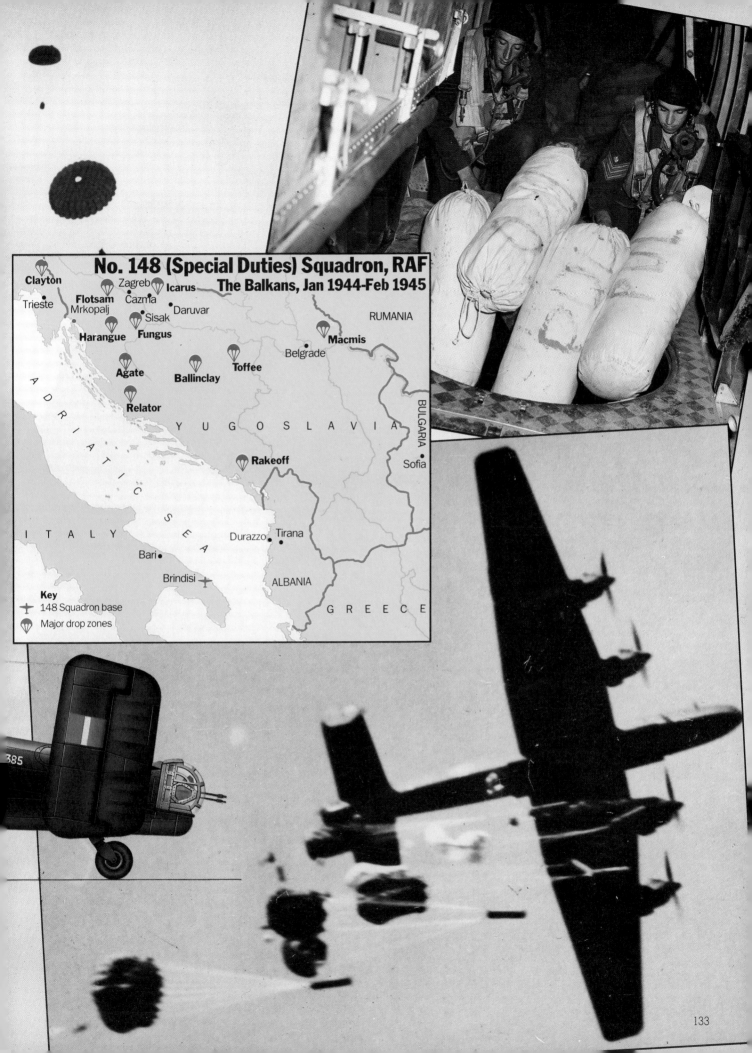

No. 148 (Special Duties) Squadron, RAF
The Balkans, Jan 1944–Feb 1945

Clayton
Trieste
Zagreb
Flotsam
Mrkopalj
Cazma
Icarus
Sisak
Daruvar
RUMANIA
Harangue
Fungus
Macmis
Belgrade
Agate
Toffee
Ballinclay
Relator
Y U G O S L A V I A
BULGARIA
Sofia
A D R I A T I C
Rakeoff
S E A
I T A L Y
Durazzo
Tirana
Bari
Brindisi
ALBANIA
G R E E C E

Key
✈ 148 Squadron base
☂ Major drop zones

385

On 1 August 1944, as the Red Army entered the Warsaw suburb of Praga, the Polish Home Army, led by General Bor-Komorovski, rose up and secured large areas of the city from the occupying German forces. Contrary to the expectations of the Poles, the Soviets made no effort to cross the Vistula River and support the uprising, and soon the Home Army was bearing the brunt of a ferocious campaign by SS units to retake Warsaw. Without Soviet help, ammunition and other needs were rapidly in short supply. To make matters worse, the Soviets refused to allow Allied aircraft to land on their territory in the course of supply missions and long round trips were necessary from distant bases.

On 4 August, seven of No.148 Squadron's aircraft set out from Brindisi to make the long and hazardous flight. One returned early, one crash-landed, one was successful and four failed to return. Warsaw was defended by heavy flak emplacements, and the dropping heights, often as low as 100ft, had made the drops extremely perilous. Back at Brindisi, only one officer pilot remained to command two flights. Another aircraft was lost on 15 August, the pilot later being reported a prisoner of war.

During August, No.148 made seven trips to Warsaw. In all, 100 tons of weapons and three million rounds of ammunition were dropped, but due to fire in the city less than half of the supplies reached the Polish Home Army. Of the 24 aircraft lost at Warsaw, five of them, with their 35 crew members, were from No.148 Squadron.

On 2 October, the Polish Home Army surrendered. Warsaw was in ruins, and when the Red Army finally took the city in January 1945, 85 per cent of the city had been destroyed and half its prewar population of 1.3 million were dead.

In October 1944 it was decided to begin daylight operations using the Sugar- or S-phone, a radio device with which an aircraft could communicate with an agent or operator on the ground. Supply missions were to be led by a special force operator in the leading S-phone aircraft, who would make contact with the ground and convey instructions to the other aircraft. All the squadron's wireless operators were given S-phone training, and the first successful mission of this type was completed on 18 November.

The squadron's operations over the Balkans were not without their adventures. On 16 October, Sergeant Edwards crashed his Halifax 100ft below the summit of a 4000ft Yugoslavian mountain. One survivor of the crash was Sergeant Bromage, who climbed down to a partisan village and picked up a rescue party. Together, they helped two more members of the crew down the mountain and eventually they all reached safety. Bromage was able to board a plane to Bari, arriving there on 8 November.

In another incident, Flight Sergeant Uttley went missing on 5 November during a mission to Yugoslavia. On the 8th he returned to the squadron. His engine had caught fire, so he had jettisoned the main load and set course for the Yugoslavian coast. Ditching successfully, the crew had paddled in a dinghy to the line of the shore. Spotting a Liberator aircraft, they had fired Very cartridges and put out florescine colouring on the water. The Liberator had seen them and stayed until an Air Sea Rescue launch arrived to pick them up.

The S-phone really came into its own in December.

Sergeant Bromley was found shot through by bullets, having been fired upon as he parachuted down

On the 26th, six contacts were made at Mrkopalj and Grabnovica in Yugoslavia, and all the drops that followed were successful. Flight Sergeant Brown, flying as S-phone and wireless operator with Pilot Officer Robinson in Halifax JP 278, reported that the efficiency of the drop was greatly increased by the detailed instructions given by the ground operator. On the 27th, three contacts were made at Grabnovica and, despite solid cloud cover, the drops were 100 per cent successful due to S-phone contact.

On 4 January 1945, Pilot Officer Walker was part of a force of seven aircraft detailed to drop supplies and one agent into Yugoslavia. The aircraft were all successful and, having seen their agent stand up and wave to the crew, Walker went on to carry out a second drop over Sisak in northern Yugoslavia. However, on the way Walker's aircraft was hit on three occasions by flak and caught fire. Ordered to bail out, the wireless operator, Flight Sergeant Rowe, was captured, and the bomb-aimer, Sergeant Bromley, was found shot through by bullets, having been fired upon as he parachuted down. Two more of Walker's crew, Sergeants Breen and Towner, were found by partisans and escorted through German lines to Cazma, a journey of about 11 hours. The next day they proceeded to Grabnovica, where they stayed until 18 January, when a Dakota flew in under an escort of P-51 Mustangs and took them to Bari.

On 17 January 1945, No.148 Squadron was requested to fly supplies to a prisoner-of-war camp containing 1000 prisoners at Lazarina in Greece. Nine Halifaxes were sent with medical supplies, blankets and clothing, only to find dense cloud from 700 to 10,000ft. One aircraft approaching the coast was thrown tail first down from 800ft to 100ft. Forced

to return by the weather conditions, the aircraft flew again on the 18th, and this time four Halifaxes succeeded in dropping supplies from 500ft between breaks in the cloud. A second drop was completed on the 19th, but on the same day a mission over Yugoslavia by 10 Halifaxes ran into accurate light flak and one aircraft was badly damaged, the flight engineer receiving a head wound.

Later in January, messages of thanks were received by the squadron for their supply work. On the 21st the Air Officer Commanding Greece thanked them for the drops on Lazarina, and a letter was also received from one of the prisoners, Sergeant Kelly, who told them that if his fellow prisoners met the aircrews they would buy them all the pints of beer they wanted. The squadron replied by saying that if it had been possible they would have included a few barrels in the drops, wishing them good luck and conveying the hope that they would soon be free.

On the 24th, a signal was received concerning the flak received on 19 January. It had been 'friendly' Soviet fire, and the message read:

'Due to this being a new drop area, all had been warned not to fire on four-engined aircraft. On arrival of the first plane, one or two scattered groups opened fire on the plane and the parachutes, thinking they were enemy parachutists. General Matetic, the Russian commander, is very perturbed and requests he be personally informed of the progress of the wounded airman. The excellent dropping caused a tremendous sensation and impressed the Russians.'

On 3 February, the Lysander Flight was asked to pick up a wounded airman: the task was given to Warrant Officer Dalzell. When he arrived over the landing zone he found it covered by snow but he landed safely, only to get bogged down in the mud. Having unloaded some 500lb of supplies, the partisans dug the aircraft out and he finally took off for Biferno in northern Italy. Following a drop of further supplies a message was received from the combat area:

'Heavy enemy attack yesterday from the north on Daruvan but successfully beaten off. This entirely due to your prompt action in answering our call from here for mortar bombs. Enemy using 100mm howitzers and artillery.'

On the 22nd a female agent had to be dropped into Yugoslavia. This posed a slight problem as pretty girls were in short supply, so an honest married captain was asked to do the job. The records do not tell us who this lucky man was. On 23 February a message arrived, informing the squadron that she had landed safely and naming her as Section Officer Sturnock of the Women's Auxiliary Air Force. Once again, No.148 Squadron had demonstrated that in no way was it to be outclassed by its famous cousins, No.138 and 161 Squadrons, in the performance of Special Duties.

THE AUTHOR Alan Cooper is an aviation historian who has written four books, one of them concerning the legendary bombing raid on the Ruhr dams by the Lancasters of No.617 Squadron, RAF.

Above left: A No.148 Squadron aircrew prepare to load supplies into their Halifax. After the drop (background), a group of partisans examine the much-needed arms and ammunition (top left) that will enable them to continue their resistance to the occupying Germans. Top: High over the outskirts of Warsaw, parachutes stream from arms canisters dropped by No.148 Squadron to the beleaguered Polish Home Army during the Warsaw Uprising.

COMBAT

READY

WING COMMANDER JOHN FEESEY

John Feesey (above) joined the RAF in September 1961 as an officer cadet, and after flying training, became a Qualified Flying Instructor.

In 1966 he was posted to No.1 Squadron, at that time flying Hunters from RAF West Raynham. Three years later, he moved to RAF Wittering for conversion to the Harrier.

After two tours with No.1, and promotion to flight lieutenant, he was posted in 1971 to No.233 OCU as an instructor on the Harrier. A move to RAF Germany came in 1974 and, as a squadron leader, he became Wing Standards Officer at RAF Wildenrath.

From 1978 to 1979, Feesey studied at the RAF Staff College, Bracknell, and was then posted to a desk job at the Ministry of Defence (Army Department) with responsibility for army-air liaison and the staffing of ground liaison officer and forward air controller positions.

His next posting was as an exchange officer with the USAF.

He attended the Air University's Air War College and, after promotion to wing commander, served at HQ Tactical Air Command at Langley AFB, Virginia. As Chief of Training, he was responsible for all the USAF's fighter conversion training units and during this time got the opportunity to fly the F-15 Eagle and A-10A Thunderbolt II.

In 1983 Wing Commander Feesey was appointed commanding officer of No.1 Squadron.

Looking back over his flying career with the RAF, he thinks that the RAF today is certainly a more professional service, but that flying is every bit as much fun as always.

A combat-tested ground-attack fighter, the Harrier GR 3 gives No.1(F) Squadron a remarkable 'dispersed-site' capability

THE ROYAL AIR Force's No. 1 (Fighter) Squadron has as its motto 'In Omnibus Princeps' – Foremost in Everything – which is not inappropriate for the first front-line unit anywhere in the world to operate a V/STOL (vertical/short take-off and landing) aeroplane. Moreover, the squadron's BAe Harrier GR Mk 3s were certainly to the fore during the Falklands Conflict of 1982, when they flew 126 sorties in support of British ground forces. Yet these achievements are already part of history. Only two of the pilots currently serving with the squadron saw action in the Falklands, although the lessons of that war have been thoroughly absorbed and have led to significant changes in the unit's equipment, tactics and training. Today, as No.1 Squadron prepares for a war role that could take it to virtually any part of the world in support of NATO or British commitments, it confidently looks to the future and its planned re-equipment with the new Harrier GR Mk 5.

No.1 Squadron is stationed at RAF Wittering in Cambridgeshire, an airfield which it shares with No.233 OCU, the Harrier Operational Conversion Unit. It operates a total of 10 aircraft, comprising nine Harrier GR Mk 3s and a single Harrier T Mk 4 two-seat trainer. There are 18 pilots on strength, organised into two flights, 'A' Flight and 'B' Flight. It is not unusual for many of the squadron's pilots and aircraft, together with their groundcrew, to be away from Wittering on various deployments at any time. The station provides No.1 Squadron with a peacetime base, but it will not be its war station.

The nature of No.1 Squadron's operational commitments requires that it be ready to deploy overseas at short notice. The squadron is assigned to NATO, and may be despatched to reinforce the alliance's air forces in West Germany, Denmark or Norway. Peacetime training deployments to northern Norway in winter provide the squadron with essential experience of Arctic operating conditions. Here, the climate is the great enemy. Aircraft are in danger of being overtaken by snowstorms when airborne, and pilots have to cope with the problems of operating from snow-covered terrain. The long hours of winter darkness impose severe restrictions, since the Harrier is not equipped for night opera-

Page 137. Above: Three Harriers from No. 1 Squadron fly over Stanley airfield during the Falklands conflict, while (below), back at RAF Wittering, four pilots of No. 1 pose beside a GR Mk 3. Left to right: Captain Dave Wallace, Flight Lieutenant Steve Fox, Squadron Leader Tony Harper and Flight Lieutenant Mark Bowman.

After taxiing into take-off position (below), Wing Commander John Feesey angles the nozzles of his GR Mk 3 down 50 degrees to obtain maximum thrust (centre left), before lifting the Harrier into the air (centre and centre right). Bottom: Back at base. One of the Harrier's drop-tanks is clearly visible under the starboard wing.

tions, although it is able to deploy in darkness. However, it is only during the month of December that it is dark for the full 24 hours of the day in northern Norway, and in other months there is always some light to fly by. Permafrost can provide a good, hard operating surface for the aircraft, but come the thaw, the Harriers must use hard standings to avoid becoming bogged down in the slush. Summer in these northern latitudes, with its long hours of daylight, also poses problems, since the squadron may be required to sustain flying operations around the clock with manpower levels intended for the much shorter daylight periods of the UK.

For the tactical reconnaissance role, the Harrier carries a nose-mounted F95 camera

Outside the NATO area, UK contingency operations could take the squadron virtually anywhere. During the 1970s, it was twice required to deploy to Belize in Central America. A residual commitment to this area continues, for although the resident Harrier unit there, No. 1417 Flight, has its own commander and aircraft, its pilots and groundcrew are supplied by No. 1 Squadron and the RAF Germany Harrier squad-

rons on detachment. The Falklands deployment in 1982 provided a further contrast in environment and operating conditions.

The Harrier's primary role is to provide offensive support for ground forces, which includes close air support, battlefield air interdiction and tactical reconnaissance missions. Its ground-attack weapons comprise BL 755 cluster bombs, 1000lb bombs, 68mm SNEB rockets and two 30mm Aden cannon. The Aden gun is a well-liked weapon and, although its rate of fire cannot compare to that of Gatling-type weapons such as the M61 cannon, its heavy shell is very effective. In addition, since using them in the Falklands conflict, the squadron has also trained with Paveway laser-guided bombs.

For the tactical reconnaissance role, the Harrier carries a nose-mounted F95 camera, angled downwards at 18 degrees. No sight is fitted and so aiming it is very much a matter of individual pilot skill. In addition, a five-camera pod may be fitted to the aircraft's centreline station and this gives virtually horizon-to-horizon coverage. No. 1 Squadron is required to train with this pod as part of its NATO commitment, but more usually relies on the nose-mounted camera.

For self-defence, the Harriers are fitted with chaff

Generally, groundcrews welcome the change from routine RAF life which overseas deployment provides. Living conditions, however, can be very uncomfortable, and even in the best conditions the Harrier is not an easy aircraft to service. Engine changes, for example, require that the wing be removed for access, and the job takes up to eight hours to complete.

In addition to the squadron's servicing requirements, specialist support in the field is needed for the tactical reconnaissance role. This is provided by RAF Wittering's Reconnaissance Intelligence Centre (RIC). The RIC's three portable cabins and generator can be air lifted by a single Hercules transport and the unit is self-sufficient. Once a Harrier has landed from a reconnaissance mission, the RIC has to move fast to produce a report from its films within 45 minutes of engine shutdown.

Film is processed at the rate of 120ft per minute and generally reaches the photo interpreters within 10 minutes. They usually work from negative film strips, although if contact prints are required, these can be produced extremely quickly.

The Harrier pilot also contributes to the final intelligence report and it is the RIC's experience that pilots are able to acquire an astonishing amount of information through visual reconnaissance. This information can be radioed back to base during the mission, so that if the reconnaissance aircraft is shot down on its return flight, not all the intelligence will be lost.

dispensers, and may also carry AIM-9L Sidewinder infra-red homing air-to-air missiles (AAMs). But the Sidewinders can only be carried at the expense of most of the aircraft's ground-attack weapons. This handicap is not insurmountable, however, as one Harrier in a four-ship formation may carry AAMs, while the other three are armed with bombs.

The skills of accurate weapons delivery and tactical flying are only acquired after a great deal of training and are constantly practised by all pilots on the squadron. A pilot joining No. 1 Squadron straight from training will begin with a work-up period of six months, flying under supervision, at the end of which he is considered combat ready. The experience of Flight Lieutenant Mark Bowman is fairly typical. He joined the RAF with a University Cadetship, and flew with the University of London Air Squadron while reading for his degree. In 1982 he began his basic flying training on Jet Provosts at the RAF College, Cranwell. There followed fast-jet training on Hawks at No. 4 Flying Training School at RAF Valley, and then a six-month course of basic combat tactics and weapons delivery with No. 2 Tactical Weapons Unit's No. 151 Squadron at Chivenor. In February 1985, Bowman began his training on the Harrier with No. 233 OCU. The course is arranged in two parts: on the OCU's 'B' Squadron, the student learns how to fly the Harrier under the tuition of Qualified Flying Instructors. He then moves to 'A' Squadron, where he is taught to fly the aircraft

tactically, covering much of the Tactical Weapons Unit course again, but on a front-line aircraft. After this training, Flight Lieutenant Bowman was then posted to No. 1 Squadron where he received further instruction during his individual work-up period. The work-up training involves advanced tactics, work on the weapons ranges, medium and low-level air combat, and such skills as inflight refuelling, which is not taught on the OCU, and the carriage and release of real weapons, which are much heavier than the practice bombs and so have an appreciable effect on the aircraft's handling. Bowman felt that his training at this stage was directed towards doing a job and not simply concerned with the 'canned solutions' of the training syllabus. There was also a tremendous feeling of having 'made it', and a great sense of camaraderie with the squadron.

But not all pilots come fresh to Harrier operations on joining No. 1 Squadron. There is a considerable amount of cross-posting between the Harrier squadrons, and pilots tend to stay within the Harrier community. In mid-1986, seven No. 1 Squadron pilots, including the commanding officer and flight commanders, had already served with the two Harrier squadrons in RAF Germany. For such experienced pilots, the individual work-up period is really only a formality, consisting of only two or three sorties. Yet for one experienced pilot, who had recently joined No. 1, there was much that was unfamiliar to be absorbed. Captain Dave Wallace of the United States Air Force (USAF) came to the squadron on an exchange posting with the RAF. His previous flying was on Phantoms, both the F-4E

Operating on a NATO mobile exercise (below left), the Harrier's camouflage paint allows it to blend into Norway's snow-capped terrain. Below left: The squadron's T Mk 4 two-seat trainer undergoes routine maintenance. Used for training, photo-reconnaissance and flying visiting VIPs, the 'T-Bird' retains full combat capability. Because of the position of the Harrier's exhaust nozzles, overhauling the aircraft can be a lengthy procedure for the groundcrew. Centre: Back in the hangar, a GR Mk 3 is given a 12,000-mile service. Below: Outside one of the hangars at RAF Wittering, 'The Home of the Harrier', three Harriers are prepared for take-off.

fighter and RF-4C tactical reconnaissance versions, and he encountered many differences between the large, twin-engine, two-seat American fighter and the small, single-engine Harrier. Yet he found the Harrier to be a very capable aircraft. The RAF's ultra-low-level operations were also entirely new to Captain Wallace, as the USAF usually flies at medium level. Exchange pilots are generally thrown in at the deep end, with little allowance made for their inexperience of RAF operational methods.

Once a pilot is combat ready, he can work towards higher standards, and after about a year on the squadron he is ready to lead a four or six-aircraft formation. There are various annual training exercises for the squadron as a whole, including a deployment to Sardinia for live-weapons training. Since the Falklands conflict, the squadron has trained aboard a Royal Navy aircraft carrier for two weeks of every year. Squadron Leader Ian Mortimer, the squadron's 'Exec' or second in command, was a former exchange officer with the Fleet Air Arm who fought with No.801 Naval Air Squadron on Sea Harriers in the South Atlantic, and thought this an excellent idea. Not only did it give the RAF pilots experience of operating from a pitching deck rather than

terra firma, but it also gave them a taste of the different environment and procedures of the Fleet Air Arm.

In order to practise 'dispersed-site' operations, No.1 Squadron deploys to RAF Hullavington, an active RAF station although its airfield is now disused. More regularly, the squadron's aircraft fly dissimilar-air-combat training sorties against the RAF's Phantom and Lightning air-defence squadrons. The Lightning pilots are considered to be especially tough opponents. RAF surface-to-air missile sites also provide simulated opposition.

A typical training sortie might take in two simulated attacks on targets off the range, using realistic tactics but with no bombs dropped. The aircraft would then make a timed attack with practice bombs on a weapons range target. If, however, the aircraft misses its allotted time slot, it will not be allowed on the range. Achieving an accurate time on target is an essential skill, especially if more than one pair of aircraft are carrying out a co-ordinated attack, and on NATO exercises aircraft from several different air forces may well be attacking the same target. The problem of accurate timing is complicated by the air-defence forces, which will position two interceptors on combat air patrol somewhere along the Harriers' route, ready to pounce. The evasion tactics needed to counter these attacks are liable to throw out the pilots' timing calculations and, if a formation

has been broken up, it will take time to re-assemble.

Even without the added harassment of interception, navigation at low level is difficult. The Harrier's inertial navigation system and moving map display are good pieces of equipment, but are comparatively old – a three-mile slippage during a sortie is a typical error. However, this equipment is not always serviceable and then navigation must be by map and stopwatch – a difficult skill in a fast, low-flying aircraft, which requires a lot of practice to master.

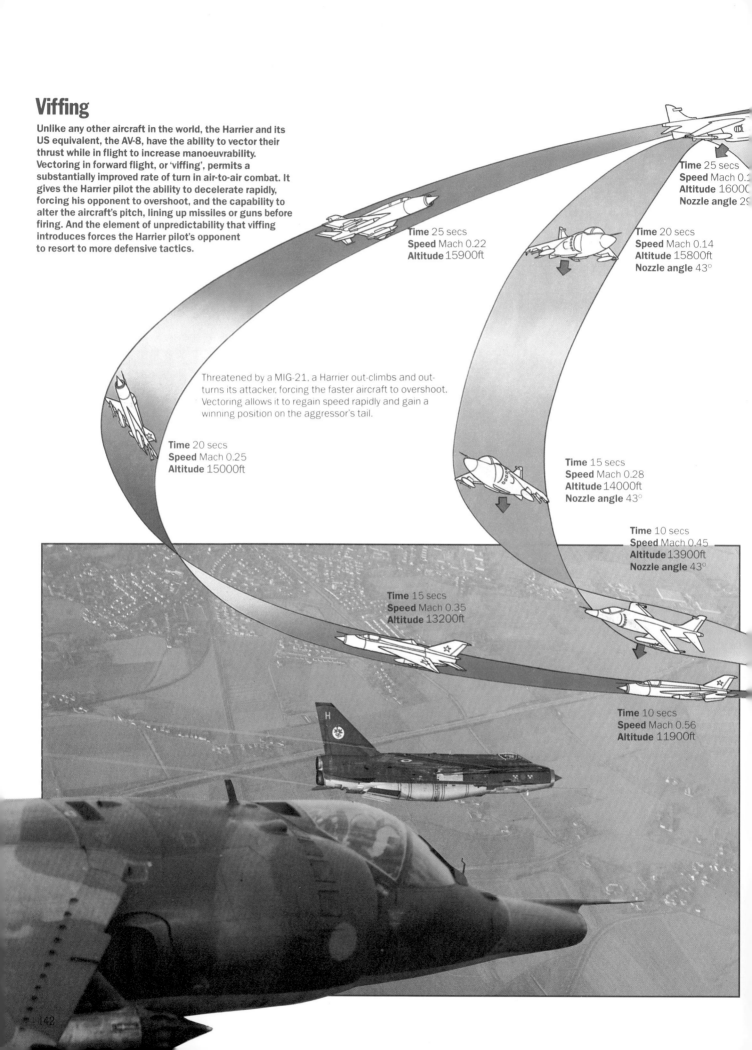

Viffing

Unlike any other aircraft in the world, the Harrier and its US equivalent, the AV-8, have the ability to vector their thrust while in flight to increase manoeuvrability. Vectoring in forward flight, or 'viffing', permits a substantially improved rate of turn in air-to-air combat. It gives the Harrier pilot the ability to decelerate rapidly, forcing his opponent to overshoot, and the capability to alter the aircraft's pitch, lining up missiles or guns before firing. And the element of unpredictability that viffing introduces forces the Harrier pilot's opponent to resort to more defensive tactics.

Time 25 secs
Speed Mach 0.22
Altitude 15900ft

Time 25 secs
Speed Mach 0.1
Altitude 16000
Nozzle angle 29

Time 20 secs
Speed Mach 0.14
Altitude 15800ft
Nozzle angle 43°

Threatened by a MIG-21, a Harrier out-climbs and out-turns its attacker, forcing the faster aircraft to overshoot. Vectoring allows it to regain speed rapidly and gain a winning position on the aggressor's tail.

Time 20 secs
Speed Mach 0.25
Altitude 15000ft

Time 15 secs
Speed Mach 0.28
Altitude 14000ft
Nozzle angle 43°

Time 10 secs
Speed Mach 0.45
Altitude 13900ft
Nozzle angle 43°

Time 15 secs
Speed Mach 0.35
Altitude 13200ft

Time 10 secs
Speed Mach 0.56
Altitude 11900ft

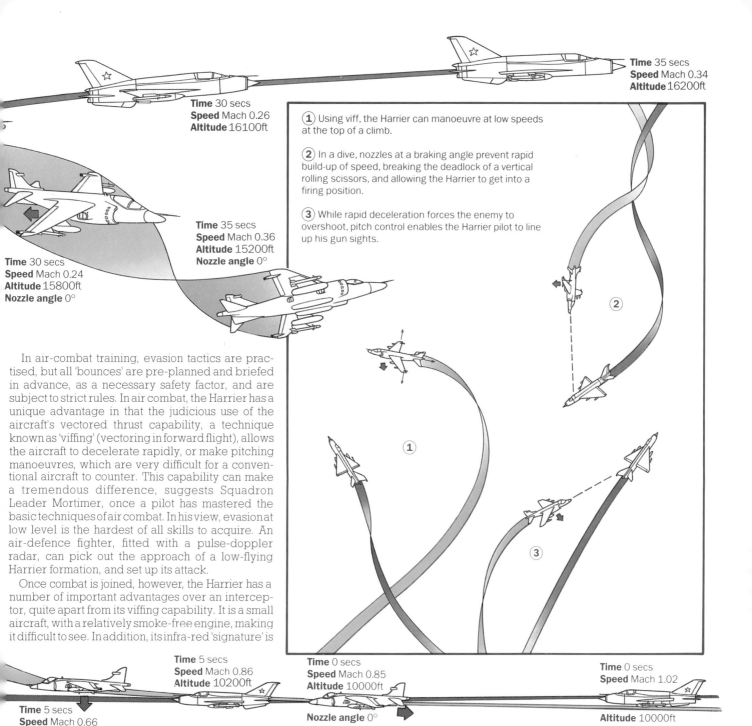

Time 30 secs
Speed Mach 0.26
Altitude 16100ft

Time 35 secs
Speed Mach 0.34
Altitude 16200ft

Time 30 secs
Speed Mach 0.24
Altitude 15800ft
Nozzle angle 0°

Time 35 secs
Speed Mach 0.36
Altitude 15200ft
Nozzle angle 0°

① Using viff, the Harrier can manoeuvre at low speeds at the top of a climb.

② In a dive, nozzles at a braking angle prevent rapid build-up of speed, breaking the deadlock of a vertical rolling scissors, and allowing the Harrier to get into a firing position.

③ While rapid deceleration forces the enemy to overshoot, pitch control enables the Harrier pilot to line up his gun sights.

Time 5 secs
Speed Mach 0.86
Altitude 10200ft

Time 5 secs
Speed Mach 0.66
Altitude 11000ft
Nozzle angle 43°

Time 0 secs
Speed Mach 0.85
Altitude 10000ft
Nozzle angle 0°

Time 0 secs
Speed Mach 1.02
Altitude 10000ft

In air-combat training, evasion tactics are practised, but all 'bounces' are pre-planned and briefed in advance, as a necessary safety factor, and are subject to strict rules. In air combat, the Harrier has a unique advantage in that the judicious use of the aircraft's vectored thrust capability, a technique known as 'viffing' (vectoring in forward flight), allows the aircraft to decelerate rapidly, or make pitching manoeuvres, which are very difficult for a conventional aircraft to counter. This capability can make a tremendous difference, suggests Squadron Leader Mortimer, once a pilot has mastered the basic techniques of air combat. In his view, evasion at low level is the hardest of all skills to acquire. An air-defence fighter, fitted with a pulse-doppler radar, can pick out the approach of a low-flying Harrier formation, and set up its attack.

Once combat is joined, however, the Harrier has a number of important advantages over an interceptor, quite apart from its viffing capability. It is a small aircraft, with a relatively smoke-free engine, making it difficult to see. In addition, its infra-red 'signature' is small, and can be further reduced by rolling the aircraft's underside exhaust nozzles away from the direction of the threat, thus making it difficult for an opponent to lock-on an infra-red guided missile.

In Squadron Leader Mortimer's view, the Falklands certainly did the Harrier force some favours. For example, ultra-low-level flying at 150ft, with the aircraft cleared down to 100ft, can now be practised. Such flying is essential in wartime, yet it simply cannot be done without adequate training, and even today it is only possible on special exercises. In addition, the new weapons and electronic counter-measures equipment introduced during the Falklands conflict provide the Harriers with far more tactical options. Arming the Harriers with Sidewinders made a tremendous difference, as interceptors are now far more wary of them. The Harrier pilot can be confident of a 'kill' if he can get his nose onto an adversary. The less tangible lessons of the Falk-

Left: An RAF Lightning flies over rural Germany. Combat exercises are an invaluable feature of No.1 Squadron's training, with the Harrier (inset left) required to carry out ground-attack missions under threat of being 'bounced' by the Lightnings and Phantoms of the air-defence squadrons. Pitted against such experienced and rugged opposition, the pilots of No.1 must use every ounce of their skill to prove their effectiveness in a combat scenario.

lands, however, are more difficult to absorb. In conflict, psychology is a very important factor, and Squadron Leader Mortimer feels that RAF tactics tended to ignore this. Combat experience makes a very big difference to the way a pilot performs, and the fears and tensions of war cannot be simulated during training.

At least once every 18 months, a stringent test of the entire squadron's fighting abilities is conducted by a team of NATO officers. Known as 'taceval' (tactical evaluation), this assessment is carried out in two phases, the first of which is sprung on the squadron with no advance warning. High standards must be achieved to satisfy the critical examiners and the result is an uncompromising pass or fail. The evaluation team arrives unannounced and requires the squadron to go onto a war footing immediately. A high rate of aircraft sorties must be generated, with the airfield under threat of air attack, and also there

Left (top to bottom): A Harrier unloads a Hunting cluster bomb unit. Each container ejects 147 bombs, which fall to the ground in a predetermined scatter pattern, hitting the target with a blanket of explosive firepower capable of penetrating heavy armour. Below: A devastating display from a Harrier GR Mk 3 as it unleashes a salvo of SNEB unguided rockets. In the event of war, the Harriers would be deployed on 'dispersed-site' operations from camouflage-netting hides (bottom), close behind NATO front-line troops. A maintenance team would be attached to each hide, enabling servicing to be accomplished in the field.

may be a threat of NBC (nuclear, biological and chemical) contamination, necessitating the wearing of cumbersome and uncomfortable protective clothing by all personnel. For the second phase of the taceval, the battle phase, the squadron will deploy to Vandel in Denmark, where a five-day evaluation is conducted under typical wartime conditions in the field. The phrase 'in the field' has a special meaning for the groundcrews, who remember Vandel chiefly for its mud. The squadron will come under air attack and ground attack, with every member ready to fight as an infantryman to repel intruders. Communications will be jammed to simulate wartime conditions, and any transmissions made by the squadron will be closely monitored for possible security lapses which an enemy could exploit.

Everyone on No. 1 Squadron agrees that with the advent of the Harrier GR Mk 5 they will be in a new world. The aircraft's avionics equipment, described by the squadron's commanding officer, Wing Commander Feesey, as 'Tornado-plus standard', will provide the most dramatic improvement in capability over the present Harrier GR Mk 3. In addition, payload/range will be doubled, manoeuvrability and V/STOL performance improved, and the aircraft will be easier to service. One clear indication of the tremendous range of improvements available from the Harrier GR Mk 5 is that three pilots chose to stress quite different aspects of its capabilities as offering significant advances. For Flight Lieutenant Mark Bowman, who hopes to remain on No. 1 Squadron for a second tour after its re-equipment, the modern avionics will make the biggest difference, taking over a lot of the 'chores' of flying and freeing the pilot for tactical decision-making. Squadron Leader Tony Harper saw the increased night and bad-weather capability, made possible by the GR Mk 5's FLIR (forward-looking infra-red) used in conjunction with night-vision goggles, as a very important extension of the squadron's role. While for Squadron Leader Mortimer, the GR Mk 5's ability to carry AIM-9L Sidewinders as well as a full offensive weapons load will make the big difference. Without doubt, No. 1 Squadron is well prepared to achieve another 'first' in RAF history with the Harrier GR Mk 5.

THE AUTHOR Tony Robinson and the publishers would like to thank the Commanding Officer of No. 1 Squadron, Wing Commander John Feesey, and all the other members of the squadron for their help in the preparation of this article.

The new GR Mk 5 (below), has been specially equipped to meet the needs of the Harrier's close-support role in central Europe. Two additional weapons stations, making a total of nine, allow the carriage of Sidewinder air-to-air missiles for self-defence and interception in addition to the Harrier's ground-attack armament. Bottom: Squadron Leader Ian Mortimer, who flew Sea Harriers during the Falklands conflict.

HARRIER DISPERSED-SITE OPERATIONS

The Harrier's ability to operate from virtually any environment, away from its peacetime bases, is one of the aircraft's unique features. However, extra support equipment and many more personnel must be provided for dispersed operations, as all of the advantages of centralised servicing are lost. Moreover, this method of operation is far more complex than flying from an established base. For example, command, control and communications are a great problem, with many miles of land-line required to link up all the various elements. Secure radios are available as a necessary back-up, but no reliance can be placed on them, since, by simply transmitting, valuable intelligence will be given to the enemy.

Yet despite these costs, the end result of dispersed-site operations is more than worthwhile in terms of survivability and of flexibility. Camouflaged sites will be far more difficult to locate, and therefore to attack, than a conventional airfield and, since the Harrier needs only a minimal take-off run when fully loaded, it cannot be grounded by cratered runways. The aircraft can be deployed where they are needed, irrespective of the availabililty of fixed airfield facilities.

With the Harrier operating from close behind the battle area, requests for air support can be met just as quickly by an aircraft 'ground loitering', with the pilot at cockpit readiness, as by a conventional aircraft already airborne. A pilot can be fully briefed while sitting in his cockpit, or during a quick turn around between sorties, via a telebrief communications link. The use of standard operating procedures reduces the time this takes to a minimum and greatly increases flexibility of operations.

FIRST STRIKE

For the air strikes launched on 5 June, the Israeli Air Force (IAF) put virtually everything it had into the air. So concentrated was the attack that out of some 200 IAF combat aircraft available, only 12 Mirages remained to protect Israeli air space during the operation. Apart from Mirage IIICs, the strike force included Super Mystère B2s, Mystère IVAs, Ouragans and Sud Vauturs. After the initial attack wave that hit 11 key Egyptian airfields, sorties continued to be flown throughout the day of the 5th to attack further Egyptian airbases, including the more remote installations on the Red Sea coast and on the Nile south of Cairo. The Israelis also launched strikes against Arab airfields in Syria and Jordan.

Israeli pilots were also involved in sporadic dog-fighting over all fronts during the war and many Arab MiGs were shot down during these aerial engagements. But the air battle had been decided on the first day of the war and, with total air superiority already established, the IAF was able to provide solid ground support for the land forces fighting it out on the Syrian, Sinai and Jordanian fronts.

The comparative air losses suffered by Israel and its Arab adversaries during the course of the Six-Day War bear testament not only to the skill and tenacity of the pilots of the IAF, but also to the superb planning and preparations made beforehand. In the final reckoning, the IAF accounted for some 350 Arab combat aircraft for the loss of only 31 of its own. Without the advantage gained by the first strike, however, things might have worked out very differently. Below: Israeli pilot's wings.

On 5 June 1967, in a masterly display of low-level flying and precision ground attack, the Israeli Air Force dealt a crippling blow to Egypt

NOT SINCE THE attack in December 1941 on the American fleet at Pearl Harbor, has the element of surprise in modern warfare been so skilfully exploited on such a scale as by the squadrons of the Israeli Air Force (IAF) on the morning of 5 June 1967. In a massive, pre-emptive air strike, 11 Egyptian airfields were attacked and by late morning, half the Egyptian Air Force lay in ruins. Two hundred and four of Egypt's inventory of 419 aircraft were smashed on the ground; among the victims were Russian-built Ilyushin Il-28 and Tupolev Tu-16 bombers, aircraft with an operational range capable of taking them to Tel Aviv and other major Israeli population centres.

In that same first blow of the Six-Day War, IAF aircraft also knocked out the Egyptian combat MiGs stationed at El Arish in northeastern Sinai, effectively neutralising the ground-attack threat to the columns of infantry and armour of the Israeli Defence Forces (IDF) as they stormed into Sinai. By nightfall on the 5th, the number of destroyed Egyptian aircraft had soared to 300, and Israel had secured total air superiority for the coming days of bitter fighting with its Arab neighbours.

But how was this resounding victory achieved? The answer lies in the potent combination of detailed planning, top-notch combat efficiency, and the first-rate hardware of the IAF. For such a bold move to succeed, the operation had to be meticulously planned, and planned well in advance. In the 19 years since independence, Israel had fought two major wars (the 1948 War of Independence and the 1956 Sinai campaign) and, living in a constant state of tension with its Arab neighbours, felt it necessary to be ready at all times to react incisively at the first sign of any outbreak of hostilities.

Bringing the Egyptian Air Force to its knees would be the key to success in the war

In the spring of 1962, the Air Force GOC, General Ezer Weizmann, summoned to his office at Air Force HQ Lieutenant-General Rafael 'Rafi' Sivron, an experienced combat pilot and a very capable operations officer. Sivron was tasked with drawing up a plan of action, to be followed in the event of the outbreak of a full-scale war between Israel and its neighbours. Weizmann's directive was simple, 'This is our strength, and we have to win!'

Sivron initiated an arduous programme of intelligence gathering; he left no stone unturned, digging deep for every available little detail and snippet of information. His primary conclusion, at the culmination of the research, was that the main effort should be highly concentrated, and directed against Egyptian Air Force runways.

Egypt's air force represented the most serious threat to Israeli security, being by far the largest and best equipped of the Arab air forces of the Middle East. Bringing this force to its knees, while it was still on the ground, would be the key factor and an essential precondition for the success of the whole war. Another crucial decision that had to be taken was the time that the attack should be launched.

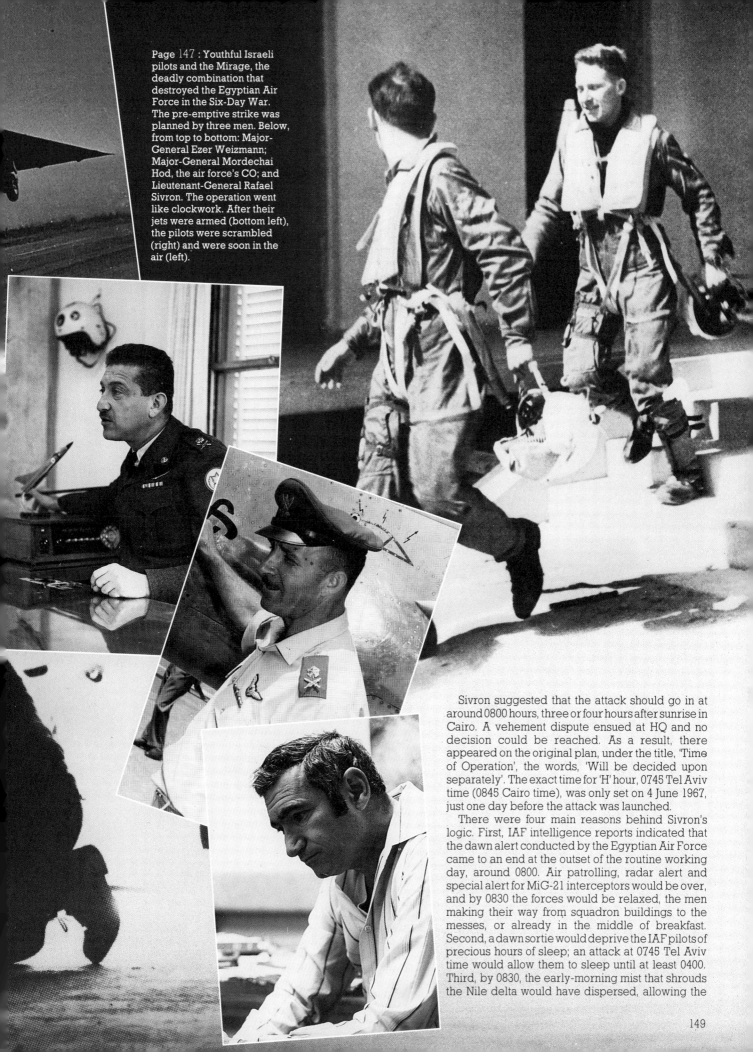

Page 147 : Youthful Israeli pilots and the Mirage, the deadly combination that destroyed the Egyptian Air Force in the Six-Day War. The pre-emptive strike was planned by three men. Below, from top to bottom: Major-General Ezer Weizmann; Major-General Mordechai Hod, the air force's CO; and Lieutenant-General Rafael Sivron. The operation went like clockwork. After their jets were armed (bottom left), the pilots were scrambled (right) and were soon in the air (left).

Sivron suggested that the attack should go in at around 0800 hours, three or four hours after sunrise in Cairo. A vehement dispute ensued at HQ and no decision could be reached. As a result, there appeared on the original plan, under the title, 'Time of Operation', the words, 'Will be decided upon separately'. The exact time for 'H' hour, 0745 Tel Aviv time (0845 Cairo time), was only set on 4 June 1967, just one day before the attack was launched.

There were four main reasons behind Sivron's logic. First, IAF intelligence reports indicated that the dawn alert conducted by the Egyptian Air Force came to an end at the outset of the routine working day, around 0800. Air patrolling, radar alert and special alert for MiG-21 interceptors would be over, and by 0830 the forces would be relaxed, the men making their way from squadron buildings to the messes, or already in the middle of breakfast. Second, a dawn sortie would deprive the IAF pilots of precious hours of sleep; an attack at 0745 Tel Aviv time would allow them to sleep until at least 0400. Third, by 0830, the early-morning mist that shrouds the Nile delta would have dispersed, allowing the

FLAGSHIP OF THE IAF

The Mirage III is a real pilot's aircraft. Lieutenant-Colonel 'G', an Israeli Air Force ace with 17 air victories to his name, had this to say about the French-built Dassault-Breguet Mirage IIIC:

'Since its appearance, and for many years afterwards, there was no combat aircraft so suited to its role as the Mirage IIIC. If you took a pilot, sat him on a chair, and then started to build an aeroplane around him according to his precise wishes – placed the buttons, placed the stick, gave him

performance – and then stepped back to see what you'd created, you'd find that you'd built a Mirage!' Originally, the Mirage was designed as an interceptor to take on strategic bombers, but the Israeli strike on the Egyptian airfields confirmed its value as a ground-attack aircraft. For Operation Focus, the Israeli Mirages mounted 30mm DEFA cannon and carried specially designed runway-destruction bombs. These 500kg bombs were fitted with a rocket and drogue parachutes to retard their speed and stabilise them during descent, and a further rocket to punch them through the concrete surface of the runway on impact. On exploding, they gouged a crater up to two metres in depth. Powered by the SNECMA Atar 9B3 augmented turbojet, the Mirage IIIC is capable of speeds up to 1386mph (Mach 2.1), and when fitted with external fuel tanks has a range of 820 miles.

incoming pilots a clear view of their route and their target airfields. The final reason for delaying 'H' hour was that the Egyptian generals, whose working day began at 0900, would all be in their cars between home and office, and thus unable to direct and co-ordinate any effective response to the attack.

It all looked very good on paper, but would it work? – that was the question. A simulation 'war game' was conducted and minor faults in the plan ironed out. The operation was codenamed Focus, or *Moked* in Hebrew, and was passed around the squadron commanders of the IAF for comments. There were none. The plan was sealed, classified 'Top Secret', and deposited in a safe. It was now the end of 1965.

Simple as the plan was, its execution was another matter. Split-second timing and perfect co-ordination were essential to the attack: the IAF would be flying aircraft of dissimilar cruising speeds from a number of different bases; if the attacks did not all go in at the same time, the element of surprise would be lost and the Egyptians would be able to put up a defence; and the necessity of flying very low throughout the mission, below the umbrella of Egyptian radar, would make navigation very difficult, and demand a considerable level of airmanship. The success of Focus would depend on the pilots.

There follows the story of one of the Israeli Mirage squadrons involved in the initial strike. Its target was the bomber base at Cairo West. For security reasons, the identity of the squadron, the officers and the pilots involved cannot be revealed.

Lieutenant-Colonel 'A', the squadron commander, recalled the preparations made for the attack:

'We actually built a wooden model of the airfield we were supposed to attack. It was a perfect model which included everything – runways, hangars and buildings. We practised the attack over the Negev desert until we'd got it perfect. Each and every pilot knew exactly which hangar was "his", what he'd have to do after the second circling

around, and so on. I could have asked any pilot to come up to the board in the briefing room and he would have been able, by heart, to draw the exact plan of the Egyptian airbase, down to the last detail. We felt that we knew all there was to know about those airfields.'

The squadron briefing on the morning of 5 June 1967 started very, very early. Not knowing for sure, but feeling that 'this was it', the pilots crowded into the briefing room. They were yet to learn the most important factor of the whole mission – the exact hour that the strike would go in. Major 'O' remembered the tense atmosphere of that briefing:

'Colonel "B", the base commander, was short, sharp and clear in his orders. His instructions were strict: all aircraft were to take off in complete radio silence, and maintain silence in flight until "H" hour. Under no circumstances, even in the event of an accident or mechanical failure, was radio silence to be broken. Any plane found not to be in working order on the ground was not to take off.

'The aircraft we were flying that day were heavy: two 500kg bombs, plus two 1000kg fuel bidons – that makes three tonnes. In the fast, low profile of the programmed flight, the Mirages were bound to behave a little roughly.'

Leaving the briefing room, the aircrews gathered at the take-off post. Major 'O' described the hectic

activity as the air force got under way:

'Everybody was absorbed in their tasks, checking and re-checking switches and navigation maps, as each man waited for the appointed time for him to get onto the runway and start his take off.

'Then suddenly, it seemed that the whole Israeli Air Force was going to take off at once. The exhaust pipes on the aircraft must have been raising hell outside with all the noise and the dust, but inside the cockpit it was surprisingly quiet. Only the hands on the instruments moved, while warning lights blinked nervously.'

Below: The Mirage IIIC, backbone of the Israeli Air Force during Operation Focus. Below centre: An ace, credited with 11 kills, prepares for another sortie over Arab airspace. Bottom right: Straining groundcrew manhandle a Mirage into postion for take-off. Bottom left: Mirages during a training exercise.

Another pilot recalls the final few seconds on the ground:

'I sat in the cockpit and prayed that the afterburner would catch. It did. The formations got the green light from the tower. The heavy configuration of our aircraft necessitated the use of the long runway. The nose was heavy and the Mirage refused to raise speed. After what seemed like a very long time, we finally arrived at 250 knots. I turned off the afterburner, gathered to formation, and turned towards the target. Then, and only then, did I begin to believe that this time we were going to go the whole way.'

The 'air armada' first flew westwards, out over the Mediterranean, but, at a pre-determined point, the aircraft turned onto a southerly heading, to cross the Egyptian shore-line from the north, the least expected line of attack. Keeping on course over the sea was extremely difficult, and the pilots had to fly by a

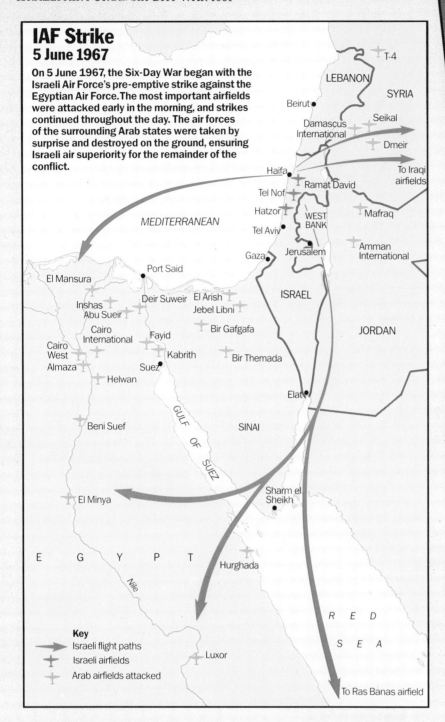

IAF Strike
5 June 1967

On 5 June 1967, the Six-Day War began with the Israeli Air Force's pre-emptive strike against the Egyptian Air Force. The most important airfields were attacked early in the morning, and strikes continued throughout the day. The air forces of the surrounding Arab states were taken by surprise and destroyed on the ground, ensuring Israeli air superiority for the remainder of the conflict.

Key
→ Israeli flight paths
✈ Israeli airfields
✈ Arab airfields attacked

method known as 'direction and time' flying, based on the highly accurate use of compass and chronometer. Major 'O' remembered the flight in:

'We were flying low and fast over the turbulent sea. It was like flying over a blue desert, with nothing to hang onto for indentification. I was very tense, waiting for the moment when we had to turn south. We turned. The route we were on took us in towards the Nile delta. We passed over some fishing boats, but the fishermen didn't even bother to raise their heads.

'Then, ahead of us, I saw the golden strip of sand on the edge of Lake Bardawill in Sinai. This was the spot where we were supposed to cross. The lake was chock-full of fishing boats and fishermen, and I remember that this time they looked up and waved as we flew by. Naturally, they had no idea as to who we were, or where we were going!

'A few seconds later, we could see the Suez

Top right: Their fuselages burnt-out after being hit in an Israeli strafing run, two enemy aircraft litter the taxiway of an airbase deep inside Egypt. Right: One of the Arab's Russian-supplied MiG-21s, its tailplane badly damaged, waits for the Israeli Air Force to deliver the coup de grace. Above right: Seen through the sight of an Israeli jet, bombs hit an enemy outpost. By midnight on the first day of the war, over 300 Egyptian aircraft had been destroyed; Israeli losses were minimal.

Canal. The scenery below changed – now it was green and cultivated, as we approached the Nile delta and Cairo West.'

The squadron commander's formation, which was to be the first to go in, had some difficulty with navigation over the delta but, finally, the target airfield came into view and the Mirages zoomed down.

In a matter of seconds, five of the six bombs dropped, crashed into the runway. All over Egypt, similar attacks were devastating other Egyptian airfields. After the bombs had been dropped, the Mirages moved in to shoot up the aircraft parked on their hard standings. This 'sniping round' set fire to eight Tu-16s, three Il-28s and three MiG-21s.

The second wave of the squadron's attack, the formation led by Major 'O', dived into action over Cairo West, but pillars of smoke, rising from the blazing Egyptian aircraft, made it difficult for the pilots to enter the battle area:

'It seemed like we were flying through a forest of huge black trees, with fire raging below. We arrived at our entry point and I broke radio silence to order, "Full power! Switches!" The formation spread to form a spearhead and we attacked.

'My heavy aircraft rose – 7000ft, 9000ft. I turned over and dived towards the runway with the rest of the formation hard on my heels.

'The light points in my bomb sight glittered like diamonds. I could see some burning Tupolevs, but, out of the corner of my eye, I detected some planes that were still intact. I pressed the bomb-release button and the bombs were on their way.

'We turned back, flying low over the desert, and came in again for a sniping round against the huge

STRIKE ON BENI SUEF

An Egyptian eye-witness at the Beni Suef airfield remembered the devastating effect of the Israeli Air Force attack on 5 June 1967: 'In those first instants of the Israeli assault everything was completely confused. Even before we realised what was happening, the attack was over. Everything was damaged. It was incredible. Despite dummy planes and camouflage, the Israelis seemed to know exactly which targets to hit. In those moments I was in terror of my life and the scream of the jets as they flew in low to attack was more frightening than the explosions of the guns. We were caught in complete surprise and had no chance to defend. The planes which were actually on the runway were completely destroyed, the buildings were burning and for

the first time in my life I saw war casualties.

'It was terrible. Blood was everywhere and people were trying to hold on to limbs that were falling off. I saw one man who was cut in half by machine-gun fire trying to scoop his intestines back into his body. Everywhere people were running around shouting orders but nobody knew what was happening or what to do. The runway had been hit many times with a special bomb. It had a delayed fuze and as soon as we tried to move them they would go off. We lost many men in human sacrifice as we tried to clear the bombs away; sometimes they would just go off when you got near them. We could do nothing. We were destroyed and we could not get operational. But above all, we were completely shocked, astonished by the ferocity and speed with which our unit was annihiliated.'

Tupolevs. I stabilised on a flat dive and fixed a shining Tupolev in my gunsights. I squeezed the trigger and a burst of 30mm cannon shells tore into the aircraft, setting it on fire. A huge plume of black smoke poured from the shattered hulk.

'After a third round, black clouds were rising all over the airfield. Our mission was accomplished.' Surprise had been complete, and its devastating effect was summed up by a young Mirage pilot on his return from the mission:

'We came over Bir Gifgafa, straight and level at 20,000ft. We took a runway each. On our first pass, we lit up two MiG-17s. Coming out of the attack, we circled back and I looked down – soldiers were waiting in line for their breakfasts, mess tins in their hands. They didn't even know that there was a war going on.'

THE AUTHOR Aharon Lapidot is a major in the Israeli Air Force and has been editor of the Israel Air Force Magazine since 1982. He has written many articles for various journals and books on the Israeli Air Force and aeronautical subjects.

SR 71

Flying the 'Black Line' during high-altitude spying missions, the aircrews of the futuristic SR-71 Blackbird have added a new dimension to intelligence-gathering

THE SR-71 is not an airplane, it is a national asset. When the national command authorities of the United States need prompt and accurate reconnaissance information, the Blackbirds of Beale are called upon to produce the goods. The Blackbird is the SR-71 aircraft, and Beale is its home base. Beale was not named after an illustrious former airman, as most US air bases have been. It bears the name of the founder of the US Camel Corps, Edward F. Beale. Beale was a naval academy graduate who, as an army general, started the Camel Corps as an experiment in long-distance, high-endurance operations. The camels are long gone. But long-distance, high-endurance, and very high-speed reconnaissance operations continue from the base that bears Edward Beale's name. Situated in the foothills of the Sierra mountain range about 110 miles northeast of San Francisco, Beale is home to the 9th Strategic Reconnaissance Wing (SRW). The 9th SRW flies two unique aircraft: the fastest and highest-flying aircraft in the world, the Lockheed SR-71 'Blackbird'; and its subsonic high-flying brother from the same stable, the Lockheed U-2/TR-1.

The SR-71 missions are flown by the 1st Strategic Reconnaissance Squadron (SRS). The crews of the 1st SRS fly their Blackbirds to collect reconnaissance information in response to requirements laid out in the Peacetime Aerial Reconnaissance programme, and are also responsible for contingency (quick-reaction) assignments. Two men make up an SR-71 crew: a pilot and a Reconnaissance Systems Officer (RSO).

A typical SR-71 crew member has more than 1500 hours flying time and operational experience in at least two aircraft before he applies to join the programme. He is in his early thirties, and has gone through a rigorous selection and training programme. Most are majors and junior lieutenant-colonels, together with a few very senior captains, and all possess superlative records. Prospective pilots and RSOs volunteer from other flying assignments within the United States Air Force (USAF), and the selection process includes evaluation of their experience and extensive checks into each man's background. Suitably qualified applicants are invited to Beale for an interview with wing and squadron officials, as well as a flight check in the supersonic T-38 Talon aircraft. About one in 10 applicants makes the grade and becomes accepted into the 1st SRS.

After they have been accepted, pilots and RSOs begin a year-long training programme that culminates in aircrews attaining operational status. Under this regime, the pilots and RSOs train and fly together as a co-ordinated team, sometimes for as long as four years. As one SR-71 crew member put it, 'Knowing the other guy and what he will do is the key to successful missions in the Blackbird.' Before they can become operational, however, the crew members must spend hundreds of hours in simulators, gaining invaluable experience in operating the Blackbird's systems and mastering the multitude of emergencies that may occur in operations at speeds greater than Mach 3 and altitudes above 80,000ft.

Prospective SR-71 pilots log about 100 hours in the simulator before flying the aircraft. Then they log at least five qualifying flights in the SR-71B with an instructor pilot in the back. The SR-71B has two pilot positions, with the instructor behind and slightly above the pilot being checked. That qualification passed, there follow two flights in the SR-71A with the man in the back being an instructor RSO. Meanwhile, the prospective RSO in training continues simulator work and flies qualifying missions with experienced pilots before being considered ready for operational status.

When both crew members are qualified, they form an aircrew and begin flying regular training missions from Beale. All crews fly at least three training missions per month, and operational missions also count as training. The duration of each mission varies with its requirements. However, with in-flight refuelling provided by the 9th SRW's tankers, time aloft is primarily limited by crew endurance. Most SR-71 crews have flown several missions that required five refuellings, and some have even exceeded that.

Successful SR-71 missions are the product of team-work among hundreds of skilled specialists

Until a qualified crew has amassed 100 hours in operational training status, they fly out of Beale Air Force Base. After achieving the required quota, they join the rotation of crews to the 9th SRW's forward-operation locations overseas. From RAF Mildenhall in the UK, and Kadena Air Base in Okinawa, SR-71s are forward-based to carry out operational requirements over Central Europe and the Soviet Union. The 1st SRS and parent 9th SRW rotate aircrews and support specialists to Mildenhall and Kadena on six-week cycles, followed by two-month cycles back at Beale. The result is about 130-180 days away from home each year, performing missions in the national interest.

Successful SR-71 missions are the product of team-work among hundreds of skilled specialists bending their energies to the smooth functioning of two men and a Blackbird flying high where no other aircraft venture. Major team-mates in the air are the KC-135Q aerial tankers; on the ground, men and women of the maintenance organisations and Physiological Support Division (PSD) are essential.

The planning for a typical Blackbird mission begins the day before it is flown. From Washington through Strategic Air Command, the mission tasking arrives at wing headquarters. The 1st SRS is then notified and a crew assigned. The maintenance chiefs designate an SR-71A aircraft that is deemed by them to be mission-ready. At the same time, 9th SRW mission planners develop the computer flight plans and mission tapes. The 'Black Line', or flight path for the mission, is drawn on aero charts and distributed to all with a need to know. At the 1st SRS,

Previous page: Once groundcrew from the 9th Organizational Maintenance Squadron have carried out last-minute checks (below), the SR-71 begins its reconnaissance mission (above). Right: While a suit technician from the Physiological Support Division (PSD) checks the full-pressure suits (right), the primary and back-up crews run over the mission and aircraft status (top right). Inset far right (above): Lieutenant-Colonel Bob Crowder is helped into his pressure suit. Inset right (below): A technician feeds compressed air into Major Ed Yeilding's suit in order to test its integrity.

THE 9TH STRATEGIC RECONNAISSANCE WING

The 9th Strategic Reconnaissance Wing (SRW) is located at Beale Air Force Base, California, and operates two unique aircraft – the SR-71 and U-2/TR-1. The wing's operational squadrons are the 1st (SR-71), and the 99th (U-2/TR-1) Strategic Reconnaissance Squadrons. During World War I, both the 1st and 99th Aero Squadrons flew combat missions in France. In 1922 the Army Air Corps formed the 9th Observation Group at Mitchel Field, Long Island. This new unit included the 1st Aero Squadron, and was converted for bomber duties during World War II. De-activated in 1948, the 9th Observation Group was periodically re-activated during the budget fluctuations of the 1950s. During the periods when it was operational, the unit flew B-47 Stratojets and was responsible for the operation of Titan I missiles. Following yet another period of de-activation, the unit was re-activated as the 9th Strategic Reconnaissance Wing during the development of the Mach 3 SR-71 Blackbird. Beale Air Force Base became the home of the SR-71s in January 1966. Personnel from the 9th SRW have set several records in the SR-71, and have earned a variety of awards and commendations. In July 1976, the 9th SRW set six absolute speed and altitude records.
Above: The crest of the 9th Strategic Reconnaissance Wing.

157

COLONEL DAVID H. PINSKY

Colonel David Pinsky (above) is the current commander of the 9th Strategic Reconnaissance Wing (SRW). He assumed command of the 9th SRW in January 1985, after 18 months as the unit's vice-commander. His illustrious career has involved flying and staff duties as diverse as tactical, training, interceptor, reconnaissance, bombing and space.

Born in Teaneck, New Jersey, on 22 December 1939, Colonel Pinsky entered active service in the USAF in October 1961, earning his pilot's wings one year later. He then served as an instructor in Air Training Command (ATC).

From the fast jets of ATC, Pinsky was re-trained in the Cessna O-1 Birddog and saw combat in the Vietnam War as a forward air controller. He flew 614 missions and was twice awarded the Silver Star for gallantry. From 1967 to 1974, Pinsky flew and instructed on the Convair F-106 interceptor. His assignments were in the USA and overseas, and included the command of an F-106 squadron. There followed a period of staff duty at the Pentagon and NATO.

Colonel Pinsky then flew the General Dynamics FB-111 'Aardvark' bomber in two wings of the US Strategic Air Command – the 380th and the 509th. In the 509th Bomber Wing, Pinsky served as the deputy commander for operations. Pinsky moved to the 9th SRW in June 1983 as its vice-commander. His decorations include the Distinguished Flying Cross and the Bronze Star for gallantry.

Below: Looking more like an astronaut than a pilot, Captain Harold 'Buck' Adams steps into the cockpit of an SR-71 Blackbird. Two weeks earlier, on 16 September 1974, Major Sullivan had flown this same aircraft from New York to the USAF base at Mildenhall, England, in the record-breaking time of one hour and 56 minutes.

the pilot and RSO go through their own detailed planning and co-ordination. They check the Black Line, translating its path into altitudes, airspeeds and headings (both magnetic and true) for each leg of the flight. Also at 1st SRS, a 'buddy' crew is designated. On mission day, its pilot and RSO will perform pre-flight activities on the aircraft – this buddy crew will be ready to fly should the primary pilot and RSO prove unable to embark on the mission.

Route planning always involves the avoidance of populated areas. The Blackbird's supersonic flight generates a sonic boom, and its routes are chosen to minimise the number of people who will hear it. The 9th SRW therefore maintains close communication with the Federal Aviation Administration on the Blackbirds' flight characteristics and route needs. To that end, SR-71 crews visit regional air-traffic control centres to liaise with controllers and to show video tapes of their aircraft.

At the 349th and 350th Air Refueling Squadrons, crews and KC-135Q tanker aircraft are designated to support tomorrow's mission. As their planning begins, they pick routes and times that will enable them to arrive at refuelling points ahead of the SR-71. In the PSD, life-support specialists take down each crew member's special full-pressure suit from its rack. They conduct pre-flight checks, then lay out the suits ready for the crew the following morning. With their own planning complete, the SR-71 crew goes into a rest period. That means no official duties for 12 hours before reporting, and several hours of sleep.

The mission take-off is scheduled for 0900 local time. Throughout the night, maintenance men and women of the 9th SRW prepare the aircraft for its mission. The Blackbird is fuelled to about half-full. It will take off at light weight, then top-up with fuel about 30 minutes after take-off. Pre-flight checks are conducted on all systems and checked off by maintenance supervisors.

MISSION PROFILE

0600 hours: Pilot and RSO visit Base Operations, receive weather briefing and file the flight plan.

0630: Pilot and RSO arrive at PSD. Cooks prepare a special high-protein, low-residue breakfast such as steak and eggs or an omelette. During breakfast, the primary and back-up crews discuss the mission and review their plans. The crew chief for the aircraft takes part in this meeting, covering the Blackbird's status. Breakfast over, the back-up crew and crew chief depart for the aircraft to perform pre-flight checks.

0730-0805: At PSD, crew members begin the suiting-up process. It begins with a cursory physical examination. Vital signs are checked: pulse, temperature, blood pressure; and so are eyes, ears, nose, and throat. After the physical examination, the men begin suiting-up. They pull on long underwear tops and bottoms – not so much to keep warm as to absorb the perspiration that they will generate during the mission. Meanwhile, a team of life-support specialists has entered the suiting room and stands ready to assist. Entering the room and sitting down, the pilot

Left: An SR-71 crew member climbs into the PSD van en route to the aircraft hangar. A life-support technician carries the portable oxygen system. Top left: As white-coated technicians integrate the pilot to the SR-71's systems, a maintenance specialist reaches down to check the status of the ejector seat. Above left: In one of the hangars, the pilot and RSO of Blackbird 17976 conduct final flight checks before a night mission.

and RSO slip their feet into the 'booties' of the pressure suits. With help from the life-support specialists, the suits are pulled up over their torsos, hands slipped into gloves, and their heads poked through the neck joints. The heavy helmets, with soft internal skullcaps, are placed over their heads and locked to the suits by specialists. The suits are now tested for functioning and pressure integrity. At operating altitude, the SR-71's cockpit is pressurised to a level of 26,000ft. Should cockpit pressure fail, the full-pressure suit automatically begins functioning when cockpit pressure falls to the 34,500ft level.

0730-0805: At the SR-71, the two men of the buddy crew walk around the aircraft with the crew chief, performing the external pre-flight inspection. Together, they mount the service stands set alongside the aircraft and settle into the cockpits. Their task is to pre-set switches in both cockpits, saving the flight crew both time and energy. Radio frequencies are pre-set, computer and sensor parameters keyed in, and the cockpits arranged to receive the pilot and RSO in a few minutes. An important control setting at this point is the 'face heat' temperature. The faceplate of the pressure suit helmet is heated electrically through a grid of fine gold wires so that it does not fog up during the mission. Each pilot and RSO has an optimum face heat setting. Around and on the aircraft, maintenance specialists continue final checks under the crew chief's expert eye.

0805-0815: Pressure suit testing complete, pilot and RSO rise. Portable cooling and oxygen boxes are connected to their suits. They walk the dozen steps to the waiting PSD van backed up to the door and climb inside. They recline on lounge chairs in their pressure suits, and the white van pulls away from the preparation area. It drives the short five-minute ride to the hangar where their SR-71A awaits. The van stops beside the open hangar door. The men rise and clump up the steps of the service stand placed alongside the SR-71 cockpits. They disconnect the portable life-support system, climb over the cockpit sill, and settle into their positions. PSD specialists integrate the men to the aircraft communication, life-support, and escape systems. They connect air hoses, communication lines, ejection-seat fittings, shoulder and waist harnesses to the crewmen and their suits. Pilot and RSO check their cockpits, then begin the engine-start checklists.

0815 Runway 15: One minute apart, the two KC-135Q tankers take off, bearing thousands of pounds of JP-7 fuel to be transferred to the SR-71.

0840-0844 Hangar: With a mighty roar and blast of flame, the special liquid chemical, triethyl borane (TEB), explodes, igniting the JP-7 fuel. The compressors and turbines of the two J58 engines start turning. Pilot and RSO check instrument displays. Everything is in order. The pilot signals the ground-crew away. The chocks in front of the three-wheeled main gear are pulled away. The SR-71 is ready to roll. The crew calls ground control for permission to taxi, using the radio callsign 'Aspen Three Zero'. From the hangar, the SR-71's black needle nose emerges. Red light flashing, a mobile vehicle leads the SR-71 while taxiing. The Blackbird rolls out, turning left to roll its nose gear onto the yellow taxi line. Two vehicles fall into column behind the SR-71: the maintenance checkout crew in a blue van and the life-support specialists in the white PSD van. The SR-71 pilot keeps the J58 engines rumbling at near-idle, so that the aircraft rolls down the taxi line smoothly and at a speed of about jogging pace. The engine noise is surprisingly low, especially when compared with fighters such as the F-4 Phantom.

0847: Aspen 30 taxis into the engine run-up area just short of the active runway, nicknamed the 'Hammer-head'. This is the last chance for checks before the flight. In turn, each engine is brought up to power and its parameters checked. Inlet and exhaust temperatures, percentage revs per minute, and other variables must meet precise criteria. Flight controls are exercised. The groundcrew watches for correct reaction from the control surfaces, such as full deflection from the two rudders.

0900: Precisely on the second, the pilot brings the two J58 engines to take-off power. As their roar rises to a crescendo, he releases the brakes and the SR-71 begins to roll. Fuel load for take-off is about half-full. This decreases weight, cuts the take-off roll, and is safer than taking off fully loaded. In less than 5000ft, the aircraft leaves the ground and arcs into the sky. The SR-71 soon disappears. The two bright exhausts are the most visible signs of its passage. In only a few seconds, even the exhaust plumes are gone from sight and the sound of Aspen 30's engines dies away to stillness.

Time Aloft: Aspen 30's crew are climbing out at subsonic airspeed towards the first refuelling. They are breathing 100 per cent oxygen. Over a period of 30 minutes, a process known as 'denitrogenisation' will rid their bloodstreams of nitrogen bubbles that could cause severe pains at high altitude. Inside the aircraft, pilot and RSO are attending to the dozens of

Bottom left: Chief Master Sergeant Donald W. Campbell (right), one of the 9th Strategic Reconnaissance Wing's top maintenance specialists, reviews the operational records of an SR-71 with Senior Airman James N. Palmer. When the U-2/TR-1 (below) was developed as an advanced spin-off of the SR-71, these new aircraft were handed over to the 99th SRS.

THE SR-71 BLACKBIRD

President Lyndon B. Johnson revealed the existence of the SR-71 aircraft at a press conference on 24 July 1964, and flight testing began five months later with Lockheed test pilot Robert Gilliland at the controls.

The project was co-ordinated by Kelly Johnson, the head of Lockheed's Advanced

Development Projects group – less formally known as the 'Skunk Works'. Kelly's team had already built the U2 strategic reconnaissance aircraft, but the development of the SR-71 posed a completely new set of problems. As Kelly Johnson later recounted: 'Everything about the aircraft had to be invented. Everything.' The lineage that led to the SR-71 began with the A-12, conceived by the Central Intelligence Agency (CIA) as a replacement for the Lockheed U-2. The A-12 first flew in 1962 and was operated by the CIA until the USAF was ready to take delivery of the SR-71.

Among the inventive solutions that led to the SR-71 were the powerful Pratt and Whitney J58 turbojet engines, designed to operate at a speed of Mach 3 and an altitude of 80,000ft. In addition, the heat-resistant titanium-alloy construction is capable of withstanding temperatures of 930 degrees Fahrenheit.

Digital computers have recently replaced the analog computer systems in the SR-71 fleet, and the primary navigation system is astro-inertial – the aircraft's position is calculated according to

There are 12 SR-71 hangars at Beale Air Force, and the doors of each are opened and closed at random times before each mission in order to confuse 'unfriendly' observers. Main picture: The red streamers attached to this SR-71 designate locking pins that must be checked before the aircraft can take off. Below: The 'Mach 3' shoulder patch of the 1st SRS.

instruments on their panels, while talking to air-traffic control centre, and flying the Black Line to rendezvous with the first tanker. Join-up can be accomplished independently of external navigational aids; both the SR-71 and KC-135Q are equipped for precise join-up. They rendezvous at 25,000ft. The tanker's boom is carefully guided into the receptacle behind the SR-71's astro-inertial navigation system. Flying a level race-track pattern with gradual turns, the tanker pumps JP-7 fuel into the SR-71's tanks for about 15 minutes. Fully loaded with fuel, Aspen 30 is now a strategic reconnaissance system ready for its mission.

The two aircraft disconnect. It is time to go supersonic. Aspen 30's pilot lowers the SR-71's nose and goes into a gentle descent. Airspeed builds up rapidly during a descent of about 3000ft. Aspen 30 soon passes smoothly through Mach 1, the pilot raises the nose and continues acceleration and climb to best operating speed and altitude. Pilot and RSO are alone with their aircraft and its systems, en route to the target area. They function as a symbiotic team, each anticipating the other's actions and reactions. The RSO, for example, must be capable of operating several different sensors simultaneously, while also attending to the precise navigation required for collection of reconnaissance information. At the same time, he and the pilot work together to cope with malfunctions or anomalies in the aircraft and its sensors.

Navigation must be precise. The Black Line governs. The navigation systems are capable of achieving an operational accuracy of 0.1 nautical miles at cruise speeds and altitudes. Such precision ensures that the specific mission requirements are met and that the aircraft is at precisely the right speed and

constant sights on three stars chosen to suit each mission.

The SR-71's maximum take-off weight is 170,000lb, with a fuel load of 80,000lb of JP-7 fuel. The engines provide a thrust of 30,000lb at sea-level with afterburn. The Blackbird's maximum speed is Mach 3 (2000 miles per hour at 80,000ft). Below: An SR-71 Blackbird from the 1st Strategic Reconnaissance Squadron (SRS).

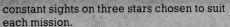

17976

altitude over the target. Although the navigation systems and the computers do much of the routine work, the RSO constantly cross-checks and monitors their performance. If the automatic systems deviate from plan, or if malfunctions occur, the RSO and pilot must take immediate corrective action to stay on the Black Line. Sensors aboard the SR-71 are capable of gathering imagery on more than 100,000 square miles of territory in each hour. That is an area larger than the Federal Republic of Germany!

Reconnaissance complete, Aspen 30 flies the Black Line out of the target area and turns for base. Another drink of JP-7 is usually needed at this point. Deceleration and descent to the tanker begins several hundred miles from join-up. The SR-71 loses altitude and airspeed, arriving at the right moment some 40 miles behind the tanker, then flying ahead to rendezvous and take delivery of the required fuel. Fuel management is imperative in the SR-71. Although headed for base, the crew wants a healthy reserve against emergencies. Besides, fuel onboard at the end of the mission can be burned in productive

training during the approach holding pattern and landing of the aircraft.

If it is a long way from base, the SR-71 may return to its most efficient high altitude and supersonic airspeed. Several hundred miles from base, the 'decel-descent' begins again. About 60-80 miles from base, Aspen 30 is subsonic at 31,000ft, and air-traffic control is handling it like any other fast jet in the system.

Approaching the base, Aspen 30's pilot and RSO prepare for 'flying the pattern', making approaches and going around again. This is required training, and is undertaken whenever fuel and time permit. Approach and landing, like all other aspects of SR-71 operation, are team efforts. During the landing, the pilot's forward and downward visibility is restricted. Both pilot and RSO are on instruments, bringing the aircraft to landing speed and height. In practice sessions, the aircraft makes a low approach and then accelerates away its landing before the landing gear can touch the runway. The pilot makes four, maybe even five, approaches before bringing the Black-

Below: Afterburner plumes glow white-hot as a Blackbird takes off from Beale. After accelerating towards an altitude of 25,000ft, the SR-71 throttles back for a rendezvous with a KC-135Q refuelling tanker (top left).

bird in to land.

An SR-71 making its approach looks like an eagle chasing its prey: nose high, reaching down with its landing gear, then touching precisely on the runway. The nose gear remains off the ground for a time, allowing the fuselage to assist in aerodynamic braking. The landing roll consumes about 4000ft of the runway. As airspeed bleeds off, the pilot deploys a huge orange parachute that brakes the Blackbird even harder. Slowed to taxi speed, the pilot cuts away the parachute, turns off the runway, and follows the blue escort van back to its hangar.

The data or imagery collected on this mission will be analysed by reconnaissance experts

In the hangar: Engine shutdown checklist is performed. The two J58s wind down to silence. Inside the cockpits, ejection seats are put on 'safe'. The two cockpit canopies rise. Pilot and RSO give 'thumbs up' to the groundcrew swarming around the aircraft. Life-support specialists reach into the cockpits to disconnect the pilot and RSO from the aircraft systems. They help the crewmen over the sills and connect the portable air conditioning units. The pilot and RSO descend the steps, mount the PSD van, and

settle into the lounge chairs for the ride back to PSD. There, they are helped out of the pressure suits and, for the first time in hours, can stretch, scratch, and begin to relax.

Now it is time for a long hot shower, fresh underclothes and flight suit, and a short drive over to wing headquarters for mission and maintenance debriefings.

Maintenance crews plug external power and communication lines into the aircraft and begin the seven post-flight checklists that comprise more than 600 items. Other specialists reach into the sensor bays. Their job is to remove the products for processing. The data or imagery collected on this mission will be analysed by reconnaissance experts and translated into intelligence information.

In other hangars, Blackbirds are being readied for the next mission. In the simulators, pilots and RSOs are continuing their never-ending training. The Blackbirds of Beale are 'Semper Paratus' – Always Ready.

THE AUTHOR Clifton Berry Jr writes from Washington on military subjects. He would like to thank the members of the 9th Strategic Reconnaissance Wing at Beale Air Force Base for their generous assistance during the preparation of this article.

Top: The sleek aerodynamics of the Blackbird have been left virtually unchanged during 12 years of service. The powerful reconnaissance equipment is located in sensor bays in the aircraft's nose cone and fuselage. Below: To reduce speed during the landing roll, an SR-71 pilot deploys an orange braking parachute. Above left: Trained for speed and altitude; two members of the 9th Strategic Reconnaissance Wing.

THE 'FIGHTIN' 36TH'

The 36th Tactical Fighter Wing was the US Air Force's first jet-fighter unit to be deployed in Europe. In July 1948 the wing set up at Furstenfeldbruck Air Base, flying F-80 Shooting Stars, and has since then become well-known for introducing new fighter aircraft types into Europe, including the F-15 Eagle in April 1977.
The history of the 36th began in February 1940 when the 36th Pursuit Group was activated at Langley Field in Virginia, flying the Curtiss P-36 Hawk. They then flew P-40 Warhawks in the Caribbean before progressing to P-47 Thunderbolt missions in Europe. During World War II the 36th earned two US Presidential Unit Citations and the nickname 'Fightin' 36th' for its wartime efficiency and endurance. Since World War II the 36th has been named one of the USAF's 'Outstanding Units' on five occasions. Its F-15 maintenance crews won awards in 1982 and 1983, and in 1984 Captain Michael Bebo was selected top fighter pilot in the US Air Force. In 1985 Major Eric Nedergaard was the first American to win the coveted International Air Tattoo Solo Trophy.
The F-15s of the 36th are currently committed to NATO control, both in peacetime and during times of conflict. The control is exercised by Allied Sector 3 of the 4th Allied Tactical Air Force. The US chain of command ensures the wing's readiness. Top control in Europe is in the hands of the US European Command (near Stuttgart) and the chain of command extends through US Air Forces in Europe (Ramstein Air Base) and the 17th Air Force, which has its headquarters at Sembach Air Base. Above: The emblem of the 36th Tactical Fighter Wing.

On 24-hour call, the 'Zulu Alert' F-15 crews of the US 36th Tactical Fighter Wing are ready to scramble at a moment's notice

SHOULD WAR COME to the central European region, the 36th Tactical Fighter Wing (TFW) of the US Air Force (USAF) will be one of the first NATO units to go into battle. The 36th TFW's mission is to ensure the sovereignty of NATO airspace by being its first line of air defence. This means that the 72 aircraft and 110 or so pilots of the 36th must be ready for air battle around the clock, all the year round.
The leading edge of the 36th Wing is represented by four F-15 Eagle air-superiority fighters. The aircraft stand perpetually cocked and ready in a special nest with a bland name. It is called the 'Roether Memorial Zulu Alert Facility'. The Facility consists of four hangars, built into a hill at Bitburg Air Base in West Germany, close to the border with Luxembourg. Apart from the protection provided by the hill, the hangar structures are specially strengthened or 'hardened' to withstand attack.
Inside, the four F-15C Eagles are fully fuelled, armed, and ready for action. To go to war, they need only for their pilots to mount, and engines to be started. Standing gleaming and silent, they are like

fire engines in a fire station, on ready alert, waiting for the alarm bell. This analogy extends to the planes' immaculate surroundings, in which machines and environs are spotlessly clean. Cords for power and communication snake purposefully across the floor and are plugged into the aircraft. No oil spots or bits of rubbish lie about to mar the 'operating-theatre' sterility of the surface.
On the fuselage and wings of each aircraft are hooked four live AIM-7F/M Sparrow and four AIM-9L/M Sidewinder air-to-air missiles, awaiting their deadly role in the skies. Near the right wing root of each Eagle, its 20mm cannon is ready to blast off a total of 940 rounds when triggered.
In the centre of the hangar area is a gleaming fireman's pole, leading to the floor above, where a functional spartan lounge area accommodates the Eagle Zulu Alert

ZULU ALERT

crews. At all times, four pilots sit waiting for the call to action, fully kitted out in coveralls and G-suits. With them are crew chiefs for each aircraft who know the armament, avionics, and other skills necessary to keep the aircraft of the alert force in top form.

Most of the time, the Zulu lounge is quiet. The pilots read, catch up on paperwork, nap, or watch television. But the placidity of the quiet scene is deceptive. It masks the energy and fighting ability that the pilots must unleash when the call comes – the call that could mean an enemy attack.

The summons to action comes at least once a day. It may be because an aircraft has wandered into the buffer airspace between East and West Germany. Or an unidentified aircraft on the screen makes a radar controller suspicious, and the NATO sector operations centre decides to scramble the Zulu Alert F-15s. Or the operations centre has no actual target, but wishes to test the alert system. The Zulu Alert crews

never know the reason why they are scrambled. For them, every alert could be the real thing.

When the scramble order comes, the calm of the alert lounge is shattered by a loud and raucous roar

Below: An armed-up F-15 Eagle of the 525th Tactical Fighter Squadron of the 36th Tactical Fighter Wing.
Bottom: Pouring dense 'contrails' behind, a flight of three F-15s streaks off to intercept a target aircraft over Germany during one of the many realistic combat training missions flown by the 36th.

from the klaxon horn. Leaping to their feet, the pilots charge to the fireman's pole and slide down. On the main floor below, they sprint to their F-15s. At the aircraft, the four airmen shoot up the ladders into their cockpits. They hook up shoulder and lap harnesses rapidly, then connect themselves to the ejection seat, oxygen, and communications systems of the aircraft. Meanwhile, each crew chief has dashed to the aircraft and put on an intercom set. The crew chief is busy pulling safety streamers from key parts of the aircraft and its missiles, and can talk with the pilot if he needs to.

As the pilot connects himself up to the aircraft, he also starts its two Pratt & Whitney F100 engines. First, the starboard engine, to generate power for the aircraft systems, then, as the crew chief pulls the ladder clear of the aircraft and moves it to a safe position, the pilot starts the port engine. His left hand moves the twin throttles to flight idle. With his right hand he punches the buttons to enter Bitburg's geographic co-ordinates into the Eagle's Inertial Navigation System (INS). Alignment of the INS computer takes about three minutes. This operation eats up the single longest chunk of time in the alert.

While the INS is aligning itself, the pilot is busy on the radio. He receives mission instructions from the 36th TFW's command post, and clearance to taxi from the Bitburg control tower.

The eight turbofan engines on the four aircraft are rumbling, ready for launch. Inside the cockpit, all is quiet. The engine noise is blocked by the pilot's headset, helmet, and the pressure seals of his cockpit canopy. The only sounds in his headphones are the whisper of his breathing and the crackle of his and other voices on the radio.

Zulu Alert force is organised in two flights of two aircraft. The first flight is cleared to taxi to the active runway. The second flight remains in the hangar.

Within seconds, the two fighters arrow into the grey overcast and disappear from sight

The lead pilot receives taxiing instructions and basic information on the intercept mission. The data absorbed and acknowledged, his gloved left hand advances the throttles. The roar of the engines builds to a heavy rumble, and his Eagle pokes its nose out of the hangar. Followed by his Number Two, the Flight Leader taxis 550yds down a special taxiway. They assume take-off positions at the end of Bitburg's 8200ft Runway, 06-24. The wingman rolls his F-15C into position alongside and slightly to the rear of his leader. On a pre-arranged signal from the Flight Leader, throttles are advanced smoothly to military power, then through the throttle quadrant gate to afterburner. The roaring shriek of the four F100 turbofans splits the air, bouncing off the rolling hills around the base – audible for miles. From the four tailpipes, white-hot exhaust streams outward.

Zulu Alert! At the call of the klaxon, aircrew race from the alert lounge, go down the pole (top left) and straight into the cockpit, closely followed by the crew chief (top centre). Emerging from the TAB VEE shelter (top right), the Eagles are airborne within five minutes of the alert warning and closing on their targets (above right). Above: A pair of Eagles returns to the runway at Bodo during a 36th TFW deployment to Norway.

COLONEL PETER D. ROBINSON

Colonel Peter D. Robinson brings some 3500 jet-fighter flying hours and 435 combat missions to his leadership of the Fightin' 36th, and he flies regularly with the wing's fighting squadrons. Born in 1940 in Ann Arbor, Michigan, Robinson went on from high school to the Air Force Academy, graduating in 1962 with a bachelor of science degree. He earned his pilot's wings in August 1963. Combat crew training in the F-100 Super Sabre led to flying F-100s for two years with the 81st TFS at Hahn in Germany. From Hahn Robinson went to Southeast Asia for his first combat tour of the Vietnam War and flew 325 combat missions in the F-100 between 1966 and 1967. After combat, he attended the University of Freiburg as an Olmsted Scholar in mathematics. Returning to a jet fighter cockpit, he made the transition onto the F-4 Phantom and went on to fly a second combat tour in Vietnam from 1970 to 1971. On this tour, he flew 110 Phantom missions with the 555th 'Triple Nickel' TFS. After a spell at the Pentagon, he returned to fighters in 1975 and oversaw the 49th TFW's conversion from Phantoms onto the F-15 in 1979. From the cockpit of the F-15 he returned to academic studies and graduated from the Royal College of Defence Studies in London in 1982. From there he went on to serve at HQ US Air Forces in Europe, but was soon back with the F-15, this time at Bitburg. Having served as second in command of the wing for nearly two years, Colonel Robinson assumed command of the 36th in January 1985.

The Eagles begin to roll – slowly for a second or two, then they surge forward, punched by 50,000lb of thrust down the runway. In the quiet cockpits, the Flight Leader keeps his aircraft aligned with the runway stripe while Number Two keeps station. Within 1000ft, the two 44,000lb aircraft leap into the air.

Less than five minutes have elapsed since the klaxon buzzed. Five minutes is the prescribed standard. Most of the time, the Eagles of the 36th break ground well within five minutes of the buzzer.

The tricycle landing gear tucks up. The two Eagles pitch up sharply. They swoop skywards in a graceful curve that steepens to near vertical as the pilots pull back on their control sticks. Within seconds, the two fighters arrow into the grey overcast, disappearing from sight, with only the sound of their engines trailing their presence.

Meanwhile, the second Zulu flight stands by in the hangars. They are ready to launch if something goes wrong with the first flight, or if reinforcement is needed.

Given the weather and light conditions in this part of Europe, nearly 80 per cent of the time the aircraft will have to launch in darkness, or into an overcast.

Number Two keeps station on Lead unless the overcast is too thick. In that case, he follows closely in trail, using his Hughes APG-63 radar to stay a few thousand feet behind his leader.

The controller at the Ground Control Intercept (GCI) radar site transmits headings and altitudes for the flight of Eagles to intercept the target. They climb at more than 500 knots, streaking upward towards the high, thin-air vastness, where the air-superiority battle will be fought. They are aiming to intercept the target track as far to the east as possible. Most tracks that cause a scramble are either aircraft that have failed to file a flight plan, or are a result of a pilot's poor navigation that has caused him to wander into the Air Defence Identification Zone (ADIZ) along the East-West German border.

The interceptor pilots watch the radar displays projected in front of them, picking up the targets at long range. Once the Eagles spot their target aircraft, the pilots manoeuvre the jets in to make a visual identification. They fly up alongside the target and rock their wings, the international signal meaning that the 'intruder' should follow the F-15s. Together, they fly to a nearby airfield. The F-15s circle and lower their landing gear to signal the target to land. Once he is on the ground, the F-15s leave.

Actual scrambles against an unidentified track are rare. Most often, the Eagles are launched to intercept a real or simulated aircraft as part of NATO forces' constant programme of training for the air defence mission. To execute the air defence role, the 36th TFW is organised into three tactical fighter squadrons (TFS): the 22nd TFS, nicknamed the 'Stingers'; the 53rd TFS 'Tigers'; and the 525th TFS 'Bulldogs'. Each squadron has 24 aircraft and 30 pilots, and an additional 20 pilots from the wing staff are available to augment the squadrons. The aircraft flown are mainly the F-15C single-seat type, with a few twin-seat F-15Ds on strength. The 'D' models are used primarily for training, but are also fully capable of the same combat missions as the F-15Cs. The F-15s of the 36th TFW are identified by the large letters 'BT' on their vertical stabilisers, and each individual squadron's aircraft are further identified by a coloured horizontal stripe: red for the 22nd, yellow for the 53rd, and blue for the 525th.

The wing trains constantly for its combat mission and the efforts of its strength of 5000 men and women are focused on keeping the pilots and aircraft ready to fly and fight, and to sustain that fighting effort for as long as it is required by the NATO authorities.

It takes about 60 days for a new arrival to become a ready frontline fighter pilot. This is true, whatever his background. Pilots arriving at the 36th come from three main sources. First, there are the young pilots who have recently earned their wings. These men have gone through pilot training, fighter lead-in training in the AT-38 Talon, and have then trained on the F-15 in the States for six months. Other newcomers, however, are more senior and experienced – fighter pilots qualified on aircraft such as the F-4 Phantom, and who have finished the training to convert onto the F-15. Finally, fully qualified F-15 pilots come to the 36th from other USAF F-15 wings. Whatever their source, pilots selected to fly F-15s in the 36th TFW are tops in the fighter field.

Keeping the Eagles in tip-top condition and ready for action is the task of the three maintenance squadrons of the 36th. Left, top: Personnel of the 36th Equipment Maintenance Squadron work on an F-15. Left, centre: Routine engine cavity maintenance. Left: An armourer loads linked 20mm cannon rounds.

All incoming pilots must first 'fly' missions in the F-15 simulator at Bitburg. The simulator time familiarises them with local procedures, radio frequencies, navigational aids, and such. They then begin progressing through the stepping-stones of preparation for F-15 missions flown in Germany. The training sequence opens with basic fighter manoeuvres (BFM), in which one aircraft takes on another from its squadron, high in the skies over Germany. From there, they progress to air combat manoeuvres (ACM), working as a co-ordinated flight of two aircraft against a single adversary. This is when a new wingman begins to appreciate his crucial role in the aerial battle: to protect his leader and be ready to kill other fighters himself. From ACM the pilots then move on to air combat tactics (ACT) – a batch of F-15s from a squadron seek out and engage other F-15s in a wider chunk of European airspace. Finally, the F-15s of the 36th fight other types of NATO and US fighters in dissimilar air combat tactics (DACT).

Intercept training is conducted at night and in bad weather, when tactics practice is not feasible. The Bitburg Eagles find targets, and manoeuvre into weapons position in two ways: either via the powerful ground-based radar at Ground Control Intercept sites, or by using their own on-board radar, the Hughes APG-63. Intercept training is usually done at medium or high altitudes. Additional spontaneous intercept training is provided through NATO's so-called 'Target of Opportunity' programme in which all military aircraft flying below 10,000ft throughout West German airspace are liable to be intercepted without warning. Every military aircraft, from the ground up to 10,000ft, is fair game, liable to be 'bounced' by any other military bird. It is excellent practice for F-15 pilots in detecting, intercepting, and identifying targets. It also offers valuable experience in protecting one's own formation.

There, in clear flying conditions, they fly combat training missions against other NATO aircraft

When a pilot is considered 'mission ready', he can expect to fly about 15 missions each month, logging some 20 flying hours. He will also be away from Bitburg for extended periods for about one third of the year.

Flying training away from Bitburg is necessary for several reasons. First is the need for pilots to be familiar with flying conditions in other parts of the Nato arena, ranging from the far northern curve of Norway to the eastern Mediterranean. Another reason is that the restricted airspace in Germany hampers freewheeling and realistic aerial combat. Finally, the poor weather in central Germany cuts the available training time because so much of each mission is spent coping with the demands of darkness, bad weather, or both.

Thus, for two months of each year, each squadron flies to Decimomannu in Sardinia for training. There, in clear flying conditions, they fly combat-training missions against other NATO aircraft. The adversaries they encounter most often in the air are the USAF 'Aggressor' pilots from the 527th Tactical Fighter Training Squadron, based at RAF Alconbury in England. The Aggressors are some of the US Air Force's best fighter pilots, already skilled in operating the F-15, F-16, or F-4, and, flying Northrop F-5Es to simulate Soviet MiG-21s, they use Soviet tactics in engagements against the F-15s from the 36th. Flying against the Aggressors is as close to real air-to-air

Three maintenance squadrons work to keep the 36th's aircraft in shape and ready to fight. These are the 36th Aircraft Generation Squadron (AGS), the 36th Equipment Maintenance Squadron and the 36th Component Repair Squadron. The 36th AGS is divided into three sub-units, each of which is linked with one of the wing's three flying squadrons. Much of the routine minor maintenance is done in hardened aircraft shelters called TAB VEEs – an acronym for the jaw-breaking title, Theater Air Base Vulnerability Shelters. These shelters are dispersed over a two-mile area and are hardened against blast to ensure the survival of the precious F-15s they harbour. Much F-15 maintenance is of the 'remove, replace, repair' concept. When a pilot or crew chief identifies a problem, the maintenance people locate the trouble and remove the malfunctioning component, replacing it with a spare. The faulty part is then taken to the workshops of either the Equipment Maintenance or Component Repair Squadron. Meanwhile, the supply squadron ships a new spare to the flight-line shelter to replace the one fitted to the F-15. When a squadron or flight deploys away from Bitburg, a group of essential personnel are sent on ahead. These people form a representative slice of the wing's maintenance and supply units and include weapons specialists from the AGS and technicians from the other two maintenance squadrons. Also deployed are specialists in transportation, supply and administrative support. Wherever the 36th is deployed, the men and women that perform the crucial back-up for the flying squadrons will be there to ensure that the wing is combat ready at all times.

AIM-9L Sidewinder

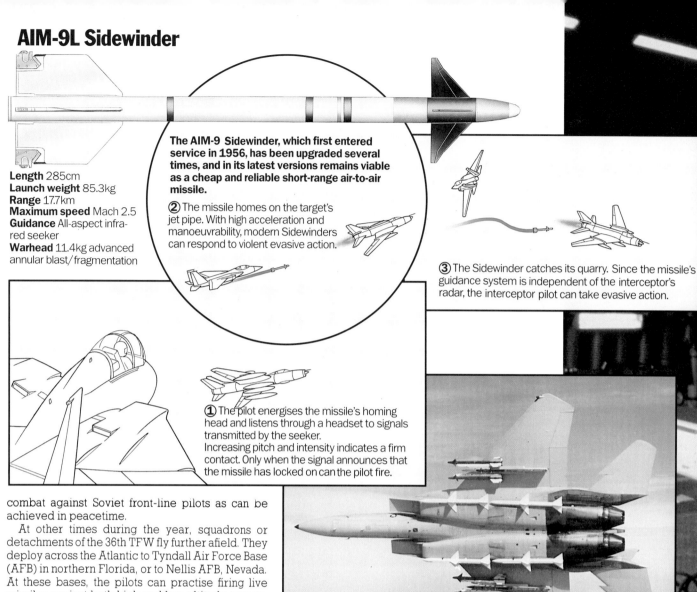

Length 285cm
Launch weight 85.3kg
Range 17.7km
Maximum speed Mach 2.5
Guidance All-aspect infra-red seeker
Warhead 11.4kg advanced annular blast/fragmentation

The AIM-9 Sidewinder, which first entered service in 1956, has been upgraded several times, and in its latest versions remains viable as a cheap and reliable short-range air-to-air missile.

② The missile homes on the target's jet pipe. With high acceleration and manoeuvrability, modern Sidewinders can respond to violent evasive action.

③ The Sidewinder catches its quarry. Since the missile's guidance system is independent of the interceptor's radar, the interceptor pilot can take evasive action.

① The pilot energises the missile's homing head and listens through a headset to signals transmitted by the seeker. Increasing pitch and intensity indicates a firm contact. Only when the signal announces that the missile has locked on can the pilot fire.

combat against Soviet front-line pilots as can be achieved in peacetime.

At other times during the year, squadrons or detachments of the 36th TFW fly further afield. They deploy across the Atlantic to Tyndall Air Force Base (AFB) in northern Florida, or to Nellis AFB, Nevada. At these bases, the pilots can practise firing live missiles against both high and low-altitude targets. Also, the 36th regularly deploys northwards, to Bodo in Norway. There, above the Arctic Circle, it performs periods of training with other NATO units.

The fighter pilots who fly the F-15s are the elite of the USAF's pilot force. The F-15 Eagle they fly is also, in its own way, elite. In more than 11 years of service with the USAF it has proved to be extremely capable. The power from its two F100 engines produces more pounds of thrust (nearly 50,000) than the aircraft weighs (44,000lb plus). With this power-to-weight ratio, the F-15 can accelerate while climbing straight up, and is capable of speeds in excess of Mach 2.5. In aerial combat it can manoeuvre at up to nine times the force of gravity, with agility.

In addition to its massive power, the F-15 is an extremely sophisticated weapon system. The on-board Hughes APG-63 radar gives the pilot the ability to locate, track and fire against both high and low-flying aircraft at distances beyond 50 miles. The radar's 'look-down' capability is coupled with the AIM-7F Sparrow radar-guided missile's ability to shoot beneath the aircraft. This means that the F-15 pilot can shoot down targets far below him, including low-level penetrators hugging the ground.

The F-15's cockpit layout, controls, and displays enable the pilot to fly and fight without having to look down at his instruments. The head-up display (HUD) and other visual representations of the situation combine to show the pilot all the information he needs about the performance of both his own aircraft

Right, above: A weapons technician works on a Sparrow air-to-air missile prior to arming an F-15. The F-15 currently carries two missile types – the AIM-7F Sparrow and the AIM-9L/M Sidewinder, mounted on points below the fuselage and wings (above). Right: A lone Eagle of the 53rd Tactical Fighter Squadron.

and the target, plus armament status. He can engage targets above and below, hitting them way out beyond visual range with the Sparrow, closer in with the heat-seeking Sidewinder, and even closer with the stream of fire from the Vulcan 20mm cannon. In the near future, the AMRAAM (Advanced Medium Range Air-to-Air Missile) will be added to the Eagle's air defence armament package.

With the East German border less than 15 flying minutes away, the men and women of the 'Fightin' 36th' know that their unit will be among the first to fight if war comes. They are ready to meet that challenge.

THE AUTHOR F. Clifton Berry, Jr. is an aerospace writer based in Washington, DC. He is an active pilot with land and seaplane ratings. He has flown with USAF units in the F-15 on training missions.

RECON

As part of a reconnaissance team, your mission is to provide friendly forces with accurate information on the enemy and the terrain he occupies. Your role is vital, and it is imperative that your team gets into the target area, conducts the surveillance, and then gets back to base with the minimum of contact with the enemy. Stealth, patience and maximum concealment are your bywords – the success of the mission will depend on your team avoiding battle and fighting only when there is no other alternative. One sure method of preventing misunderstandings while out on a mission is to practise the arm and hand signals that you intend to use. Sound travels, so you must keep talk down to a minimum.

Once the field commander has asked for intelligence of the enemy, the reconnaissance team will be called upon to deliver the goods. The brief may be narrow – pinpoint the enemy's Achilles' heel, for example. This type of mission is generally referred to as a point reconnaissance and surveillance. An area reconnaissance and surveillance, on the other hand, usually requires detailed information on the terrain of one or several regions. Are the banks of streams too high to be negotiated by armoured vehicles? Is there any evidence of minefields in the area? These are just two of the questions you will be expected to answer.

The type of mission will dictate the size of your patrol, though a minimum of two men is always essential. If contact with the enemy in the target area is a strong possibility, it may be necessary to augment the reconnaissance element of the team with an assault, security and support element. Assuming that you have been authorised to engage the enemy only as a last resort, arms should be limited to individual weapons and grenades in order to ensure that the team's mobility is not threatened. Make sure, however, that one of your colleagues is equipped with an automatic weapon in case of unavoidable contact. Clean and test-fire the weapons before setting out on patrol.

Whatever the mission, and however small the reconnaissance team, there is a number of items that you must carry when out on patrol: a pencil and notebook for making notes and sketches of the terrain, two compasses and watches, day and night binoculars, wire-cutters, two maps of the target area, flashlights and communication equipment. Other necessary equipment may include a camera, night-vision devices, lightweight radar, booby traps and demolitions. The latter may prove invaluable should you be forced to clear a landing zone before the reconnaissance team can be extracted by helicopter.

Before leaving base camp, your commander will make it clear whether he considers it appropriate for the patrol to fight, if necessary, to accomplish the mission. He may, for example, decide to authorise reconnaissance by fire as a technique for locating and determining enemy strength. A technique used only as a last resort, this involves designated patrol members firing on suspected positions in order to draw return fire that will reveal the enemy.

Whether you are being inserted by land, sea or air, one of the keys to effective reconnaissance is careful map study: en route to and returning from an objective, make sure you always know your patrol's precise location. This will enable you to avoid known

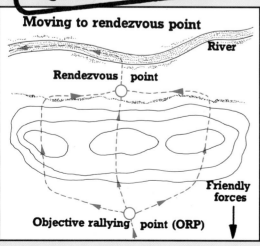

Moving to rendezvous point

River

Rendezvous point

Friendly forces

Objective rallying point (ORP)

Above: The secret of successful reconnaissance is to collect the information you need without alerting the enemy to your presence. The camouflage uniform of this member of a Danish reconnaissance troop allows him to blend in with his surroundings, and binoculars enable him to survey the terrain in his brief without needing to move in close. If there is a danger of the sun betraying your presence by flashing off your glasses, conduct your watch from an area of shade.

danger areas and make contingency plans for artillery support in case of ambush. Keep a watch on the other members of your team. Is anyone suffering from a cold, however slight? You are about to go behind enemy lines, where the noise of an involuntary cough could jeopardise the mission.

Moving cautiously through the area to be reconnoitred, your patrol must be ready at all times to counter an ambush. Watch out for dead foliage and brush that has been tied down, as this could be enemy camouflage or a possible firing lane. Rotate the man on point and always have your gun pointing in the direction in which you are looking – otherwise, the split second it will take to bring your weapon to bear could prove fatal.

Place trust in your senses, and use them to the full. The aroma of cigarette smoke can be detected from up to a quarter of a mile away, for example, and may give you a fix on an enemy troop location or possible ambush site. By the same token, avoid the use of such items as soap or insect repellent in areas where the indigenous population do not use them. During counter-insurgency operations in Malaya, the British learned that the smell of these could be detected by guerrillas from a considerable distance. Listen out for the abrupt cessation of normal wildlife sounds – this could indicate that the enemy is nearby.

At some point during the reconnaissance patrol it may be necessary to sleep. Men on guard should kneel rather than sit to ensure that they stay awake. Patrol members should sleep close enough to touch

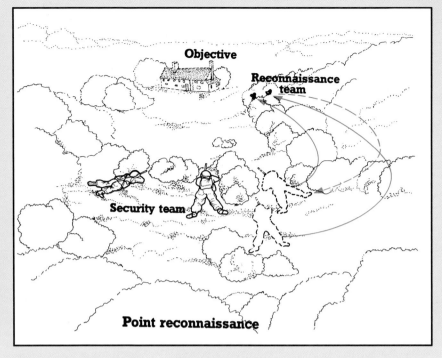

Objective

Reconnaissance team

Security team

Point reconnaissance

Below: In order to conduct a reconnaissance unobserved in flat terrain, it is best to make use of even the sparsest cover: from a distance the outline of your head will be broken up into a less recognisable shape. Left: Your reconnaissance completed, it is advisable to make immediate radio contact with headquarters to ensure that your data reaches its destination. If the radio waves are being monitored, however, first move away from enemy lines as technicians will be able to pinpoint your position.

COMBAT SKILLS Of The Elite

each other, and make sure that the mouths of noisy sleepers are covered with a cloth of some sort. Recon patrols in Vietnam had great success with a 360-degree defensive position that ensured all fields of fire were covered. If your mission takes place under the cover of darkness, remember that sounds carry further at night and reduced visibility will necessitate a closer approach to the objective.

The intelligence you pick up during the reconnaissance patrol may take many forms. If you locate an enemy gun position, try to ascertain the type of gun, its field of fire and the number of enemy troops that man it. The details of any vehicles you observe should be noted in full, as should any large concentrations of enemy troops. Once the objective of a point reconnaissance mission has been reached, be it a building, encampment or weapon site, the patrol must designate a rallying point and then conceal itself. This allows the leaders of security and reconnaissance teams to decide on the best possible positioning of the men under their command. The security team is responsible for securing the rallying point and providing early warning in the case of an enemy approach.

Once the men are in position, the reconnaissance element goes into action, moving towards the objective using the way that is best suited to exploiting the camouflage potential of the terrain. One, perhaps two, reconnaissance teams must work their way towards vantage points close to the target and carry out their intelligence gathering mission. The teams will then either move back to the rallying point or proceed forward to a rendezvous that had been agreed upon in advance. Use the latter method of assembly when it is necessary to avoid moving through the same area twice.

In the case of area reconnaissance, the extended nature of the mission means that each team within the patrol should comprise both reconnaissance and security elements. Whatever the mission, however, all information gained must be disseminated to every patrol member as soon as the reconnaissance has been completed. This increases the chances of getting the intelligence back to base in the event of an ambush. If radio contact is possible, make a preliminary report at the first opportunity.